THE PSYCHOLOGY OF DEATH

Robert Kastenbaum, PhD, completed his doctoral studies in clinical psychology at the University of Southern California in 1959, a year that also saw the publication of Herman Feifel's pioneering book, *The Meaning of Death*, to which Dr. Kastenbaum contributed the chapter: "Time and Death in Adolescence." From that time to the present, Dr. Kastenbaum has been studying the encounter with death in many of its forms. These studies include a major research and demonstration project with hospitalized geriatric patients, the National Hospice Demonstration Study, and, currently, explorations of deathbed scenes in reality and in fantasy. He has worked closely with terminally ill, grieving, and suicidal people and their caregivers, and served as director of a geriatric hospital. Dr. Kastenbaum has been honored for his contributions to death education and research by the Association for Death Education and Counseling, and the National Center for Death Education. He has served as president of the American Association of Suicidology and held offices in the American Psychological Association and Gerontological Society of America. Dr. Kastenbaum is editor of *Omega, Journal of Death and Dying*, senior editor of *Encyclopedia of Death*, and author of numerous articles, chapters, books, and plays. He is a professor in the Department of Communication, Arizona State University.

The Psychology of Death

Second Edition

Robert Kastenbaum, PhD

SPRINGER PUBLISHING COMPANY
New York

Springer Publishing Company, Inc.
536 Broadway
New York, NY 10012

        95 96 / 5 4 3

Library of Congress Cataloging-in-Publication Data
Kastenbaum, Robert.
    The psychology of death / Robert Kastenbaum. — 2nd ed.
        p. cm.
    Includes bibliographical references and index.
    ISBN 0-8261-1922-0
    1. Death—Psychological aspects. I. Title.
BF789.D4K372   1992
155.9'37—dc20   91-33877
                                                                      CIP

Printed in the United States of America

Contents

Preface

The death that is inside this book is not the same as the death that rode with "surgically precise" aerial attacks in the Persian Gulf area. It is not the same as the man-made death that most frequently ends the lives of young Americans—accidents, homicides, suicides. It is not the same as the most recent form taken by catastrophic death, AIDS. It is not the same death that one court of law ordains and another court forbids. And it is not the same death that takes a life that has barely started or that eases the last sigh from a person who has nurtured three generations.

This is only a book about death.

But this is a book about the death that is in our minds, our interactions, our conversations, our silences, and our averted glances. Spending a moment with the history of this book will also recall for us how our shadow dancing with death has both altered and remained the same over recent years.

FROM INTRODUCTION TO FIRST EDITION (1972):

A "psychology of death" is both premature and overdue. The prematurity will quickly become evident as the limitations of present knowledge, methodology, and conceptualization are exposed on these pages. No topic in psychology has been more neglected through the years—yet one might contend that psychology originated in thoughts about death.

Preliterate man achieved his closest approximation to a definition of mental life when he considered death. The "soul" or "spirit" was regarded as that-which-departs from the corpse. . . . The more sophisticated Greek concept of *psyche* was in large measure an elaboration of that-which-departs. . . . The anticipated loss of one's most intimate and treasured possession—his own "psyche" or "soul"—generated not only the discipline of philosophy, but also its offspring, psychology. Were death unknown to man, we would not have become so aware of our own mental life, so self-conscious. . . . Nevertheless, we are struck by how little our own field, psychology, has contributed to the understanding of death.

PREFACE TO CONCISE EDITION (1976):

Death has always been in our lives, but it has not always been represented clearly in our minds. The authors of this book became acutely aware of their own inadequate preparation as they entered into intimate contact with men and women who were living within the shadow of death. Very little in our educational background could be called upon for guidance. The fact that we were psychologists and therefore presumed to be expert in human thought, behavior, and interaction served only to emphasize our ignorance.

It was obvious that "book learning" would not have been sufficient, even if it had been available. . . . But it was evident that our learning process would have been greatly facilitated had we the advantage of a broad, integrative book on the topic. No such book was to be found at the time, so we wrote one for ourselves. . . .

The Psychology of Death turned out to be a long book—long in preparation and long in the distance from front to back cover. It was also a complex book. Try as we might, some of the problems and issues could not be neatly packaged without risking oversimplification. Premature answers, glib generalizations, and easy sentimentalisms were not the sort of material we found helpful as readers, and so we did not knowingly engage in this kind of writing ourselves.

Awareness of death has increased noticeably in our society over the past few years. The taboo has been at least partially lifted, as witness the development of death education courses throughout the United States and more sensitive recognition of death-related problems by the media. We hope this book will prove a useful guide to the person whose view of life encompasses the phenomenon of death. As noted in the original preface, this book is neither the first nor the last word on the subject, but rather an invitation to *continue* the dialogue—with our best minds forward.

BACK TO THE PRESENT

Times have changed. Hospice care has become a welcome alternative for dying people and their families. Peer support groups have developed in response to a variety of death-related stressors. The Widow-to-Widow program, innovated by Phyllis Silverman, and Compassionate Friends, created by Reverend Simon Stephens, are among the most notable examples. The Association for Death Education and Counseling has taken its place alongside the American Association for Suicidology as organizations devoted to education, research, and the improvement of services. Death education is no longer "the latest thing." The frothy thrill-seekers have gone elsewhere. But death education has taken many valuable forms in our society, although still resisted in some quarters. Students of nursing, social work, and counseling have been afforded greater opportunities to consider death-related issues in their studies; medical schools have lagged behind, but even here one can identify outstanding efforts to sensitize students to the human dimensions of mortality. There are useful journals, text books, monographs, video documentaries, and the entire panoply of scholarly and pedagogical endeavor.

Times have not changed that much. Evasion, resistance, and denial have become more subtle. Death is sometimes "covered" in both senses of the term. The new license to speak about death-related topics has often been put to dubious use. For example, skilled manipulators of the media first promulgated a "war on cancer," and then followed with "surgical strikes" on military targets. This massaging of metaphors would not have surprised Orwell or McLuhan. It seems as though everytime the public is ready to face the facts of mortality, we are rescued by the impulse to transform death into an externalized enemy upon whom it is both possible to wage war and win. For another example: the five stages described or invented by Kübler-Ross at first contributed to the awareness that the dying person is still a living person who should not be excluded from the human community. Before long, however, many people were treating the stages as though they comprised a formalistic ritual or a string of rosary beads. The unique reality of each dying person's experiences and needs were veiled by the observer's or caregiver's tendency to use the stage theory as a personal anxiety-reduction mechanism.

Micro-loops of evasion and self-deceit can also be found in many other corners of our lives. In some respects the taboo has been lifted, but in other respects it remains alive, well, and more resourceful than ever. Academic psychology is by no means an exception. Although no longer scarce, death-related studies often are narrow, attentuated, and—well, what's a euphemism for mindless?

So what was to be done for this new edition? What would be worth a serious reader's attention today? There were several givens:

(1) I would be preparing this book solo. Dr. Ruth B. Aisenberg, co-author of the first edition, has since pursued other interests, currently serving as Director of Psychological Services and Training at Westboro State Hospital (Westboro, MA).

(2) There would be no point in presenting material that is already well represented in the abundant literature that has come into existence in recent years. For example, there are a number of competent textbooks that provide topical introductions to death-related thoughts, feelings, and behaviors (or "psychosocial thanatology" for those who prefer resonant phrases). With a variety of reliable books available at the introductory level, I did not see the need to impose the constrictions that come with that genre. This meant that chapters could be organized around themes, issues, and controversies rather than standard topics (e.g., "Dying," "Grief").

(3) Not feeling compelled to "cover the waterfront," I could select those questions that seem most to require attention today—or, perhaps, simply those I find most interesting. I would not propose to offer *A Psychology of Everything That Has Something to Do with Death*, nor *A Psychology of Everything We Really Know for a Fact About Death*. Instead, we would have *A Psychology of Some Pressing Issues About Death That We Still Do Not Understand Very Well*. This latter was not a title calculated to win favor with a publisher whose patience I have long tested, and so we have folded this thought into the already familiar *The Psychology of Death*.

(4) There would be a tighter focus on psychological processes. The original edition explored some significant topics that are not usually considered to be within the province of psychology (e.g., social policy and its impact on mortality). This is no longer necessary, as many contributions have been made in important areas at or beyond the fringe of psychology. I still see psychology as an approach more than a domain, but most "fringe" material has been expunged.

(5) Obviously, the revised edition would be informed by research and clinical contributions that have been made since the publication of the previous editions.

This latest edition of *The Psychology of Death* retains only about 25% of the material included in the first edition: just the steering wheel, hood ornament, two hub caps, and a few other trinkets to which I may have become overly attached. The first two chapters are completely new and derive from my current research activities. They form a matched set: DEATHBED SCENES confronts us with one of our most powerful and palpable encounters with mortality. By contrast, A WORLD WITHOUT DEATH explores what our minds do when we are (hypothetically) set free from the expectation of finitude. Also new, the third chapter is reflective, if not inquisatorial. THE PSYCHOLOGIST'S DEATH examines the implicit choices that this discipline has made in approaching or avoiding death.

It is not until the fourth chapter that we return to previous material. HOW DO WE CONSTRUCT DEATH? A DEVELOPMENTAL PERSPECTIVE examines the development of death-related ideas, especially in childhood. Here, the classic sources that provided valuable information in the first edition remain classic, augmented by more recent contributions. With DEATH ANXIETY IN THE MIDST OF LIFE we plunge into not one, but two intersecting hazards: the academic's cosy garden patch of empirical studies and the clinician's wilderness of observations made under conditions of stress and desperation. Some of this material is recycled; some is new; my approach to it all has been modified and perhaps improved.

A WILL TO LIVE AND AN INSTINCT TO DIE? is a longish chapter where previously there had been just a few pages. Does anybody want to read about a failed theory? I hope that I am not the only person who suspects we can learn more from Freud's rejected theory than from many tidy little successes.

The final chapter, also new, comes a little sooner than I would have preferred. There are several other issues I would have liked to address in this book. The publisher is confident that *you* would not have been deterred by a volume twice this length, but is not so sure about potential readers. Dr. Ursula Springer is seldom mistaken about such things, and so we move directly from the theoretical enterprise to the necessity of GETTING ON WITH LIFE. This is a new chapter in which I try to offer a little guidance while not going (too much) beyond what we actually know.

I appreciate your patience with these introductory comments and admire your willingness to consider a book that must present many questions if any useful answers are to be discovered.

1

Deathbed Scenes

The dying man's clothes are ripped off, an intern has slammed her fist into his chest as hard as she can, and now she starts to push down on the dying man's breastbone, rhythmically breaking his ribs. A medical resident sticks a metal hook in the man's mouth and lifts his head and neck off the table with the hook as he places a large tube in the man's throat. Another intern sticks a large needle into the dying man's chest, just below the collar bone; then, cursing, he pulls it out and sticks it in the dying man's neck. All the while there is shouting, maybe even laughing. . . .

—James S. Goodwin & Jean S. Goodwin

I had been out of the room just a moment. I was coming back from the kitchen with fresh water, just in case he wanted another sip. And then just like that he died. One moment he looked peacefully asleep. The next moment he was gone. It was almost as though nothing had happened, but now it was all over. The first thought you had was that now nothing more could hurt him, and then you found tears running down your face like they would never stop.

—Daughter of an elderly hospice patient

I die the death my parents and grandparents died
and I die the deaths my children will die.
I die all the deaths I have heard of and can imagine.

—Joseph A. Amato

1

Psychological studies of death have all too often taken the guise of trivial pursuits. Apply simplistic methods to artificial questions, run some numbers through the computer, and rush the manuscript into the mail! The emptiness, however, must be filled somehow. And so we continue to rely on assumptions that have been worn thin by the fingers of time, and on personal experiences whose gradients of generalization remain obscure. There has to be a better alternative than losing ourselves either in numbers or in reveries.

Perhaps deathbed scenes can provide that alternative. Four of the most direct and profound ways in which death presents itself to the human mind are integral to the deathbed scene: (a) a pointed reminder of our common and personal mortality; (b) the observable transition from life to death; (c) the person become a dead body; and (d) the pain of separation and loss. To put it another way: Death is no longer theoretical.

It is true that a participant in the scene might choose to respond as though nothing momentous has occurred (e.g., a ward clerk who blank-facedly starts the process of clearing out all signs of the deceased person to make way for the next patient). The ritual of routinizing both life and death is itself, however, a process so bizarre (although not so rare) that death understands what a tribute has been paid. For those whose humanity has not been sacrificed to personal or institutional anxieties, the deathbed scene is the border, the edge, the precipice. What strengths do we possess as individuals, and what strengths can we draw from companions and culture that can offer comfort and meaning as the deathbed scene runs its course?

We begin this book, then, with an exploration of the deathbed scene. Psychological aspects will be emphasized, but not to the neglect of major physical, sociocultural, and spiritual factors. At the least, this venture will help to remind us that the psychology of death is not primarily a set of academic exercises, but an encounter with both the outermost limits and potentials of the capacity to be human.

DEATHBED SCENES AS SYMBOLIC CONSTRUCTIONS

Deathbed scenes are enacted in our minds both before and after they occur in the "real world." Anticipated scenes. Remembered scenes. We may anticipate a deathbed scene for days and remember it for years—and yet feel detached or disoriented during the actual episode. Deathbed scenes are symbolic constructions that draw on both idiosyncratic personal experiences and culturally available themes, events, and meaning fragments. In this sense, the deathbed scene is comparable with a variety of other occasions that bring people together to observe or participate in a shared event. There is no scene quite like a deathbed scene, but all human societies have established scenes with which instructive, if limited comparisons can be made (e.g., initiations, graduations, weddings, retirements, etc.). Our interests here center on the deathbed scene itself, so we will forego the comparisons. Instead, we start with one example of the way in which the many elements and events that occur during a period of time become transformed into a deathbed scene.

Creation of the Story of a Death

One person is dying. Others are providing care, making observations, communicating, undergoing stressful experiences, and so on. All these anticipations, observations, communications, and stressors do not of themselves constitute a coherent "story of a death." Furthermore, the participants may not have a firm sense of the deathbed scene while it is in progress, and the "same" death might be represented very differently during a period.

Here is one typical sequence that I have noticed, primarily from reviewing hospice case histories with the assistance of the nurses who were most closely involved in their care. There is no magic about this sequence: It is not the only way in which deathbed scenes are constructed, nor is it necessarily the way we should construct them. It is simply a sequence one discovers fairly often when people have been looking after a family member who is in the end stage of a terminal illness.

1. The dying person is characterized as rejecting nourishment by mouth. Respiration labored. Low-grade fever. Urinary incontinence. Questions raised about adjusting medications: effective symptom control in one sphere might produce side effects in another. Family tense, subdued, looking to each other and to staff for clues as to how to respond. Many isolated observations such as these are made, noted in the record, sometimes shared among the caregivers.

2. The guiding principle emerges that the dying person will quietly and painlessly ease from life—slip away. The family now has a firmer sense of its role: "We should *keep watch*, while professional caregivers preside and consult." Be available. Be caring. But, mostly, watch and wait.

3. No: that's not what is happening at all. An alternative interpretation has appeared. "There's *crisis* just ahead. Something terrible might

happen that we would never forgive ourselves for. But something marvel-ous might happen also. And it can all depend on us." This change in the story line can be prompted by either a positive or negative development (e.g., the dying person has become more alert and communicative, or the medications no longer seem to be effective in controlling symptoms). The family must be at full alert and see to it that the health professionals are also prepared to do all that can be done to influence the course of the struggle.

4. These alternative constructions—slipping away versus crisis— also take their turns as alternating constructions of the situation. If there are many participants in this scene, we may find some who favor one interpretation and some the other, with a few "swing votes" who alter their views whenever there is a new real or apparent development.

5. Several months after the death, most of the family have agreed on a fairly stable and consistent construction of the events and their mean-ing. Contributing to this stability is the fact that "it is over," thereby providing most of the elements needed for an enduring mental represen-tation. (This stability can be challenged, however, if some discordant and unexpected fact turns up later.) Furthermore, the family survivors are liberated from the pressure of the ongoing events with their ambiguities and uncertainties. Everybody can reflect on the deathbed scene, no longer being seized by it as an urgency of the moment. (The professional caregivers who were involved will have achieved their own sense of closure, usually more rapidly.)

This sequence started with a set of factual observations that did not add up to much. Things were happening. Assessments were being made. The dying person was behaving like this; people were feeling like that. There was no dominant story or construction, however. (We are focusing now on the experiential state of the family; the pattern often would differ for the professional caregivers.)

We are seldom at our best when forced to function in a demanding situation without the guidance that a persuasive story, belief, or myth can offer. In this early phase of the sequence, the family is more likely to have difficulty in reconciling "deathbedness" with their ordinary life routines. There is a lack of clear delineation and definition. How should I behave differently? In what ways can I continue to go on with my normal life while "this" is going on? The family at this point is likely to be cautious and inhibited for the most part because the signals are that not clear to them. (This prevailing tendency may well be interrupted occasionally when peaks of anxiety occur.)

The "no story" situation seldom lasts very long. We need stories. And we are gifted in the making of stories. The particular sequence described here continued with the emergence of two competing interpretations of the situation. (These are not the only types of interpretation that arise during and subsequent to a deathbed scene, but are among those most often discovered.) Some of the observed and agreed-on facts loaned themselves to either version. Once the main story lines had been formulated, however, the participants could emphasize observations that favored either the slipping away or the crisis interpretation. Furthermore, each new development could be evaluated within the frame of both competing stories as the dying person's physical, emotional, and communicational status changed. Given a story—given two radically different stories—the family tends to be more active and purposeful, taking life into its own hands again, even if sometimes at cross-purpose with each other and even with themselves.

The deathbed scene as such does not exist until it has been breathed into life by the story maker's imagination, whether one especially persuasive individual or the totality of a group's experience. The *elements* of the deathbed scene are real enough: labored respiration, fever, impaired communication, and so on. It requires an act of narrative imagination, however, to create the overall construction of the deathbed scene. In the sequence we have briefly considered here, the competing stories were seen as though emerging from the participants' ongoing observations and experiences. On further analysis, however, we would discover that the central ideas had been preexistent. Our shared culture had already provided the participants with usable symbols and meaning modules that include *keeping watch for a slipping away* and being *on guard during a crisis*.

Suppose that we met a family member some time after this deathbed scene. Expressing our interest in the experience, we would be likely to hear a coherent narrative in which many of the elements have been preserved. Some aspects and some moments would be given more prominence than others. There would also be a sense of development, conflict, and destination or denouement. The multitudinous observations and experiences would at last have added up to something: to a compact and meaningful symbolic structure. This "package of meaning" would be easier to recall and to share with others, as distinguished from the unstable mixture of elements and experiences that one processes while the events are in progress. In this sense, the "true deathbed scene" emerged after a preliminary period of selection, choice, and refinement.

Let us take this process one step further. A colleague at work reveals that a person in his or her family has a terminal disease and is not expected to live much longer. The person who has already experienced a death in his or her own household may now be in a position to be helpful in many ways (e.g., as a good listener and companion). In particular, though, the survivor who possesses an authenticated deathbed story (e.g., "this really happened to us") might choose to offer it as a model for others. The colleague who has had an experience with a dying family will then be alerted to certain deathbed scene anticipations. Whether for better or worse (or a little of both), this person may view subsequent developments from a particular framework—and attempt to behave in accordance with this model.

Consider, for example, the daughter of an elderly hospice patient who was quoted at the beginning of this chapter. Her long-absent sister had charged back into the home with the conviction that a deathbed scene was a crisis that must be managed like a five-alarm fire on an oil tanker. This view had been inspired by what she had been told (or what she had taken from) another person's report of a deathbed scene. This "raging inferno" view of the dying process did make things more exciting at home, and stimulated thoughts and feelings that might not otherwise have surfaced. Nevertheless, after a period of competition between story lines, the serenity of the dying person and the low-key competence of the hospice personnel moved the balance toward the slipping away version.

Deathbed scenes are not simple, peripheral, or inconsequential. As symbolic constructions, they enshrine emotionally significant facts and values and become an enduring part of our memories, hopes, fears, and dreams. Additionally, these symbolic constructions can have vital implications for actions that are taken while the dying person is still with us. We will explore this process subsequently through the question: Who owns the deathbed scene? First, however, we will find it useful to establish a more balanced approach to deathbed scenes—the quasi-objective perspective that so captivates behavioral scientists. (This, too, is a symbolic construction, of course, but we will pretend not to notice.)

DEATHBED SCENES AS BEHAVIOR SETTINGS

Place

A deathbed scene occurs in a particular place. The more carefully we identify and observe this place, the better our opportunity to understand what is happening and perhaps even why. Consider this set of alternative descriptions:

- Geriatric facility
- Intensive care unit (ICU) of geriatric facility
- Private side room on ICU of geriatric facility
- Bed screened off by curtains in private side room on ICU of geriatric facility

Although all are very brief descriptions of the same behavior setting, they differ markedly in the information provided. I have known many people whose physical deathbed scene could be described by any or all of the preceding. In the memory of G. S., here is the way in which one person's place of death could be reconstructed.

For the purposes of the death certificate, it was sufficient to state that G. S. died at Cushing Hospital. For public notice, a local newspaper reported that she died in a nursing home (not quite correct and chose not to include the name of the particular geriatric facility.) This briefest of behavior setting specifications (either Cushing Hospital or "nursing home") was as much as the public expected or required. There was a psychological subtext, though:

"Who dies?"
"Old people."
"Well, that's a relief. Where do they die?"
"Some place else. Not in our homes, not in our beds."

Bare-bone descriptions, then, suit us well when we do not really want to know too much, and when our main interest is that the scene occurred some place else. For most people, the most significant thing was not the precise scene itself but its location: right across from the town dump, where old age and death could be sequestered behind a chain-link fence. Physical boundaries and barriers. Psychological boundaries and barriers.

For contrast, consider the most elaborated of these brief descriptions. The expanded information tells us that G. S.'s death had been expected by the staff or, at least, had not come as a surprise to them. She was at three removes from most other residents of the facility: (a) transferred to ICU, (b) moved to the side room, and (c) screened off. Each of these boundary markers also could be regarded as road markers on the final steps of her life's journey. Separately and accumulatively, they had the double function of providing specialized care for G. S., but also of protecting the hospital community at large from her "deathness." Many others would die in the weeks, months, and years ahead. It was thought necessary and proper to encapsulate the acute deathness of G. S., however, and thereby keep the rest of the hospital an (illusory) death-free zone. The relatively differentiated description of her physical deathbed scene tells us, then, of a death anticipated, a specialized staff available to provide comfort and care, and an attempt to divide the hospital community into the living and the dying—just as the general community tended to view the facility itself as the place where old people went to die.

At this point it might be tempting to move away from G. S.'s death place. It is not a very appealing physical setting: small, clinical, sequestered, apt to make us feel claustrophobic and ill at ease. But isn't that precisely what we must try to identify and understand? The narrow confines of the ICU side room and the space-taking equipment and supplies severely limit the number of people who can be present. Furthermore, the location—deep within the medico nursing core of the hospital—make it difficult for potential visitors to approach. It is not a casual place, like the day rooms on "home wards," or the "Times Square" sector with its recreational facilities, coffee shop, and other amenities. One must pass through a boundary of tension into a specialized area in which "civilians" are neither welcome nor comfortable. The location and the parameters of the physical setting often convey information about how the deathbed scene is conceived, who exercises control, and what types of actions and communications are to be countenanced.

We change the setting now. Here is a family home. A man is dying too soon: He was a vigorous person in his early 60s. Nobody in the large, multigenerational and multi-in-lawed family had been prepared for his rapid decline and, now, his imminent death. Let us ignore everything else—as we would not do in the actual situation—and focus on one physical element. He is dying not just at home but in the guest room often used by visiting grandchildren. And he is dying not just in that room, but in a bed that has taken on heirloom status after use by several generations of children and grandchildren. Unlike G. S, L. L. was in a physical setting that made it easy for people to come and go. It was a familiar location, and "house rules" rather than "hospital rules" applied. He remained integrated into family patterns of interaction, communication, and affection until the end.

But now he has died. And there is that bed—the bed in which he died. What is to become of it? When the family returned home after the funeral, discussion eventually turned to the bed. There was a general feeling that they would have to get rid of it. In fact, the "kids' room" itself had become the "where-Dad-died" room and emotionally off limits. A surprising thing happened that night. Two of the "kids" decided to sleep in the death-tainted bed that had now been returned to the death-tainted room. The next morning they reported that they had felt that Grandfather had been close to them and liked having them there. The kids also ate a good breakfast. This action had the effect of decontaminating both the room and the bed. They would remain part of the family's shared memory of the deathbed scene, but they had overcome the risk of being exclusively the physical setting of the deathbed scene.

One further example will introduce the concept of "placeness" as a psychological complement to place. The following passage is excerpted from a young woman's depiction of the deathbed scene as she expects it to occur after she has had a long and fulfilling life:

> My death, as I picture it, occurs in my own bedroom, not a hospital room. The surroundings are comfortable and familiar. It seems foolish to me to consider the decor of the room, however that's what pops into my mind first. This I believe reflects my desire to die content. The bed, higher than the average, has a beautiful floral spread with matching sheets and lace pillow cases. The carpet, drapes, and wallpaper are softly colored and create an open and fresh feeling. The atmosphere in the room will be accented by the weather outside. The season is mid Spring, a sunny morning with a light, warm breeze and birds singing outside. The importance of the type of day to me signifies a sense of freedom or the lifting of burden.

The loving attention to detail is obvious. This young woman is describing a well-imaged scene. Her sense of herself as an individual is affirmed by the particularities—the colors she has selected, the type of day it must be. The place itself, however, is unknown, indeed, unknowable. She cannot predict where she will be living many years from now (and with a husband she has yet to meet). But she does have a well-developed sense of placeness. The deathbed scene is both located ("my bedroom") and indeterminate (what part of the world?). What really matters is "placeness," the comforting and individual quality of the scene—wherever it might happen to be.

Time, Timing, and Sequence

A deathbed scene moves through time at a particular time. Again, we can choose to notice little or much as the following set of brief examples indicate:

- W. B. E. died at 10:30 a.m., September 8, 1985.
- W. B. E. died at 10:30 a.m., September 8, 1985, *after a long illness.*

- W. B. E. died at 10:30 a.m., September 8, 1985, after a long illness, *culminated by a farewell scene of nearly 24 hours.*
- W. B. E. died at 10:30 a.m., September 8, 1985, after a long illness, culminated by a farewell scene of nearly 24 hours *that came at the right time (for W. B. E., wife, and friends, Mr. & Mrs. B.) and also prematurely (for visiting hospice nurse).*

The first of these reports establishes a coordinate between W. B. E.'s death and the matrix of public or social time. It is the moment he has left the company of the living and the moment that a particular behavior setting has become a place of death. This report satisfies bureaucratic requirements for converting W. B. E. into a statistic but accomplishes little else. The second report indicates that there had been an extended passage, a period in which W. B. E. lived with his dying. Possibly some or all of this time was shared with others. Possibly there was a scene of parting at the end. Possibly.

Most reports of a death are limited to the first or second types that have been exemplified. This is true not only of routine newspaper reports but also of the records maintained by health care providers. Occasionally we will learn that a newsworthy person has died peacefully in the company of three of his or her ex-spouses, a press agent, and Waldo, the wonder pig. Typically, however, the temporal pattern of the death and what might or might not have made it a scene are ignored.

I have reviewed thousands of "closed" as well as current hospital and nursing home charts. Seldom can the reader reconstruct even the most basic elements of the (possible) deathbed scene. Who was with this person as he or she died? Anybody? What type of communications occurred? Did the dying person attempt to speak? Did a nurse—or perhaps a custodian who just happened to wander in—take the dying person's hand? Did a relative pause in the doorway and then turn away with tears in her eyes? Who was there and what happened? It is rare that questions such as these can be answered from the available documentation. I have noted this lack of documentation in celebrated research hospitals as well as underfunded and understaffed nursing homes. Despite its impressive record of health-related research, the Veterans Administration quietly backed away from its promise to conduct a preliminary self-study of deathbed scenes. Left to itself, the U.S. health care system prefers not to notice how people think, feel, and communicate at the point of death. Hospice organizations are not necessarily exceptions to this rule. Although often much more sensitive to the needs of the dying person and the family, hospice staff are apt to feel under pressure to do paperwork necessary to comply with regulations, and have little incentive or training for observing the deathbed scene as such.

The expanded time-of-death descriptions given earlier are seldom available from medical records and similar sources. We usually learn about deathbed scenes only by having been there ourselves or by managing to do research despite the numerous obstacles. Some years ago we discovered that a modified psychological autopsy method could help us understand how the last moments might be related both to personality and lifestyle, and to the circumstances and events that a person had moved through as the end approached (Weisman & Kastenbaum, 1968). The many nurses, physicians, and other caregivers who participated in this investigative process shared with us in our growing appreciation for the end phase of human life. We realized (sometimes too late) that having known the person a little better previously could have helped us to offer more sensitive and appropriate care at the time that a behavior setting was becoming a deathbed scene.

Let us continue with the more recent example of W. B. E., to see how closer attention to time, timing, and sequence can alert us to the significance of a deathbed scene.

The hospice nurse was taken aback when he crossed W. B. E.'s threshold for the first time. An enormous polar bear rushed at him, toothy jaws agape. Fortunately, the bear's attack was restrained by its placement in the wall. W. B. E. had been a vigorous and independent-minded man who spent many years hunting, trapping, and prospecting. Now in his mid-70s and exhausted by his battle with cancer, he had become housebound and reconciled to death. "I've had a great life," he told the nurse, "no regrets." Following the initial examination, W. B. E. had first one and then another request for the nurse. "Can you talk my doctor into letting me drink a shot of whisky now and then?" This was quickly accomplished. "Thanks. Now I want you to promise that you'll take a last snort with me when I croak." The nurse, a very light drinker, agreed that he would join the clan (patient, wife, and another couple who had been friends for years) in a "last snort" if circumstances permitted. ("I prayed it wouldn't be in the early morning hours when so many seem to pass away: a shot of whisky at that hour might finish me, too!")

Consider what has already been brought foward in this situation: The dying person has conceived of his own deathbed scene and is making plans for it. This is not to be a scene in which the central player intends to be unaware or passive. Furthermore, he has a devoted "supporting cast." Wife and friends indicate that they are with him all the way. There *is* to be a deathbed scene, and it is to be scripted or constructed in advance. It is to be a sort of celebration—of the way one man has chosen to live and end his life, affirmed and amplified by his closest companions. Ensuing contacts made it clear that the old friends had moved in with the couple for a "last house party" that would signify the end of an era for all of them. Everybody seemed ready for W. B. E.'s death, except the nurse. Impressed by the patient's resilience and, perhaps, not yet willing to let him go, the nurse believed that he would hold on for some time yet.

All too soon (from the nurse's perspective) his beeper signaled a call from W. B. E.'s wife. They had been gathered around the dying man for nearly 24 hours, telling the old stories together, but it looked as though there was not much time left. The old man was pleased to see that the nurse had returned to keep his promise. "Fix the drinks, lover." As his wife placed a drink in every hand, all except the nurse burst out with an X-rated toast to the good life. The old man winked and died.

This concluded the deathbed scene as anticipated. But there was more to come. The nurse performed the obligatory ritual of checking the man's vital signs and confirming his death (to be later certified by a physician). Another action remained to be taken. Unlike thoughts and communications about death, a deathbed scene results in a corpse, and something must be done with it. The nurse placed a call. Sometime later, two men arrived at the door, their business vehicle parked outside. As they approached the bed and started to place hands on the corpse, the deceased's "good old buddy" halted them: "Say, what's the rush? Can't you see he hasn't finished his drink?" Sure enough, there was the shot glass still in the dead man's grip, and still containing whiskey. "A man in his condition needs a little extra time to finish his drink. You can see that for yourself!" The two men retreated in confusion and sat in their van for a while. When they returned, they noticed that there was now only a drop left in the whiskey glass. Again they started to take the corpse, but again were angrily confronted by the buddy. "One last sip—can't you wait for his last little sip! What kind of guys are you, anyhow!" After a longer interval, the two men ventured to return again, saw that the glass was now empty, and removed the corpse without further incident.

The rough humor of this incident was viewed by W. B. E.'s wife and friends as a bonus or encore facet of his deathbed scene that he would have heartily appreciated and approved of (a view not likely to have been shared by the corpse handlers). Whether the reader responds with outrage or amusement to this incident, it represents a broad type of deathbed scene, one that is at least partially crafted in advance and requires the willing participation of others. Time is important in the prepared deathbed scene, time to anticipate and prepare. Timing and sequence also matter. Had the hospice nurse entered the picture a little later, for example, he might not have become so much a part of the unfolding scenario. The deathbed scene, like any other, is vulnerable to unexpected events, coincidents, breakdowns, and so on. It is also subject to variant interpretations: for example, the death coming too soon from the perspective of the nurse, but not the man and his companions; and the total scene appearing either appropriate (insider's view) or bizarre (outsider's view).

Satisfaction with the knowledge that "W. B. E. died at 10:30 a.m., September 8, 1985) would have deprived us of the opportunity to "witness" this rather elaborate and unique deathbed scene.

People

A deathbed scene could involve only one person. Many people have died alone, whether far from others or socially isolated. Usually, we do not know what was experienced by the person who died without companionship. Occasionally, however, we are given access to some of the person's last thoughts:

Lay in bed . . . all day.
Life? is so boreing. Back into the same rut. No lights in Chev. Joe has got car. Truck wont start, stereo quit, caint sleep. Women left me. I feel like shit.
(Leenaars, 1988, p. 237)

and

My love for you has always been the deepest and hopefully I'll see you again. You are my miracle. I have accepted the Lord Jesus as my saviour but I know that he wouldn't condone this. I accept the just dues and pray that maybe you won't hurt anymore. Make our kid something! You and Jesus I pray can forgive me for copping out. . . . If I see mom I'll see that Joe is taken care of + I will try to be with him too! . . . Eternity is the best way of saying how long I (?) love you. . . . May the Lord bless + keep you + forgive me for something I have no earthly rights to do. (Leenaars, 1988, p. 241)

These suicide notes tell us that their authors were not entirely alone. They may have been the only visible person in their behavior setting, but in their minds they were playing scenes that involved one or more other people. Both facts are significant: (a) the person was alone; (b) the person thought and experienced as though interacting with others. The second note is especially rich with its inclusion of "you," "our kid," "Jesus," "mom," and "Joe." If all scenes are symbolic constructions, then all begin in the mind, whether or not they also "play" in shared time-place.

Reports of near-death experiences (NDEs) often describe interactions that seem to have been locked within the individual's private experiences (e.g., Moody, 1975; Ring, 1980). The individual later may report encounters with his or her own unresponsive body or with a "spiritual being of light." Even if other persons are operating within the same physical setting, they will not have detected and probably will not have suspected that this vivid scene had been enacted.

There have been numerous reports of people emerging from a deep and sometimes prolonged period of unresponsiveness. Sometimes one has the impression that they did have interactions and experiences within their own phenomenological spheres even though these were denied expression. Sacks (1968) has described dramatic examples of this type among people who were stricken by encephalitis at the end of World War I and then regained their minds when successfully treated many years later. A study of our own that was reported in previous editions of *The Psychology of Death* is also germane. Three student research assistants made two daily observations for a 3-day period on more than 200 hospitalized geriatric patients. Four types of low-level behavior syndrome were established on the basis of these observations. The lowest level syndrome was characterized by the following set of observations:

Type I

1. In bed
2. Supine
3. Mouth open
4. Eyes closed or with empty stare
5. Head tilted back
6. Arms straight at side
7. Absence of adjustive movements, fidgeting, speech, verbalizations, and so on
8. General impression of having been placed or molded into position

As can be seen, there was virtually no behavior to describe. People who consistently fit into this category appeared to be static objects within their behavior settings.

A simple behavioral intervention was carried out for patients in all of the low-level behavior categories. One member of the observational team would slowly approach the patient, then take the patient's hand and hold it gently, introduce himself or herself, and speak to the patient by name. This intervention was repeated twice a day for three days. Nearly half of the Type I and Type II patients responded to such an extent that they were reclassified into a higher category; a "priming effect" was observed in which the repeated brief contacts seemed to increase the patient's readiness to respond to a subsequent contact. Apparently the prolonged lack of interpersonal stimulation had contributed to their nonresponsive orientation, although all were also neurologically impaired as well.

Of particular interest here was a transitional phenomenon that was not mentioned in the earlier report. In "coming up," some patients behaved as though they had been engaged in a continuing interaction with the contact person. We had the impression that a kind of "shadow play" interaction had been occurring, at least sporadically, within the minds of these previously unresponsive people before their "awakening." For example, an old man who had not been known to speak in the past several weeks responded to a research assistant's hand embrace on her third visit. He pressed her hand, stared at her for a moment, and then spoke to her comfortably as "Irene." For several minutes he nodded and chatted with perhaps the same Irene he had been visiting with previously in his clouded reveries.

Often we have no way of knowing whether or not an unresponsive person is still experiencing life at some level. It is virtually impossible to rule out the null hypothesis: Lack of responsiveness does not prove lack of phenomenological experience. We do know that many people have reported having had experiences while apparently nonresponsive after they have recovered from a life-threatening condition. Awareness of this possibility has prompted some nurses, physicians, and other caregivers to speak with a nonresponsive dying person as though this person were still capable of experiencing and understanding. Many of us who have had experiences with anesthesia can recall that "in-between" state of mind in which our thoughts and interactions move across an unstable boundary between fantasy and reality.

A dying person may also experience private or phenomenological deathbed scenes in addition to events that actually occur in shared time-place. An old woman (in the same geriatric hospital) was as lucid and well oriented as ever despite her declining health. Two days before her death, she said her good-byes to her visiting sister and brother-in-law while I also happened to be with her. She set aside their objections that she was not about to die by reporting a dream from the night before: Mother, father, and the whole family had been there by her bedside, which was also, at the same time, the old family homestead in Wyoming. Everything was going to be fine. They were keeping a place for her. This woman had also a more expansive and heartening deathbed scene on the level of dream-experience.

Nevertheless, when we think of a deathbed scene we are most likely to visualize one or more intimate companions gathered around the dying person in "real" time and place. Being with the right people is often specified as the most desired component of the deathbed scene. Terminally ill people who have selected the hospice care option give high priority to having the companionship of one or more people who are precious to them (Kastenbaum, 1991). Sometimes there is a core person whose presence is sought on a continuous basis; others are to be seen, farewelled, and then encouraged to depart. It is not unusual for a terminally ill person to express the wish that a certain person *not* be included ("How can I die in peace if _____ is strutting around, giving orders and putting on airs?").

The best available study of farewelling was conducted by Australian sociologists Allan Kellehear and Terry Lewin (1988–1989). They found that 81 of 100 terminally ill cancer patients expressed the desire for a leave-taking opportunity with people who were significant to them. Not everybody intended to wait for the last minute; some had already said their farewells or were planning to do so well before the end. Those who preferred a relatively early farewell scene were usually motivated by the desire to do so while they were still in relatively good health. Another advantage seen in the early farewelling was the opportunity to give little gifts and remembrances: One woman, for example, made many small dolls while she lay abed and gave these to friends on their last visit.

The classic version of a farewell scene in their final hour, however, was contemplated by most (73) of Kellehear and Lewin's respondents. They most often wanted to have their very last words with their spouse, children, and closest friends. But why did some people prefer not to have farewell scenes, either early or late? Mostly, they did not want to upset themselves or other people: "From these persons' viewpoints, final farewells would make 'the end' too intense and dramatic, overdrawing attention to the fact of imminent death" (Kellehear & Lewin, 1988–1989, p. 285). Two respondents felt that there was no point to having a farewell scene because they would be meeting each other again in the afterlife. As though agreeing with this logic, two other people who described themselves as nonreligious declared that that was no point in saying good-bye because they would not be saying hello again.

The individual differences reported in this study are worth remembering. If we assumed that everybody wants to have a deathbed scene, we might inadvertently force this arrangement on some people who would prefer to close out their lives without a conspicuous final scene. It is also possible that some people would discover that they really do want the comfort, affection, and companionship of a farewell scene after they have had the opportunity to express and revise the negative scenario that has been troubling them.

A thorough discussion of the people dimension of deathbed scenes would also consider such factors as the following:

- Barriers to being together (e.g., a roomful of bulky and noisy equipment; intrafamily conflict; competing responsibilities, such as child care; travel time and expense, etc.)
- Unresolved problems in the relationship between the dying person himself or herself and others (e.g., disapproval of the other person's life-style, recriminations about past misdeeds, etc.)
- Place of the dying person within the entire family and friendship configuration (e.g., Is this the king or queen pin of the entire network, or somebody who had been "written off" by the family many years ago, etc.?)
- Personal meanings and implications of the death for the survivors (e.g., Is this person dying of an illness to which others believe themselves vulnerable? Is this person's suffering perceived as a foretaste of what others will undergo when their time comes?)

We will give further consideration to the people dimension of the deathbed scene in much of what follows below.

WHO OWNS THE DEATHBED SCENE?

This question offers us a way of looking at some of the uncertainties, ambiguities, and conflicts that arise around deathbed scenes today. Paradoxically, it is when life and death become most concrete, palable, and immediate that fantasies, imaginings, and dogmas are also likely to escape their leash. We can talk at great lengths about life and death. Our usual decontextualized discourse, however, has little to do with what we experience when we are actually with a person who is at the very edge, here and now. The drawn face resting on the pillow is real and immediate in a way that "death talk" is not.

Let us consult several deathbed scenes and give particular attention to the related concepts of perceived control, efficacy, and comprehension, all of which figure mightily in the contest for ownership of the deathbed scene. We are especially keen to grasp control when we feel it slipping away, to demonstrate efficacy when we sense helplessness, and to proclaim understanding when we are but a gasp away from bewilderment. Everything that the deathbed scene threatens to take away from us—composure, security, comfort, power—we may seek to replace through culturally available compensatory devices or idiosyncratic improvisations. The deathbed scene also tempts those who would take advantage of another person's helplessness for the sake of their own ego gratification. A few examples follow.

Moral Claims

Deathbed scenes have had a long association with religious beliefs and practice. The episode summarized below owes much to the residual effects of a darkening of tone within Christianity. The early Christian message had emphasized triumph over death. By the thirteenth century, however, the dread of damnation had become more vivid to many believers (Aries, 1981). The Day of Judgment appeared disconcertingly close to that moment at which a person's soul left the body. The deathbed scene became regarded as a crisis. Would the poor sinner be condemned to unremitting torment or was salvation still possible? "Life's final moments . . . took on a new intensity" (LeGoff, 1984). The fundamental idea of the deathbed scene *as* a scene owes much to this intensification of fear-hope dynamics some eight centuries ago. The deathbed scene was no longer simply the expected and natural "tag end" of life, but had become more of a "final exam."

This view had retained its power 400 years later when Jeremy Taylor wrote his classic *Rules and Exercises for Holy Dying* (1651/1977). His basic exercise was more formidable than any latter-day aerobic work-out program: We must think each day of that moment when our life will end and become subject to divine judgment. "He that would die well, must all the days of his life lay up against the day of death." Specifically, he recommended that as we lie down to sleep at the end of each day we conduct a diligent examination of our actions, "the disorders of every day, the multitude of impertinent words, the great portions of time spent in vanity."[1] Each day was a life in microcosm, and each evening a rehearsal for the last fall of darkness. The expected deathbed scene had become perhaps even more salient in our minds than the final scene itself.

Our major example here comes from a point less distant in time. We are in 19th-century London, already a tumultuous city caught up in the expansive industrialism of its times. John Warton, doctor of divinity, will publish a set of three posthumous volumes entitled *Death-Bed Scenes*

(1826). He is on his way to one of them now. Warton does not know Marsden, nor has the dying man invited him, but this is of no consequence for he knew himself to be "a humble instrument in God's hands for the accomplishment of his gracious purposes of love and mercy."

Warton observes that Marsden's "nose was pinched, as if by the hand of death; and, if he had been still he might well have been supposed to be a corpse. But there was something at work within him, which would not let him rest for a single moment. He turned his face from side to side . . . and his eyes betokened enquiry and alarm."[2] This "piteous sight" instantly convinces Warton that the dying man had either been abandoned by wife and daughter who must have fled from his forbidding countenance, or that he had banished them himself. (Neither hypothesis has to be checked against reality: As usual, Warton understands a situation perfectly the moment he beholds it.)

The interaction begins with Warton's comment, "I am truly sorry, Sir, to see you in so deplorable a condition." Marsden answers immediately and sternly: "Why to be sure, this room is not a fine one, nor am I lying in a fine bed." Impregnable to ironic humor, Warton delivers a verbose explanation of what he had meant, concluding with reference to "this grevious disease, which seems to have brought you almost to death's door, and this uneasiness of mind which again makes you so restless."

These solicitous comments enrage the dying man who snaps: "You know nothing about my mind, whether it is uneasy or not. What business have you here, to make observations upon *me*? Who sent for you? I'm sure I didn't—what you are come for?" These foolish questions do not provoke the gentle doctor of divinity. He offers to forgive the dying man for his intemperate response and adds that "at such an awful time as this . . . the mind should be set quite at ease with respect to all worldly affairs; and every moment should be devoted to the thinking of God, and of your Saviour, and of the world to come which will have no end."

Marsden, whose heart is proving as "impenetrable as the granite-rock," does not leap to the invitation offered by his unscheduled visitor. In fact, he mutters to himself, "They pretend that you have a right to plague us, when we might die quietly without you." Warton just keeps on talking. When he pauses for breath a moment, the dying man seizes the opportunity to speak his own mind: "Now you have had your say, now you may go; I want none of your help for body or soul."

For a moment, Warton is too shocked to reply, but he recovers and warns Marsden of his "terrible danger," "fearful precipice," and a plunge into an "eternity of woe." He even favors the dying man with one of his favorite phrases: "O think, whilst God spares you time to think, think what it is to die, and *he* your enemy!" Surprisingly, Marsden does not warm to these comforting words. "None of your preaching, away with it! You would be kind to me, you say; be gone then! That is the only kindness for which I will thank you. Go to those who will listen. . . ." Warton responds valiantly to this challenge. He speaks lovingly of fire and brimstone, gnawing worms, stinging scorpions, and furious devils "exulting in the torments which they will inflict upon you." This impassioned oration has a tremendous effect—on Warton himself who bursts into tears at the beauty of his words. Marsden? "Have done with your whining and your jibber-jabber. I hate all your trumpery." No such ingratitude can deter the doctor of divinity once he is well launched into his mission, however. He continues to barrage the dying man with visions of the judgment that God will surely bring against him and the horrible suffering that will follow. Warton works diligently to "make him condemn himself out of his own mouth" a technique that is "generally product in the end."

Warton's account of his word barrage against the dying man goes on page after bruising page. Marsden never gives in, so Warton eventually turns away "slowly and reluctantly from the sickbed." Still persistent, he confronts the wife and daughter, doing his best to bully them into awakening the fear of God's retribution in the dying man. He reports partial success with this strategy because, after a while, "Mrs. Marsden trembled exceedingly." Continuing to give unstintingly of himself, Warton returns to belabor the dying man and his family again until the very moment of his death ("He expired with a single but a terrible groan!"). Warton uses this occasion to fall on his knees and ask grace "for ourselves, that we may live well, and die happily."

Warton offered testimonies such as these to posterity, firm in the conviction that his moral claims justified any strategem one found necessary to employ in the deathbed scene. It was proper to wear the dying person down with long, convoluted, and impassioned argument. It was proper to shame, threaten, and condemn. It was proper to ignore the dying person's or family's own ideas, values, experiences, and needs— what could these matter when compared with the "dreadful spectacle" of eternal torment? Although many of the other dying people visited by Warton also resisted his advances, he never seemed to pause for once and wonder, "maybe this person's right; maybe I should respect his or her own wishes."

Warton's example may appear extreme, but he is not the only person who has been armed with the belief that he or she possesses the right, and the obligation to change other people's lives as they lay dying. He is valuable to us today as the protagonist of a cautionary tale—to what excesses moral arrogance can lend itself. A person as steadfastly locked inside his own beliefs as Warton would not find welcome in a hospice organization or any other program devoted to care of dying people and their families.

We will see in a moment that religion has no monopoly on the claim for ownership of the deathbed scene. Furthermore, the construction of the deathbed scene as a crucible for moral values does not necessarily lead to the grotesque kind of behavior we have sampled from Warton. The ministers, priests, and rabbis of my acquaintance would be among the first to reject this approach. A recent small sample interview study by Schneider (1990) has found a high degree of self-reported religiosity among women who provide care for terminally ill people through hospice organizations. Although these women frequently used prayer as a means of seeking strength for their own continued caregiving efforts, they did not introduce prayer or other religious practices to their interactions with patients and family members. Occasionally a patient or family member felt moved to pray together, and the hospice caregiver would participate. In strong contrast to Warton's invasive and bullying approach, these caregivers were scrupulously careful in refraining from imposing their religious beliefs and practices on the people in their care. This pattern accords well with the hospice philosophy of helping people to preserve their own values and life-style to the fullest extent possible rather than targeting the deathbed scene as the proving ground for any outsider's moral (or ego) agenda.

Professional, Bureaucratic, and Legalistic Claims

Ownership of the deathbed scene has been passing from the moralist to the professional and the bureaucrat. Unlike Warton, today's "proprietors" seldom lecture or proselytze. They just "run the show," and hope to do so as smoothly and efficiently as possible. Their practices are supported at certain points by law, more often by hospital regulations, and even more commonly by "standard operating procedure": this is how we do things around here. The social psychology of the deathbed scene has somewhat less to do with shared cultural values and techniques of persuasion, and somewhat more to do with principles of organizational communication and behavior. The individual psychology has shifted from the personality and motivation of the caregiver to the ability to cope with time-sensitive situations and frequently conflicting demands.

Consider one common behavioral sequence: A nurse enters the hospital room of a terminally ill patient and proceeds to read all the machines before even looking at the patient's face. Does this mean that this nurse values technology and bureaucracy more than people? Does it perhaps also mean that this nurse has deep emotional conflicts about relating to dying people? Probably not. People who relate more to machines than to people and who are unable to care for those in great need usually are not attracted to bedside nursing. It is far more likely that this behavioral sequence is but one of many in which the nurse must cope with situational and institutional demands whether or not these suit his or her personality. The priorities and pressures of the health care system impose themselves on almost everything the nurse does. Individual differences remain important, of course. Some nurses "vote with their feet" by abandoning their careers because they experience too much stress or find themselves too often in conflict with the standard operating procedure. We would often be far wide of the mark if we interpreted the behavior or nurses (and others) in the deathbed scene in terms of their individual motivation and personality dynamics when, in fact, they are responding to an intensive "field force" of organizational and physical pressures.

Here are a few further examples of the ways in which professional, bureaucratic, and legalistic claims influence the contemporary deathbed scene.

Workable Dead

A paramedic recounts some of his recent experiences.

. . . a suicide in Sun City. He was about 73 years old. He'd had a very extensive history of chronic obstructive pulmonary disease. He took a 44-magnum, stuck it in the roof of his mouth, and just splashed his entire skull all over the headboard and the wall of this home. The wife had called us. There was a fire department on the scene who had started cardiopulmonary respiration on the gentleman. They had not done any of the advanced skills because they didn't have paramedics. But they called us; we landed (our helicopter) in the street. We go in there. I mean: this guy is dead. I mean, he is big time dead. They had been doing CPR on him for 35–40 minutes and we had no choice at that point but to continue to put IVs in him, intubate what was left of his head, and all of the other things that we had to do.

This paramedic estimates that he had been in similar situations "hundreds, hundreds of times." Sometimes these were deathbed scenes in the literal sense; however, people also die on the highway, in restaurants, and many other places. Whatever the location, the paramedic may be required to start or continue futile interventions. Several of the paramedics we interviewed have described these people as "the workable dead." There is no doubt in the paramedic's mind that this person is dead. There is no fantasy about heroic measures, either at the site or at the hospital, that might restore life. Yet the paramedic is obliged to carry out procedures on "the workable dead" or risk serious legal repercussions. Many a person who has died at home in bed has become subject to postmortem interventions at the hands of paramedics who fervently wished they did not have to perform them.

"People panic, and they call us," another paramedic commented. "By the time we get there, they realize that their husband or grandmother or whatever is dead, and they are starting to adjust to it. The wife will scream, 'Don't do that to him.' But I have no choice about it."

This bizarre-sounding concept—"the workable dead"—represents an extreme interpretation of the situation in which some people pass from life to death. We often think of denial as a defensive strategy that is resorted to by individuals who are faced with overwhelming stress. Here is a form of denial, however, that is supported by law, regulations, and the standard operating procedures of sophisticated health care providers—and that requires the enactment of ritualistic behavior on a corpse. The fact that there is a reason for "working the dead" does not obscure its bizarre features nor its psychological effects on those who must perform and those who must witness the procedures.

And the reason? Choose between "don't let the slightest chance for recovery slip by"; "we have the equipment and personnel, so we have to use them"; and "prevent malpractice suits." All these influences operate to prevent or sharply reduce the exercise of good judgment by the people who are actually on the scene. Laws and regulations are tailored for the general pattern of human behavior: but we die as individuals in unique situations. Whenever a general rule gains priority over informed judgment within the situation, there the dying person and his or her companions lose a significant degree of freedom.

Code Blue

This chapter opened with an excerpt from a vivid description of a medical team's attempt to save the life of a dying man. Goodwin and Goodwin (1985) portray the "code blue" scene as it really is: not a cool, orderly demonstration of medical science but a noisy scramble in which a crowded roomful of people seem to be engaged in violent assault on a defenseless victim. This type of scene is both more and less distressing than the paramedic's encounter with the workable dead. Family members or passersby may be disturbed by the sight of paramedics carrying out procedures in full view. The measures taken by physicians and nurses after cardiac or respiratory arrest may be even more invasive and violent, but there is no audience of laypeople to be traumatized.

There is irony here. For many years, hospitals were feared as places in which it was all too easy to die. Today, and especially in major medical centers, it can be very difficult to die. The deathbed scene is becoming an option that must be exercised in advance. The living will came into existence as an instrument for avoiding aggressive and invasive interventions that have little likelihood of prolonging sentient and meaningful life (Scofield, 1989). Some physicians and ethicists now advocate that we devise advance directives that are more specific than the living will and therefore might improve the likelihood of the individual's wishes being respected at the critical time. For example, a physician might order insertion of a feeding tube even though the patient has completed a living will document. Providing water and nutrition to a dying person is regarded by some health care providers as an attempt to prolong life; others regard it instead as a way of making the final days more comfortable. Because of such ambiguities, a person may not experience the deathbed scene that had been envisioned, but, instead, become embedded in a prolonged life-support operation. Furthermore, advance directives may be overlooked entirely in the haste of the moment and with new people on the scene.

What is the psychology of crisis intervention here? Why do physicians, nurses, and technicians rush to perform emergency resuscitation procedures? Why is a person deprived of the comfort and serenity that seems to be provided by a traditional companionate deathbed scene? We do not have an adequate answer to these questions, but I would suggest systematic attention to the following components of the situation:

1. *Excitement of crisis.* Emergency room personnel and paramedics often speak of the "high" or "rush" they feel when called on to exercise their skills in life-or-death situations. This direct psychophysiological reward—a sense of being intensely alive and challenged—may help them to continue with an otherwise stressful occupation. Some health care rofessionals much prefer routine work. Some, however, become "hooked on crisis." They are not necessarily indifferent to the outcomes of their efforts, but the intensity and excitement of all-out intervention can become an overriding factor.

2. *Element of suspense.* Will this person live or die? The question may be indeterminate for a brief and eventful period of time. Mere spectators become engrossed in observing a sporting event or a detective film because the outcome is not known in advance. How much more involved we become when we ourselves are active participants, and the

suspense centers around the life or death of an actual person who is here in our midst. The fact that a person sometimes *is* brought back from the brink of death establishes a pattern of anticipated reinforcements that is highly resistant to extinction. Did this patient die despite our best efforts? Have all emergency resuscitation efforts failed in the past few weeks? These negative outcomes will not stand in the way of response to the next code. The emergency response team knows that some people have been saved and others will be saved: No succession of negative outcomes is likely to undermine the staff's aperiodic reinforcement schedule.

3. *The wrong place.* The hospital is not regarded as an appropriate location for a deathbed scene. Technology and economy have both dictated that hospital stays should be brief. Emphasis should be given to assessment and treatment procedures that qualify under the prevailing cost guidelines. The modern hospital is no place for a person to be. It is a place of passage, more comparable with an airport terminal than a home. With a few exceptions, the hospital is not hospitable to any scenes (and those exceptions are largely under the control of the hospital itself). Staff is apt to feel either roleless or in role conflict if a family bedside scene develops. A deathbed scene just does not compute in the elaborate system of authorized services and fees.

Additionally, it should be acknowledged that some people who are the subjects of resuscitation efforts would not have had anything resembling a deathbed scene even if these efforts had been withheld. For example, a person might be recovering from a surgical procedure, but then suffer an unexpected cardiac arrest. Even more unexpectedly, a code-blue situation might arise while a person is undergoing routine diagnostic testing. In situations such as these, there may have been no basis for assuming the person's life was in imminent danger. There was no reason for the family to draw together around the bedside. Without emergency interventions, the person would have died immediately from a sudden collapse of vital functions. The intervention may or may not succeed, but, in either event, it was not the intervention but the sudden onset that deprived the individual and his or her family of the opportunity for a time together.

Attenuated Life, Attenuated Death

The paramedic's encounter with "the workable dead" can occur any place in the community; the code-blue emergency procedure is enacted within a hospital room. In both instances, strenuous interventions are central to the scene. There is seldom time or opportunity for anything resembling a traditional deathbed scene. Many other people die "sceneless," however, although there has been an abundance of time and opportunity for human interactions and a final leave taking. The specific circumstances differ appreciably, but a common element is the attenuation of both life and death. The person is seen as being markedly impaired and in a nonreversible situation. The confused old woman in the nursing home will never again be young and vital. It is just a matter of when she will finally draw her last breath. The young man who left home on his motorcycle has been gone for weeks; it is only his body that receives the benefits of the respirator and the intravenous feeding.

There are three obvious reasons for the fact that most people in such situations do not have deathbed scenes: (a) they are most often placed in a hospital or custodial care facility rather than kept at home; (b) their actual or perceived inability to communicate tends to reduce the inclination of other people to interact with them; and (c) their plight could continue for an indeterminate period.

The geriatric patients who were classified as exhibiting "low-level behavior syndromes" have had millions of counterparts throughout the nation during the succeeding years. An institutionalized aged person may be deprived of the opportunity for a deathbed scene even if he or she is not unresponsive or confused. All too many reside in facilities whose staff has little training, time, or incentive for meeting the psychological and spiritual needs of the residents. The inadequate patterns of resident-resident, resident-staff, and resident-visitor communication do not provide a foundation for developing any meaningful scenes including the final scene of life.[3] There are more exceptions to this rule today, thanks to an influx of enlightened directors and staff and to a greater awareness of the needs of dying people. Nevertheless, each day many old men and women slip away without a companion at their bedsides.

Some people are maintained on life-support systems for a relatively short period at some point in their treatment. They recover, fully or partially, and go on with their lives. It is not accurate, then, to equate intensive life-support procedures with a hopeless "persistent vegetative state" (the term in most common usage for an individual whose vital functions are maintained but who has no apparent potential for recovery). Deathbed scenes appear to be rare for those who die after a period of intensive life support. It is more typical for the person's death to be discovered during a routine visit by a nurse or technician. For other people, it is more a question of medical judgment and discretion: a nonresponsive patient is certified as dead this morning, a decision that could have been made yesterday or postponed until tomorrow.

There is a greater opportunity for a deathbed scene when a decision has been made to withdraw or forego life-support procedures. The outcome is not always as expected, however. This can be illustrated through two young women and their families whose tragedies attracted national attention, influenced public opinion, and came under judicial review. Karen Ann Quinlan did not recover consciousness after she lapsed into a drug-induced coma (a preliminary diagnosis that was later disputed and never fully resolved). Her parents maintained hope for recovery for nearly half a year, although the young woman had suffered severe brain damage and wasted away to about 60 pounds. Eventually they accepted the counsel of a priest who declared that it is not morally necessary to employ extraordinary means to prolong life.

At this point, the Quinlans were psychologically prepared to take leave of their (adopted) daughter. They had absorbed the shock of her sudden incapacitation, drawn support from their religious faith, and started the preparatory process known as anticipatory grief (Rando, 1989). The Quinlans asked the physicians to turn off the respirator. Instead of an interminable period of attenuated life–attentuated death, there could now be a time-limited, decisive ending. The Quinlans could be with Karen Ann as she slipped away and then fully grieve her death. Their request was denied, however. This refusal was based on the observation that Karen Ann was not "brain dead" (Kastenbaum, 1991). There was still some electrical activity that could be detected through electroencephalogram tracings, although this activity was very weak. She was described as existing in a persistent vegetative state (and, for the first time, this term was introduced to the general public). The Quinlans then asked the courts to override the physicians' judgment and in doing so invoked an argument based on religious freedom. The court decided that medical knowledge and opinion should prevail. And so, Karen Ann remained on the life-support system and the Quinlans were faced with a continuation of their own stressful situation.

Who owned the deathbed scene in this instance?

- The person whose own life and death was at issue could not make her own claim because of severe incapacitation.
- The family had brought its claim forward, only to be rejected by two sets of authorities: the medical and the legal establishments.
- Freedom of religious expression had also been rejected as a decisive claim, although this right is considered basic to the American way of life.
- Although nurses provide most of the services and carry out most of the interactions with total care patients, there is no evidence that

the experiences, thoughts, feelings, and opinions of the nurses were even given a hearing.

In this landmark case the ownership of the deathbed scene had been determined at two levels. The physician seemed to be confirmed as the rightful owner because of (assumed) superior knowledge. The judge, however, emerged as representing an even more basic power: It was the court that decided in favor of the physician. Less visible but not less active behind the scenes was the hospital administration. I consider the hospital administration and the health care system to have been the real victors at this point. All theory aside, the potential deathbed scene was a small part of the total sociophysical environment that comprised the hospital. The court decision had the effect of affirming a variation on the right of the landlord. When admitted to a hospital, a person should abide by the prevailing laws and regulations of the realm. Health care administrators (and their lawyers) around the nation could breathe a little easier: Their prevailing policies seem to have been supported in this first court test.

This conclusion, however, was not to remain conclusive. An appeal was made to the New Jersey Supreme Court. This time, the judiciary found a different basis for decision. It was no longer the question of whether or not some flickering signs of life remained. The critical question was whether or not Karen Ann had a reasonable chance of regaining consciousness. The respirator could be removed, with court approval, if physicians agreed that the young woman could not recover consciousness. This was not the only change, however. More than a year after she lapsed into coma, Karen Ann was removed from the respirator. Now, finally, there could be a true ending, a final being-with the lost young woman, and the belated opportunity for the Quinlans to move on with their own lives. Everybody's assumption was proved wrong: Karen Ann did not die. Although she remained as unresponsive and incapacitated as ever, her vital functions continued after the respirator was removed. There was no deathbed scene, no closure. Transferred to a skilled nursing home, Karen Ann remained in a vegetative state for more than 10 years until succumbing to pneumonia (June 11, 1985). Both her life and her death had become so attenuated over so long a period that the final cessation passed virtually without notice.

Many other people have been trapped in persistent vegetative states since the Quinlans' ordeal began. Their stories have had various conclusions, but have frequently generated questions about ownership of the deathbed scene and complications in the grieving-mourning process. We will consider only the recent case of Nancy Cruzan. Victim of an automobile accident on January 11, 1983, this young woman had been attached to a life-support system for almost 8 years. Physicians were in agreement that she would never recover consciousness and, as with Karen Ann, Nancy had also wasted away and developed contractures. The family asked to have her feeding tube removed; the request was denied. For the first time, the United States Supreme Court accepted the challenge of ruling on a right-to-die situation. By the closest of margins (5–4), the court rejected the family's appeal to override the opposition of the local hospital authorities and the state of Missouri. As in previous court rulings, sympathy was expressed for the family members. The court held, however, that there was not sufficient evidence that the young woman had ever expressed her wishes regarding termination of life-support efforts. The overall decision confirmed the validity of advance directives such as the living will but at the same time rejected the argument that others knew what Nancy Cruzan would have wanted done.

Again, a court decision did not result in the most expectable outcome. A local probate judge decided that there had been enough information brought forward to indicate that family and friends knew what Nancy Cruzan would have herself chosen in this circumstance. He gave permission for removal of the feeding tube. Attorneys for the state of Missouri chose not to contest this decision. Others did protest, however. A throng of protesters, not identified by the media, entered public areas of the Missouri Rehabilitation Center to demand that the feeding tube be reinstated. Some kneeled and prayed; others blocked a fire exit stairwell and were arrested. The philosophy of the protesters was not clearly articulated through media reports including television coverage. Nevertheless, it was apparent that they were acting on religious convictions and regarded the proceedings as an immoral assault on the young woman and the deprivation of her right to live. Nancy Cruzan did die a few days after the feeding tube had been removed. Family members and friends reportedly were in attendance with her until the end.

Changing Perceptions of Deathbed Scene

The ordeals of the Quinlans, the Cruzans, and many other families have had a growing influence on both the reality and the image of the deathbed scene. The psychology of the deathbed scene is in a transitional state at present. Among the obvious factors involved are the following:

1. Increasing awareness that one's self or loved ones might be caught in a situation in which critical life-or-death decisions must be made.

2. Increasing awareness of the end phase of life in general, a topic from which most people have shielded themselves.

3. Increasing interest in learning more about the available options to make advance decisions (request for living wills material escalated greatly after the Supreme Court's Cruzan decision).

4. Increasing communication among family members, friends, and health care professionals.

5. Intensified but varying interpretations of the psychological status of the person who is in either a comatose or a persistent vegetative state. For example, a person without experience in critical medical situations might be horrified by seeing a patient connected to a respirator, an intravenous tree, and a feeding tube. Gaspings, tremblings, and other behaviors might be interpreted as signs of suffering, and the entire scene as one of indignity, inhumanity, and humiliation. By contrast, an experienced critical care nurse might judge that the patient is actually experiencing little or no discomfort. There is some room for differing opinions, so the observer's frame of reference contributes much to the interpretation of the patient's psychological status (whether on a life-support system or not).

6. Pursuing a series of negotiations and partnerships among all the people and special interests who contest for ownership of the deathbed scene. I have never met anybody who is on the side of pain, suffering, or extended vegetative existence. Situations have placed some people at odds with each other who would have preferred to reach common cause and be of mutual assistance. We are just starting to see productive attempts to bridge the gaps between the frameworks and interests of hospice administrators, attorneys, physicians, nurses, families, clergy, and public advocates. At least some of the potential conflicts over ownership of the deathbed scene may be avoided through enlightened communication.

We do not want to overestimate the prevalence of heightened awareness, communication, and decision making. Many people remain outside the circle. Furthermore, this increased attention to the right-to-die situation has not necessarily led to careful thought about deathbed scenes in general. There is a discernible movement, however, toward integrating the thought of the deathbed scene into our system of values, beliefs, and prospects. It is not likely that profound changes will occur swiftly and easily in our perceptions of the deathbed scene. More probable is an extended period in which as individuals and as a society we experiment with the idea of our death and our selves.

ANTICIPATED VERSUS ACTUAL DEATHBED SCENES

We can offer some limited information on the present relationship between deathbed scenes as rehearsed in the mind and as actually experienced. Students of two university courses focusing on death were asked to write detailed descriptions of their own deathbed scenes (Kastenbaum & Normand, 1990). They were instructed to envision this scene as it was *most likely* to occur. Respondents were invited to think of this scene as it might be filmed for a movie of their lives, thereby encouraging enough detail to guide the director, actors, and cameraperson.

After describing this scene, the respondents were asked to make any one change that would result in a happier scenario. Next, they were asked to alter the scene again by making one change that would result in a more distressing scenario. "Happier" and "more distressing" were both to be defined by their own thoughts, feelings, and values.

We found that most of these college students located their deathbed scenes in old age or very old age (more than 100 years). In fact, "old age" was given as the commonest cause of death, followed by accidents. The typical respondent expected to die at home, although it was not uncommon to anticipate death in a hospital or in transit. Almost everybody (96%) expected to be alert, lucid, and aware of their imminent death. Except for those who expected to die in motor vehicle accidents, the respondents almost invariably expected to be surrounded by accepting, supporting, even cheerful loved ones. About one person in five specified that the deathbed scene would occur within the context of a large family reunion. Family members were the people most frequently mentioned as being on the scene; women were much more likely to mention the presence of friends than were men.

What about the dying process itself? Almost all respondents expected to die within a few minutes, hours, or days. Only one person described having experienced several months of coping with a specific illness (cancer). The dying process was not only brief, it was also almost completely free of distress. Very few expected to have pain or other symptoms. Four out of five respondents did not report any type of distress as part of their deathbed scenes, and only 6% expected to experience pain. Nausea and diarrhea or constipation were never mentioned in the total sample. (Male respondents never mentioned bleeding, loss of consciousness, numbness, head throbbing, or weakness; these symptoms were mentioned occasionally by female respondents.)

The anticipated deathbed scenes were offered in more detail by the female respondents. The scenes reported by the male respondents tended to be more generalized and less attentive to physical surroundings such as furnishings, music, time of day, and weather (spring and sunshine were the conditions most often specified by the women). Overall, deathbed scenes were portrayed in more personal and vivid ways by the typical female respondent, but the genders did not differ in most substantive respects.

It is interesting to note what possible events were *not* mentioned. There were very few deathbed scenes in which last words or parting gifts were exchanged. Life reviews on the deathbed, for all their popularity in tradition, folklore, and film, were seldom mentioned. References to an afterlife were also rare. (Most respondents separately reported having a belief in afterlife, but, for reasons unknown, few integrated this belief into the specifics of their deathbed scenes.) Furthermore, most respondents did not mention having any thoughts regarding other people as they were dying, and many did not report on their own emotional state.

About one person in six expected to die in an accident. These accidents were seen as happening in the near future, often within the next few months. Like those who died in old age, death by accident was expected to be quick and without pain or other symptoms; furthermore, they also expected themselves to be alert and aware of their situations.

What about their self-revised deathbed scenes, for the better and the worse? The respondents found it much easier to create a more disturbing scenario. The commonest additions were pain, time, and being alone. It was evident that the respondents were well aware of the possibilities they had rejected while preparing their original deathbed scene descriptions. Although respondents could always think of a more distressing deathbed scene, they could not always think of one that was more comforting or satisfying than the original. The most popular addition was the presence of a particular person; also mentioned was the sharing of personal feelings with another person, and the further reduction of the time it would take to die. The few who had previously seen themselves as dying in a hospital now took advantage of the revision opportunity to relocate themselves to their home. Either as part of their revised deathbed scenes or as comments made afterward, many said that they could not really improve on the first version because "I guess I imagined it as I wanted it to be—even though I was supposed to imagine it as it would be."

The results of this small study suggest that an interest in death-related topics does not necessarily mean that a person is ready to think about his or her own personal relationship to death on a reality level. The students included a number of active health care professionals as well as others who were preparing themselves for human service careers. Basically, most of them "knew better" but felt the need to shield themselves from the more disturbing possibilities inherent in a deathbed scene. I doubt that a more realistic set of descriptions would be created by samples drawn from the general population, although this possibility has not yet been tested.

Direct studies of dying people and their experiences differ markedly from the anticipated deathbed scenes that have been summarized here (e.g., Levy, 1987–1988; Mor, Greer, & Kastenbaum, 1988). Dying people do experience a variety of symptoms including some that were rarely if ever mentioned by the students. Thanks mostly to the hospice movement, there have been significant advances in pain relief and other types of symptom control. The fact remains, however, that the dying person is often exhausted after a long struggle with illness and disability, and may have to contend with a variety of other problems.

College students have difficulty integrating these facts into their own life-and-death expectations. Typically, they "forget" that the dying person's body is no longer a pleasure machine. This tendency is often revealed when discussion turns to the last days of one's life (apart from the deathbed scene assignment). Young men, in particular, may boost their spirits by speaking of sexual adventures; it is not unusual for both men and women to imagine that they will be able to do things they have not had the opportunity to do before (e.g., sail a yacht, hike the Grand Canyon). While spinning out these scenarios, they express a kind of euphoria and innocence that is difficult to attain without denying the realities of debilitating illness. Are college students alone in this evasion? Probably not. Fantasies about "healthy dying" (Kastenbaum, 1979) have floated above the difficult realities of terminal care ever since the emergence of the death awareness and hospice movements.

These fantasies go far beyond the basic goals and objectives of people who are knowledgeable in the care of dying patients. At an extreme, enthusiasts seem to believe that dying is somehow more pleasurable, exciting, or meaningful than our days of health and well-being. Some people have also melded reports of NDEs into this belief. A person who has recovered from a life-threatening condition might report having had an experience of transcendence, serenity, and mystical enlightenment. Uncritical thought fails to distinguish this transient and distinctive experience from the day-by-day experiences of a person whose body is slowly but surely failing. Expectations for the deathbed scene may ignore most of the realities in favor of a moral or mystical outcome that even our friend Dr. Warton might consider unlikely. Despite his personal agenda and dogged insensitivity, Warton did spend time with dying people and knew very well that angelic choirs were in short supply.

We will have an opportunity to consider the practical significance of expectations now as we turn to several types of deathbed scenes that have come to my attention.[4]

SOME TYPES OF DEATHBED SCENES AND THEIR IMPLICATIONS

I will not attempt to offer either a comprehensive catalog of deathbed scenes nor to specify their prevalence. Such an effort would be premature and perhaps even stultifying. "Types," "stages," and similar organizational devices too often distract us from the challenges of unique people in unique circumstances. Instead, I hope simply to illustrate some of the many situations that develop around the deathbed scene in a way that might be useful to those who are interested in making their own further observations.

Red Towel Deaths: Anxiety Crescendo

Think of a cohesive family that is attempting to cope with the impending loss of one of its members. It is a multigenerational family that has managed to stay close despite competing and distracting responsibilities. Now the patriarch is dying. He is nearly 80, but was active and vigorous until felled by recently discovered cancer. There has been time for the family to adjust somewhat to the prospect of losing him. Most of their energies, however, are being devoted to making him as comfortable as possible for the time that is remaining. One of his daughters had heard about hospice care. After a family conference with the physician, it was decided to seek the help of a local hospice organization with the objective of helping him to end his life at home and without unnecessary medical procedures.

How are they doing? On the surface, the family is coping well with this challenge, supported by visits from the hospice nurse and a volunteer. Both the nurse and the volunteer, however, detect an escalation of tension within the family. "They're going, each of them, into their own separate little shells," observes the volunteer. "I don't know why; I can't see anything that's happened to upset them, anything that wasn't expected." One day the nurse receives a call from one of the primary caregivers, the older daughter. It is an unusual contact because the daughter does not seem her usual well-centered self and does not seem to have a compelling reason for making this call. Visiting the home later that day, the nurse wonders aloud if something is troubling the daughter. After a momentary, "No, I'm just a little tired," the daughter becomes tearful and agitated. Yes, she and the whole family are worried sick. About what? "About Dad . . . bleeding out."

It turns out that one of the family members had been told by a friend of a scene that she had been told about: a man dying in the hospital with blood just pouring out of his nose and mouth. The family now feared that the same might happen with Dad. Until this time, the family had kept its anxiety under control through its caregiving activities and confidence in the hospice, but also through its expectation that the final scene would be peaceful and dignified. Now it appeared, however, that every member of the family was tormented by the vision of Dad hemorrhaging and suffering. Nobody wanted to dwell on this possibility, yet it could not be dismissed. This fear had not only became a personal burden to each person but also made communication more difficult because of the tacit agreement that this terrible scenario should not be discussed.

The hospice nurse is in a position to offer information as well as emotional support. She assures the daughter that terminal bleeding is very unlikely, given her father's condition and the care he is receiving. Uncontrolled bleeding is even more unlikely. There are occasional "bleed outs," but in her own several years of hospice experience, the nurse has never seen one. The daughter relaxes. The family relaxes. Attention can once again be given to Dad as he is rather than as what might happen to him and to mutual support among family members. His wife, both daughters, and a son-in-law are present as he slips from consciousness into coma and beyond over a period of hours. There is no bleeding.

"I brought a red towel with me, though, just in case," the nurse later reports. Red towel? "To absorb the blood without showing it by changing color . . . to make the last scene less stressful for the family."

Families and the dying persons themselves can have a variety of fears about the deathbed scene. Bleeding out is the fear that has been commonest in the cases I have studied, but other fears might be commoner in other samples. From a practical standpoint, it is advisable to provide opportunities for people to express whatever fears, doubts, and worries they might have about the deathbed scene. Sometimes, as with the "red towel" scenario, it is possible to provide informed reassurance. In other circumstances, the fears might lead to identification of certain actions that should be taken or avoided. In any event, open communication will tend to reduce anxieties that could interfere with the relationship between the caregiver and dying person.

Fire Dreams: Suffering and Terror

Hospice doctors and nurses often have state-of-the-art skills in providing relief for pain and other symptoms. This is accomplished in part by contributing to a socioemotional climate of security and trust. It is not unusual for pain control to be a major priority. Furthermore, it may be necessary to try several methods of control before adequate relief is achieved. What *is* unusual—and extremely stressful—is to discover that nothing works.

A woman in her late 40s learns that she has cancer of the breast. After diagnostic studies and treatment efforts it becomes clear that the disease cannot be halted. She may have only a few months. Experiencing great pain, she and her husband call on the services of a hospice. The usual medications seems to have no effect. Dosage is increased. Dosage is increased again. Other methods are tried. The woman continues to be wracked by pain. There is also a sense of terror associated with her suffering. Hospice continues its efforts. Hypnosis. Guided imagery. Relaxation exercises. Her suffering continues unabated.

As far as hospice staff can determine, the patient's home situation is strong and supportive. Her (second) husband is devoted to her and very willingly takes time from his business activities to look after her. She is a practicing Catholic of strong faith, and together they have served as foster parents for an abused child. Her memories of childhood are painful: She herself had been abused by her alcoholic father while raised as a strict Catholic by her mother. Basically, she does not like to speak of her troubled life before finding happiness with her second husband.

Month after painful month goes by. She holds on to life although the pain is relentless. An entire year passes—an unusually long period for a hospice patient. Still trying to find a way to ease her pain, the hospice staff now wonders if she has "a need to suffer . . . the pain is hard to explain."

And now the dreams begin. It is a persistent, repetitive dream. There is a fire, and she's running, running, trying to get away. Her husband hears her screaming at night, presumably during these dreams. She awakens in exhausted terror. More than once she reports, "it's like the fires of hell. I will be punished. I am being punished." The fire dreams become more frequent and intense. Meanwhile, she is feeling much weaker. "Am I dying? What's happening? Am I dying?"

Although the hospice team includes one chaplain and has access to others, it happens that another clergyman becomes a visitor to the home. Apparently, he is a good listener and a strong personality. She tells him of her dreams—yes, there had been a real fire incident in her childhood, and somebody had died, but that was not the fire in her dreams. More and more, she feels that these are the flames of retribution. She must have been a bad person, going back many years ago; now she is facing the punishment.

After disclosing her fears to the pastor, she experiences a different kind of dream. Three angels appear at her bedside. The first angel calls her by name and tells her, "It's going to be OK." The second angel adds: "You're going to see somebody soon." The third angel concludes the contact by declaring: "You're not going to have any more pain. You're not going to need any more pain medication." The next morning she wakes up relaxed and refreshed, for the first time in more than a year. Her husband brings the medications. She refuses them. "I don't need them any more." He insists. She insists. Then it becomes clear to her husband that she really does not have any pain. "The pain is over," she reports. "I'm going to have a great day."

The couple have two good days together. She is not only pain free, but also serene and relaxed. The tense and drained husband benefits much from this reprieve as well. A hospice nurse is with them when she dies: "After all that pain, she had one of the most peaceful deaths!" The hospice staff is still astounded by the sudden cessation of pain after "the mound of medications she had been taking."

This experience suggests that intense and unresolved problems of long duration may contribute to alarming visions of the deathbed scene. Did the little girl who was abused by her father so many years ago somehow blame herself, as some victims of abuse do? Did her subsequent divorce lead her to feel uneasy as a "good Catholic"? Did the theme of punishment help to make sense of being stricken with cancer when at last she had experienced happiness? Questions such as these cannot be answered definitively. It is clear enough, however, that psychological or spiritual problems make some of us vulnerable to suffering that is in excess of our physical conditions alone. It is also clear, as indicated by her experience with the pastoral visitor, that a mature interpretation of religion can have the power to overcome anxieties generated by immature interpretations.

Suicide: Death as Preventive Medicine

Earlier we described how W. B. E. and his wife and friends had cocreated a deathbed scene that was in harmony with their wishes. A key to this outcome was the fact that the dying man felt he had lived one hell of a life and was ready to take his leave. There are many other ways, however, in which people attempt to exercise control over their deathbed scene. Here are two examples of an approach that employs death itself as a form of preventive medicine.

L. V. was an unmarried nurse in her 30s. Her life had centered around her work and several close friendships. She had more than the usual knowledge of terminal illness and care. The idea of becoming a hospice nurse or director appealed to her, but she was very much involved in her current position in a hospital. This, however, is the way things had been. Now, incredibly, she was dying. With the help of friends she had been able to remain at home. By saving up her energies she could write letters, read, converse, and even continue working a little on a project she had started before her illness.

One day she asks her two best friends if they would do a couple of errands for her. These errands happen to be in different directions, and each will take at least an hour and a half. They return to find L. V. dead. She has somehow managed the very difficult feat of (a) acquiring a lethal supply of morphine and (b) rigging up the intravenous line to deliver the drug into her own veins. There was a note asking their forgiveness for this little trick. She wanted to quit before life became unbearable.

The friends experienced a very strong and very mixed response: surprise, sorrow, relief, anger. The anger was still there months later. "It was as if she didn't trust us." They had no difficulty in understanding why this strong-minded person would want to control her own destiny, especially because she knew better than most people about the probable future course of her illness and debility. They felt, however, that a bond of mutual trust had been broken when L. V. had not informed them of her plans. One did observe, though, that the "suicide machine" had been rigged with the outside possibility of rescue: She had used a hemalock device that would have made it possible to quickly shut off the flow of morphine had either friend returned earlier and noticed the setup. Many suicide attempts include an "escape hatch," enabling the individual to share a little of the responsibility with friends, family, or fate.

By contrast, J. J. did not conceal his suicidal intent. He told the visiting hospice nurse that he had his own way of treating his condition—and then produced a large handgun from beneath a pillow. Life was hardly worth living any more. They had already told him to stop smoking and drinking. What would they want to take away next? He was not going to keep lying around until he rusts out, and the doctors could keep their knives and pills for some other sucker. The nurse secured his agreement to speak with the hospice social worker about his suicidal intention, and, in the meantime, would he not like to feel a little better? The social worker responded promptly to her call. The nurse put the intervening time to good use and even persuaded J. J. to shave for the first time in weeks. He was looking more comfortable and relaxed by the time the social worker showed up.

After a brief conference with J. J. and his wife, the social worker left their home with the gun inside a plastic bag. The weapon would be held for him in a locked security box. J. J. had the receipt. Hospice had his promise that he would give them a chance to support the quality of life remaining to him. J. J.'s wife, who had hardly spoken during the whole visit, nodded approvingly to the social worker: "You're all right."

The next morning's hospice team meeting devoted considerable attention to J. J. and his wife. A little later they learned that he had killed himself with his other gun (most probably brought to him by his wife).

In both examples, the two people chose to select the exact time of death that would likely have occurred within a few weeks. Neither person was experiencing much pain at the time, and both had intimate companions for support; however, they thought to spare themselves from increasing dependency and helplessness. L. V. chose a mode of suicide that was consistent with her profession and also somewhat more characteristic of women, by contrast J. J. selected the "blast off" method that has long been more characteristic of male suicides. Officially, these deaths were similar in being suicides. The "floating off" morphine ending with its respiratory failure and the abrupt punctuation of a gunshot, however, could hardly be more different in their expressions of individual personality. Their actual deathbed scenes were prompted by expectations of the kind of death that would await them after a further period of discomfort and decline. Would they perhaps have died as peacefully as the fire dreamer if they had achieved her sense of trust and acceptance? This we will never know.

Selection of Moment: Loving Withdrawal

Here are two examples in which the dying person seems to select a "right time" to depart this life.

B. T. had been a widow for many years. She declined most offers of assistance from family members scattered around the nation. Before being afflicted by her final illness, B. T. seemed to be deriving most of her satisfaction from the ability to function independently and just as she chose. There were two good friends in the picture, and she maintained contacts with the family through telephone, correspondence, and occasional visitations (usually by coldfleeing relatives during the mild Arizona winters).

Now, at age 72, she found herself fighting a losing battle with cancer. She bore up well for a while and had some periods of relatively good health. As time went on, however, the treatments as well as the disease exhausted her. The two friends—women about her own age—did what they could to make things easier, such as running errands and transporting her for blood transfusions. Eventually the widely dispersed family members learned of the serious nature of her illness. B. T. held off as long as she could, but then accepted the offer of assistance from one of her nieces, Becky. The older woman recognized that she had become "a standoffish kind of person," and that she resented having to become dependent on anybody.

The decision to seek hospice care was made by B. T. herself. She could see that her condition was not improving and, putting various pieces of information together, judged that she did not have long to live. Her physician tried to dissuade her from this move. From his viewpoint, there were still more treatments that could be tried. B. T., however, had become more sophisticated about medical matters, and thought she was not being properly informed by her physician and that perhaps her physician had not kept himself properly informed about her condition either. A turning point was her observation that the nurses were having increasing difficulties with her frequently punctured veins, and the physician's unwillingness to admit or discuss this problem. "Mrs. B. T. was a fighter," the hospice nurse later recalled. She continued to look for treatment possibilities even after enrolling in the hospice program. She was also a realist, however, and, increasingly fatigued, decided against a possible trip to a "miracle clinic" in Mexico.

The most unusual development occurred in the relationship between B. T. and her niece. Becky was a spontaneous and high-spirited person, fond of pranks and teasing. The older woman had a serious, no-nonsense mien and a streak of compulsivity. "They should have driven each other crazy! But somehow they hit if off beautifully." Becky seemed immune to the dark clouds and frowning features that greeted her arrival and, by and by, B. T. found herself enjoying her niece's lively company. It was difficult to stay gloomy around Becky.

For nearly a month B. T. seemed to be participating in some of the most rewarding interactions of her life. She appeared to be "younger mentally" and not beyond the occasional prank herself. Nevertheless, life was becoming more and more difficult and her functioning ever more limited. There was not much pain to contend with, but she felt drained of energy. The hospice nurse recognized that "I-want-to-die" look.

With what seemed to be her last reserve of energy, B. T. thanked Becky for all that she had done and commanded her to go back to her own family ("They need you, too. Your life is with your own children"). Becky obeyed. A few hours after her departure, one of the older woman's friends contacted the hospice. The friend and a hospice volunteer by now well known to B. T. sat by her bedside, each holding one of her hands. B. T. remained conscious but silent, then sighed and expelled her last breath.

K. M. was a successful businessman who was also known for his community activities. Orphaned in childhood when both of his parents were killed in an automobile accident, he was especially responsive to the needs of children and could be counted on for contributions of time, energy, and money. After helping transport materials for a junior high school science fair, he experienced what felt like a flare-up of an old back injury. It was shocking to discover that he had cancer, and at an advanced stage. K. M. was not in the habit of paying much attention to aches and pains.

Passing through the gauntlet of diagnostic and treatment procedures, K. M. learned that his illness was terminal. He seemed to adjust to this grim prospect more readily than did his family, business partner, and many friends in the community. For a period there was division within the family, with the majority either urgently favoring continued treatment efforts or persisting in the belief that the doctors had made some kind of mistake. "We're all on the same page now—I think!" he told the hospice nurse. After another short stay in the hospital to stabilize his condition, K. M. returned home where family members were with him almost every hour of the day. The hospice nurse recalls that, "They were there for him, but for themselves, too. They were all jealous of their time with him. He meant so much to that family."

During the 3 weeks following his entry into a hospice program, K. M. participated in many interactions that could have fulfilled a scriptwriter's every need for a deathbed scene. His often abrasive and smart-alecky business partner broke down and cried. Grandchildren sat on his bed and presented him with their crayon drawings. Even a girlfriend from high school days (almost 40 years ago) showed up. There was time alone with his wife, each of his three children, and several others. Had he died during or after one of these interactions, the survivors would have had a coherent and meaningful deathbed scene to remember.

What actually happened was a little different. Rapidly tiring, K. M. also observed strain and tension on the part of others. He confided to the hospice volunteer that his family was becoming "frazzled" and neglecting their other needs. It was K. M. who suggested that he be placed in a respite care facility. "I love you all, but I just need to rest for a few days.

So do you." Reluctantly, the family agreed, but only with the provision that they could visit him and that he would come back home soon. Despite their hesitancy about having him leave their home and care for even a few days, the family immediately started to reorient itself toward some of its other pressing concerns (including an impending graduation). Satisfied that K. M. was comfortable in the respite care facility, his wife and a son allowed themselves to be shooed away for a while. He also asked a member of the respite care staff not to be disturbed for a while; he needed his sleep. That was his last communication. Apparently he died in his sleep within an hour or so after taking leave of his wife and son.

B. T. and K. M. had taken advantage of multiple opportunities to communicate with the people who were important to them. They did not have rushed, emergency farewells to make: Both had been in steady contact with family and friends. It seems likely that they did not feel a compelling need for a final interaction to convey messages or construct meaning. Possibly, some deaths require a "scene" more than others. Both of these people had, in effect, said their good-byes. They appreciated the loving care they had received and, in return, seemed to pick the right moment to leave.

Last-Minute Rally: One More Time at Bat

The last "type" of deathbed scene we will illustrate here is one that many others have noticed over the years. It is easier to describe than to explain.

In his youth, S. P. had a short career in professional baseball until felled by breaking pitches and his own resistance to taking advice. He had made a good living as a skilled construction worker, and liked nothing better than to demonstrate his talent and knowledge, especially in carpentry. His family had long since adjusted to the fact that he was "not much of a talker," although he could be an attentive listener if there was no televised sporting event as competition.

With the onset and development of his terminal illness, S. P. became sulky and difficult to live with. He made what seemed like constant demands for personal services and resented having his wife leave his bedside for any reason at all. Consequently, the family had to cope not only with the prospect of his death, but also with the tensions and unpleasantness of everyday life in the home. S. P.'s wife was not much of a talker either, but she understood that her husband's demanding behavior was an expression of his fear. She tried to assure him by her actions that she would not abandon him, but his fear-driven pressure was relentless.

By the time that hospice entered the scene, S. P.'s condition had deteriorated markedly. He was bedridden, haggard, tense, and minimally communicative. It was determined that he had been in pain for some time without telling anybody. After the hospice evaluation, S. P. was given new medications that relieved his pain and may have contributed to his somewhat more relaxed appearance. Nevertheless, he would respond to hospice personnel and volunteers with only monosyllabic utterances, and sometimes not even that. S. P.'s wife and a daughter-in-law received instruction and guidance in caregiving procedures from hospice and carried out these responsibilities in a proficient manner. The daughter-in-law apparently was the voice of the household and brought the family's anxieties and questions to the hospice staff. The family caregivers seemed to benefit most from knowing that they were not alone with this challenge and not remiss in their services.

S. P. had stopped complaining but had very nearly stopped communicating as well. There were times when he did not recognize family members. His mind was adrift. The medications were reviewed on the possibility that they were responsible for the decline in his mental state, but this conclusion did not appear justified. Apparently his longer and longer periods of sleep and drift would continue to lengthen until he was not there any more.

After several days of only minimal interactive response and very little intake of nourishment, S. P. was lying in a curled-up position with his face to the wall. On entering his room, S. P.'s wife at first wondered if he was still alive. Assuring herself that he was still drawing breath, she found herself saying: "Sunday's your birthday. Would you like a party?" She had not meant this as a sick joke; it was just a bizarre thought that popped into her mind and out of her mouth. No response, of course.

On her next visit to his bedside, however, she discovered her husband with his eyes open and searching. It was S. P. who started the conversation: "Bacon. Balloons. All the kids." And so the family decided that the next morning would be his birthday (moved up a day). The dying man remained alert and attentive to the proceedings. He proved able to take his small portion of bacon and eggs at the family table. After a rest he was again wheeled out to the dining room, which had been festooned with balloons, ribbons, and baseball memorabilia. Somebody had even fashioned a baseball medallion in the frosting of the birthday cake. He observed the comings and goings of two young grandchildren with special interest, one of whom was especially taken with the wheelchair. The candles were lit twice so each grandchild could take a turn in blowing them out.

S. P. was not a smiling sort of person and nobody observed him smiling on this occasion either. After some eating and drinking had been accomplished, he looked across the table at his wife and said simply, "That was good." She could not remember the last time she had heard a compliment from his lips. Again exhausted, S. P. was gently returned to his bed. He survived the night, called for his wife in the morning (she was there already), and died.

Known as "premortem clarity," this type of temporary recovery from withdrawal and confusion was observed several times in connections with our psychological autopsy studies and has also been reported by numerous physicians, nurses, and relatives. It would be speculative to explain these awakenings on either purely psychological or purely physiological grounds, nor can it be assumed that all instances have the same cause. It is probable, however, that heavy medication and a lack of opportunity for meaningful social interaction are both conditions that would work against premortem clarity. For S. P., his final scene can be thought of as occurring during the birthday party when his mind was again in focus and most of his family on hand. For some other people in similar situations, the deathbed scene is enacted while its principal player is mute and perhaps inattentive.

REVIEW AND PROSPECTUS

Deathbed scenes are narrative constructions that help us to preview or preserve mental representations of our most direct encounters with mortality. As mental representations (or symbolic structures), they are subject to all the influences that shape all of our expectations, memories, and interpersonal communications. Unlike most other expectations and memories, however, the deathbed scene takes us to the very limits of our knowledge and experience. I learned this from the first old man who I saw gazing into the distance and gesturing just before he died. I could see him but not what he saw.

On the behavioral and overt level, the deathbed scene can be described, analyzed, and even quantified should we choose to do so. The behavioral analysis of the deathbed scene can encompass the people, the place, and the sequence and timing of events including communications and other interactions. I believe that we can learn much of practical as well as conceptual value by attending both to the deathbed scene as an objective behavior setting and as a set of competing symbolic constructions.

It is the choice and the competition among symbolic constructions that I would like to emphasize at this point. Whoever is most persuasive in telling the story of the deathbed scene is also likely to be most successful in claiming ownership. We have seen that religious, medical, legal, and bureaucratic establishments have been among the major competitors. Psychological, poetic, and mythic versions can also be powerful and, at times, the most persuasive. There is a highly variable relationship between enfranchised and narrative power. Hospital administrators and their attorneys have a strong power base that lends strength to whatever vision of the deathbed scene they happen to endorse. The bureaucratic vision does not have to be especially insightful, comprehensive, or compelling—but it will be influential simply because it is the symbolic structure that has been erected by the "ruling class." By contrast, the pastoral visitor who listened so skillfully to the fire dreams had no enfranchised power. Yet he somehow helped this woman to relieve her own existing symbolic structure of its torment (painful death as punishment becoming angelic safe conduct).

I think we will continue to see a lively competition for the most persuasive interpretations of deathbed scenes. If we look closely, we will also see that these interpretations tend to justify courses of action that have been advocated or already taken. Agree with an aggressive physician that every last intervention must be attempted, and we increase the likelihood of ending up with a code-blue scene or reasonable facsimile. Agree with the Alaskan prospector that a life belongs to the person who has lived it, and we increase the likelihood of holding a drink in our hands while good old buddies end their relationship with a hearty final blast-off. Symbolic constructions and their fate in the marketplace of human communication are significant for their consequences as well as for their intrinsic substance and form.

We have also seen that our thoughts are tempted by both the muse of fantasy and the implacable bill collector of reality. College students and working health care professionals in good health often succumb to wishful thinking when confronted with the prospect of their own deathbed scenes. Many others have embraced the chimeric concept of healthy dying. People who have been active in the death awareness movement for many years have learned to recognize a type of enthusiastic recruit for whom dying and death provide an emotional rush, and the answer and compensation for all that has previously gone awry with their lives. Fortunately, many who jumped on the band or hearse wagon as an escapist adventure have since found other fads to enjoy. There are certainly many ambiguities and uncertainties as we move toward the deathbed scene, and many occasions that can be spiced and illuminated by imaginative thinking. There are times, however, when both the individual and society are better served by hard and resolute attention to reality.

On the positive side, as a society we seem to have overcome some of our reluctance to acknowledge the reality of the deathbed scene. It has become a less frequent standard operating procedure to ostracize and conceal the dying person, although this practice is still encountered in some nursing homes and hospitals. A perceptive and deepening dialogue on the nature of the deathbed scene has started to replace the anxious insistence that people leave the tidal pool of life without making a ripple.

Let us take two further thoughts with us as we move to other sectors of the psychology of death.

1. Although subject to external and unexpected influences, the deathbed scene takes much of its character from the long-term pattern of interactions between the dying person and others. The deathbed scene is worth attention as a special situation, but should not be regarded in isolation from the values, conflicts, and relationships of all the people involved.

2. We often relate both to the dying person as an individual and to the dying person as an advance version of ourselves. Through this person's experiences and through this person's final exit we may undergo a vicarious death—and one that is either reassuring or threatening. By comforting the actual dying person in his or her actual deathbed scene, we are also comforting the potential dying person within ourselves. In a sense, the dying person is a medium through which the vibrant life forces of hope, fear, faith, and doubt reach toward the unknown.

NOTES

1. You might enjoy reading this remarkable passage in its entirety. Taylor unrolls a 235-word discourse on the foibles and failures that characterize a single day in a person's life—all in one flowing and spicely cadenced sentence. The concluding phrase calls on us to "call ourselves to scrutiny every night when we compose ourselves to the little images of death." Reprint editions of this classic come and go. In a facsimile reprint of an 1819 edition by Arno Press (1977), the quoted material is found on pp. 46–47.

2. The example given here is found in Vol. 3. This case and several others are included in a chapter entitled "Obduracy"—a term that seems to describe Warton's bull-headed stubbornness as well as it does Marsden's determined resistance. A kindly librarian provided me with a photocopy of *Death-Bed Scenes*; I have not learned of any reprint edition.

3. Glaser and Strauss (1968) provided a valuable description of the communication patterns that accompany various "trajectories" of dying, although they did not focus on the deathbed scene itself. The number and variety of *lingering* trajectories has increased markedly since their study. Relatively few of these

people are served by hospice organizations with their emphasis on social support as well as symptom relief. Consequently, it is possible that even more people are dying without benefit of a companionate deathbed scene, despite the good work done by educators, hospice caregivers, and others.

4. Several of the cases summarized are drawn from a sample made available by the Hospice of the Valley (Phoenix metropolitan area). This is a retrospective study in which data collection has no influence on the care provided to the patients and their families. Several other cases are drawn from information made available by staff members from a variety of other hospice programs in the United States and Canada. I am grateful to all the individuals and programs that have been cooperating in this project, and impressed both by their high quality of professionalism and their devotion to the well-being of patients and families.

REFERENCES

Amato, J. A. (1985). *Death book: Terrors, consolations, contradictions and paradoxes.* Marshall, MN: Venti Amati.

Aries, P. (1981). *The hour of our death.* New York: Knopf.

Glaser, B. B., & Strauss, A. (1968). *Awareness of dying.* Chicago: Aldine Publishing.

Goodwin, J. S., & Goodwin, J. M. (1985). Second thoughts. *Journal of Chronic Diseases, 38,* 717-719.

Kastenbaum, R. (1979). "Healthy dying': A paradoxical question continues. *Journal of Social Issues, 35,* 185-206.

Kastenbaum, R. (1991). *Death, society, and human experience.* 4th edition. New York: Merrill.

Kastenbaum, R., & Normand, C. (1990). Deathbed scenes as imagined by the young and experienced by the old. *Death Studies, 14,* 201-217.

Kellehear, A., & Lewin, T. (1988-1989). Farewells by the dying: A sociological study. *Omega, Journal of Death and Dying, 19,* 275-292.

Leenaars, A. A. (1988). *Suicide notes.* New York: Human Services Press.

LeGoff, J. (1984). *The birth of purgatory.* Chicago: University of Chicago Press.

Levy, M. H. (1987-1988). Pain control research in the terminally ill. *Omega, Journal of Death and Dying, 18,* 265-280.

Moody, R. (1975). *Life after life.* Atlanta: Mockingbird Press.

Mor, V., Greer, D. S., & Kastenbaum, R. (1988). *The hospice experiment.* Baltimore: The Johns Hopkins University Press.

Rando, T. A. (1989). Anticipatory grief. In R. Kastenbaum & B. Kastenbaum (Eds.), *Encyclopedia of death* (pp. 12-15). Phoenix: Oryx Press.

Ring, K. (1980). *Life at death.* New York: Coward, McCann and Geoghegan.

Sacks, O. (1968). *Awakenings.* New York: Dutton.

Taylor, J. (1977). *The rules and exercises of holy dying.* New York: Arno Press. (Original work published 1651)

Warton, J. (1826). *Death-bed scenes* (3 Vols.). London: John Murray, Albemarle Street.

Weisman, A. D., & Kastenbaum, R. (1968). *The psychological autopsy: A study of the terminal phase of life.* New York: Behavioral Publications.

2

A World without Death?

Fear death?—to feel the fog in my throat,
The mist in my face . . .

—Robert Browning

But happiest beyond all comparison are those excellent
Struldbrugs, who being exempt from the universal calamity of
human nature, have their minds free and disengaged, without
the weight and depression of spirits caused by the continual
apprehension of death.

—Captain Lemuel Gulliver (Swift)

The woods decay, the woods decay and fall,
The vapours weep their burthern to the ground,
Man comes and tills the field and lies beneath,
And after many a summer dies the swan.
Me only cruel immortality
Consumes . . .

—Tithon (Tennyson)

Deathbed scenes mark one extreme of the human encounter with mortality. An invisible wave seems to pass swiftly across our companion. The
face that has displayed so many emotions is now fixed in an expression
that does not seem intended for the living. We press the hand we have
been holding; there is no response. Yes, there is a response. Our own inner
harbor of expectation, security, and illusion has been violated. This
feeling may be quelled immediately by an efficient "damage-control"

system, but we will never be quite the same once pierced by an intimate encounter with the death of another person. Perhaps the dying person and the companion both experience the same passing thought: "So—this is death!"

It may be different the next time we find ourselves at the life-death border. We have been through this before. We know that the transition is neither horrifying nor undignified. We have improved either our self-anesthetizing technique or our ability to integrate death into our view of life. Maybe a little of both.

This brief chapter takes us to another extreme position in the human encounter with mortality. We have already seen that coming to close quarters with death—in either actual or imagined deathbed scenes—often inspires us to evasive and compensatory inventions. What, then, if we indulged this need to avoid death? What if we presented our skittish minds with the grandest of gifts: *Here is a world without death—enjoy!* I have made this offer in several ways as part of research studies and learning exercises. Here are some of the findings that are of most relevance.

REPEAL OF DEATH SENTENCE

Purpose and Method

There have been three main purposes in my studies of "a world without death."

1. Clarify the significance of death in the structure of individual thought and sociocultural dynamics by supposing a world minus death
2. Establish a counterpoint to observations of human thought and behavior in which death is an immediate reality or prospect
3. Provide the opportunity for respondents to monitor and evaluate their own values and belief structures through this thought experiment

Respondents are given the following instructions:

Suppose that the world is just as we know it, with one exception: Death is no longer inevitable. Disease and aging have been conquered. Let us also suppose that air and water pollution have been much reduced through new technologies.

Take a few minutes to consider the implications and consequences. What will happen? How will people respond to this situation, individually and as a society?

How will the quality of life change?

Think first of the effects of the no-death scenario on the world at large. Write down the changes you think would be likely to happen.

Next think of how the no-death scenario would influence *your own* thoughts, feelings, wishes, needs, beliefs, and actions. Describe some of the major ways the no-death situation would be likely to influence you. (Kastenbaum, 1991)

Findings

The information summarized below is based on the responses of more than 600 men and women who attended conferences, workshops, or enrolled in courses focusing on death.[1] Women predominate in this set of samples.

The world at large did not improve with the repeal of the death sentence. Only 1 of 20 respondents portrayed the general consequences as prevailingly favorable. Most respondents (approaching 70%) did not find *any* positives. Let us start, however, with the some of the commonest positive general consequences of a world without death.

1. Society would be able to keep its wise and experienced people. ("We could have Gandhi's living example still with us." "Great minds could get even greater.")

2. Money would not be tied up in life insurance or wasted in funerals. ("People could use their money for life, not death." Similarly, "We wouldn't have to worry about cemeteries for all the new people dying. There are a lot better things to do with land.")

3. Societies could become more flexible and sensitive to each other and to their own subgroups because more people could learn more about alternative ways of life. ("We would all have time to learn Chinese, and the Chinese to learn English." "You could have a dozen different careers and really learn how the other guy lives.")

4. Religious institutions would have less social power (but see later discussion). ("Churches like to say they are here to save us. But there wouldn't be anything to save us from, except, I guess, ourselves." "Those hell and brimstone preachers would have to go back to selling used cars or something.")

5. Some career opportunities would improve. ("Sounds good to me. I'm a leisure studies major, and people would have lots of leisure!" "That should really help adult education. There'll be lots of time to study this and that, and that means new jobs for teachers.")

The most frequently mentioned negative general consequences of a world without death were the following:

1. Overcrowding and its effect on the quality of life. ("Full time turf wars." "Everybody'd get sick and tired of being jammed so close together." "People every place—it would be a zoo!")

2. Birth control would be enforced. ("There wouldn't be much room for the next generation." "You'd have to get a license to make babies." "It would be so depressing, not to see babies and little boys and girls all around.")

3. Discrimination, elitism, and power politics would become even more oppressive. This threat was often seen in relationship to the projections already described. ("Only people in power could have a little private space to call their own." "And who do you suppose would be approved to have children? The poor and powerless?")

4. Society would become overly conservative and lose its adaptability. ("There'd be more old people than anybody else; society would get stuck in its ways." "We'd be controlled by the past." "New people and new ideas wouldn't have much of a chance. It would all be 'Now, in my day, this is how we did it.'")

5. Economic structures and processes would change drastically, and mostly for the worst. ("There would be no more inheritance, because nobody would die." "Jack Benny wouldn't have had to take it with him—he wouldn't of had to go." "There wouldn't be life insurance companies to invest money in new construction." "I can't imagine what would happen to the idea of saving up money. Or of spending on impulse, either.")

6. Moral beliefs would be undermined, with destabilizing effects on major social institutions. Although some respondents considered that a decline in the influence of religion would be a positive development, others considered this to be extremely demoralizing. ("Society would be like a ship without a rudder, if it isn't already." "What would stop people from sinning all the time? Would people even think of sins as sins if there wasn't punishment after death?") Marriage was seen as an especially vulnerable institution. ("People would think, hey, what's the point of being married to just one person forever and ever. Everybody'd either screw around a lot with everybody else or maybe just get tired of it after a couple of thousand years and play video games instead.") The (arguable) deterrence value of capital punishment might be lost. ("I can see people—some of them—lining up for the electric chair. People might get tired of the mess they make of their lives, and try to get themselves killed, one way or another.")

There was no doubt about the prevailingly negative portrait of a world without death in its general or societal aspects. What about the personal side?

Again, the prospect of a world without death evoked many doubts and fears. The balance was tilted toward the negative but not as drastically. About four of five respondents did acknowledge the temptation of life released from its death sentence. Nevertheless, most concluded that they would be more distressed than pleased. Slightly more than half of the respondents spontaneously offered their own judgment against a world without death. Analysis of the remaining responses found some in which a clear balance could not be determined. Where a preference could be established based on content, nearly two thirds of the respondents expressed a balance of anxiety and disapproval.

The shift in perspective—from general to personal—seemed to be meaningful. Society would be crippled by many of the side effects (overcrowding, etc). There was not much good to be said for retiring death if one hoped for social progress and a high quality of life for the individual. There was something to be said about holding on to one's own life, however.

Three ideas predominated in the positive reaction toward a personal world without death. The last two themes appeared with approximately equal frequency.

1. Liberation from the fear of death. This was by far the most frequently acknowledged benefit. It was said in many ways. ("I would just give a real long sigh of relief. I would just be able to live and not think that one of these days I wouldn't be living any more." "I have to admit I've always been scared to death of death. I'd be free to enjoy life a lot more without that dark shadow hanging over me." "It would be the most amazing present anybody ever got, other than life itself, to be able to just live and not keep stabbing yourself with thinking, 'Hey, I'm going to die someday and leave all this.'"

2. Preservation of valued relationships. ("I hate good-byes, even at airports when you're going to see them again in a few months." "I have the greatest husband. I'd like to keep him forever").

3. Opportunity for continued personal growth. ("I'm a marketing major, so I'm going to get filthy rich, ha-ha. But I more enjoy nature photography. If I didn't have to die, I could do both things, and maybe even more." "I have become painfully aware of how little I know about almost everything, like the Orient, like even American history, like even how a car works! I could spend just centuries learning and learning!")

The most frequently expressed negative themes center around the meaning of life. Respondents often added either the second or third of the following themes to the first.

1. Abundance of time would sap motivation and take the edge off pleasure and achievement. ("I hate the pressure of time, but I need it. If I had forever, I'd probably take it." "I'd put things off and put things off and put things off." "I'm terrific in getting things done at the last minute. But there wouldn't be any more last minutes if I had all the time in the world." "I love stolen pleasures and stolen moments. If I had time for anything I wanted, I don't think life would taste as sweet.")

2. Religious faith and guidance would be undermined. ("Would there still be heaven, and how would you get there?" "Jesus died for us. What would that mean now?" "I'm a good Christian, basically, though far from perfect. I just don't know what would happen to my beliefs that are so important to me if life on this earth was all that we would ever have.")

3. Death is necessary as part of God's plan. Although obviously related to the preceding theme, this variant represents an affirmation of faith rather than a fear that faith would be undermined. ("We were meant to die. I think we should try to prevent diseases and treat diseases, but I don't think we should try to defeat God's plans for us." "I don't fear death. I know there's more to come . . . and (this) is what I live by." "I know that death is part of God's grand plan for us; we shouldn't even think of living forever because that would make us little imitation gods ourselves!")

4. Prolonged life would lead to continued aging and deterioration. This distinctly different fear was mentioned by a smaller proportion of the respondents. ("I've worked in nursing homes. Spare me! I'd never want to be so helpless and dependent on others." "I'd enjoy the peace of mind about living into old age and accomplishing all that I want to accomplish. But after that, I wouldn't look forward to just getting older and older.")

Implications

The most obvious implication is that presenting people with the prospect of a world without death also presents a stimulus for doubts and concerns. There was not a rush to embrace life without end. Most respondents found themselves trying to balance positive and negative consequences.

Does this pattern of response surprise us? It should surprise us, if we favor the hoary bromide that survival is the number one priority of all living creatures. Even those most pleased at the prospect of a world without death seldom accepted it without reservations and qualifications. The more usual response was to decide that the opportunity to be relieved of the fear of death was tainted by serious flaws and dangers. Our little thought experiment is a long way from being a definitive test of the "drive to survive." It certainly suggests, however, that caution is in order. If dying and death are really so repellent, then why should so many quibbles be raised?

We might also be surprised if we are cognizant of the many and varied evasive maneuvers that people take when confronted with death. In our exploration of deathbed scenes, for example, we noted that the law requires paramedics to carry out futile procedures with the "workable dead" instead of respecting the palpable and obvious facts. We also saw how even a geriatric hospital can labor to protect itself from death by a sequence of progressive sequestrations. These institutional patterns of evasion interact with individual tactics such as "forgetting" that dying people experience physical distress, or reducing our contacts both with dying people and their relatives. Lying ahead of us is an entire chapter focusing on death-related anxiety, which is one of the major topics that has attracted the attention of "thanato-psychologists." It would have been reasonable, then, to expect a great collective sigh of relief on learning that there would be no more deathbed scenes, no more obligation to enact code blue or look into the eyes of parents whose child has just succumbed to an incurable illness.

What we have found suggests instead that many—perhaps most—of us are entrapped within our own symbolic constructions and emotional dispositions. Death pains us whether presented directly to our senses or represented in the theater of our minds. Yet we cannot easily imagine a world without death: More specifically, we cannot easily imagine ourselves understanding and enjoying a world without death.

Perhaps as individuals we need death as a map needs boundaries, as a game needs rules, as beginnings seem to need endings. Our society also behaves as though requiring the integrity of its "death system" (Kastenbaum, 1972; 1991) for the continuation of economic, social, and symbolic traditions. This can be seen clearly in the consequences of increased average life expectancy. Hand wringing over the economic challenge of responding to the continued existence of older men and women has become one of the most popular nonaerobic exercises for our policy makers. The more petulant of this breed seems to be offended that public health advances have tampered so capriciously with the birth-death "population loop." Yet, what does our abundant crop of elders signify but the sharp reduction of premature death?

We fear death but we count on death. Death: We can't live with it or without it!

PARADOX OF AGING

"Consider the alternative" has become a frequent riposte when a person is asked how he or she feels about growing older. This paradox, already touched on, is worth a little further attention here.

Jonathan Swift placed Captain Lemuel Gulliver in several bizarre lands that distortion-mirrored some of the bizarre policies and practices of contemporary Europe. Among the Luggnaggians, Gulliver felt "inexpressible delight" on learning that occasionally "a child happened to be born . . . with a red circular spot in the forehead, directly over the left eyebrow, which was an infallible mark that it should never die" (Swift, 1726/1963, p. 216). As we noted in the opening quotation, Gulliver assumed that those "excellent Struldbrugs" would be the happiest of all beings, with their minds "free and disengaged, without the weight and depression of spirits caused by the continual apprehension of death" (p. 216).

Gulliver was quickly set straight by his hosts who told him the Struldbrugs were "not only opinionative, peevish, covetous, morose, vain, and talkative, but uncapable of friendship, and dead to all natural affection, which never descended beyond their own grandchildren" (p. 216). Rather than being perceived as exemplars of excellence, the Struldbrugs were forgetful and aphasic incompetents who were thoroughly "despised and hated by all sorts of people." The evident moral here is that, liberated from both death and the fear of death, people tend to curl in on themselves. We become our own worst habits. Our graveyard is our own aged self.

Tithon's lament, also excerpted at the beginning of this chapter, emphasizes physical rather than psychological or spiritual deterioration. His story represents a genre that has flourished in myth and folktale: The risky liaison between mortal and immortal lovers. The more customary plot turn confronts the immortal with the decision of joining the loved one as a vulnerable mortal or abandoning joy for never-ending life. (A charming example is the Russian story of *The Snow Maiden*, set to melodious music by both Tchaikovsky and Rimsky-Korsakov. The spirit of love triumphs for but a moment, chosen over perpetual youth without fulfillment.)

Tithon (alternatively, Tithonus), however, seems to benefit from a ploy by his immortal lover. Aurora, goddess of dawn, persuaded her father, Jupiter, to keep the young prince forever young. Unfortunately, she neglected to ask for eternal youth as well. Many years later, Tithon despairs that "Me only cruel immortality consumes." He comes to realize that humans cannot and should not escape their natural fate. It was folly to have ever supposed otherwise.

This poem is one of the keys to its poet and, through him, to the paradox of aging and death. Tennyson was a young man whose prospects in life appeared singularly unpromising. His precarious grip on survival was shaken by the death of Arthur Hallum, his best friend. Both young men had often discussed suicide as a way out of the problems that beset them. Now Tennyson felt an intensification of his sense of "death in life" (Martin, 1980). Perhaps suicide was the best solution after all. Instead, Tennyson created a small but distinguished gallery of verbal portraits: three old men, each of whom had survived their precarious youth. Through his evocations of old Tithon, Ulysses, and Saint Simeon Stylites, the young man was able to transcend his own crisis (Kastenbaum, 1989). It was with Tithon as his "advance scout," that Tennyson could come to terms with his fantasies of somehow eluding both aging and death.[2] There could be no magic of this sort. Through Ulysses, Tennyson could personify his own spirit of questing for knowledge and experience. Ulysses was old, he was mortal, but he had a compelling reason for going on until his powers finally end. Saint Simeon, portrayed as an outrageous and ludicrous character, represented the obstinately foolish (Struldbruggian) self that one becomes if whims and fantasies are allowed to multiply. Taken together, this trio of elders pointed the way for a young man to continue with his own life, face risk, accept age, and, finally, venture toward death without misgiving.

We have seen that some respondents were unsettled by the world without death scenario because it implied prolonged physical deterioration. Swift's Gulliver discovered that the moral-spiritual-psychological deterioration could be no less distressing. Tennyson created one kind of solution. Aging is not deterioration if one has a purpose, a destination (even a destination that can only be approached, never fully attained, like the ever-receding far horizon). The sense of death in life is more debilitating than the natural course of aging. A hesitant, frustrated, morose young person may live in death more than a clear-eyed, centered, purposeful old person who is ready to accept life at whatever terms it presents itself.

It is not just aging that is at issue. The larger question is our own basic identity. Who are we? Who do we seek to become? What do we want to bring to and receive from the human community? What is the life we would choose to experience in a world with or without death?

The answers to these questions will not be found in the back of the book, nor are these questions suitable for multiple-choice examinations. Directly or indirectly, however, much of the psychology of death is concerned with questions of this type. "To feel the fog in my throat" (even in imagination) is one of the more effective ways to draw our attention to death and, therefore, to the life that still possesses us.

NOTES

1. The combined sample of 629 respondents is comprised of 482 women and 119 men, in addition to 28 who did not report their gender. Educational programs centering on death-related topics almost invariably attract fewer men than women. The world without death exercise was given early in the proceedings to eliminate or reduce the possible effect of the lectures, discussion, and audiovisual materials.
2. At latest (unconfirmed) report, Tithon has taken the form of a cricket who continues to chirp his lament. Perhaps this is one and the same cricket who counseled me from a corner of my study while preparing this chapter.

REFERENCES

Amato, J. A. (1985). *Death book: Terrors, consolations, contradictions & paradoxes*. Marshall, MN: Venti Amati.

Browning, R. (1975). Prospice. *Browning: Poetical works, 1833-1864*. London: Oxford University Press. (Original work published 1864)

Kastenbaum, R. (1972). On the future of death: Some images and options. *Omega: Journal of Death & Dying, 3*, 306-318.

Kastenbaum, R. (1989). Old men created by young artists: Time-transcendence in Tennyson and Picasso. *International Journal on Aging & Human Development, 28*, 81-104.

Kastenbaum, R. (1991). *Death, society, and human experience* (4th ed.). Columbus: Merrill Publishing.

Martin, R. B. (1980). *Tennyson and the unquiet heart*. Oxford: Clarendon Press.

Swift, Jonathan (1963). *Gulliver's travels*. Boston: Beacon Press. (Original work published 1726)

Tennyson, A. (1895). *The works of Alfred Lord Tennyson* (Vol. 2). Boston: Lauriat.

3

The Psychologist's Death

Number of editions of the *Annual Review of Psychology* before the first review of death-related topics: 27.

Of the 1,128,000 words in the *Handbook of General Psychology*, 166 are devoted to death-related topics. This is .0001 of the total coverage and is limited to mention of the death-feigning behavior of opossums and the attitudes of elderly adults toward death under "Selected Areas." No death mention occurs under such major sections as The Human Organism, Perception, Learning, Language, Thought and Intelligence, or Personality.

Number of words related to death in E. G., Boring's classic text, *A History of Experimental Psychology*: 0.

Death can teach us more about psychology than the other way around. Let us see what the psychologist has made of death. This will tell us some things about psychology that we might not have otherwise observed. Furthermore, each of us can then decide for ourselves whether or not we accept these constructions as a basis for our own orientation toward death. The psychologist we are thinking of here is the one who will be most familiar to most readers of this book: a U.S.-born and educated person who is fluent only in English, holds membership in the American Psychological Association, and disagrees with many fellow psychologists on many issues. We would be missing the mark if we persisted with stereotypic notions that this person is a threat to decent folk everywhere because of a secret mission to gain control of our minds through the application of outrageous theories and cunning techniques.

Today's psychologist does not care much for theories—especially Grand Theories. He or she has read little of Freud or Jung and nothing of Kant, Bergson, or Foucault. Oriented toward techniques and measurable results, the psychologist will use specific contributions from innovators as diverse as Gustav Theodor Fechner and George Kelly, but take no interest in their theories and world views. All too prosaically, our protagonist is more likely to be found jogging, recycling newspapers and cans, and supporting environmental causes than carrying out diabolic schemes against The American Way of Life. This does not mean that today's psychologist is innocuous. He or she influences us in many ways. Psychology's message comes to us directly from the lectern and the textbook, but also indirectly through all the media that compete for our attention and allegiance. What the psychologist says—or does not say—about death tends to be absorbed by our acquisitive nervous system along with a motley of other influences. In constructing the psychologist's construction of death, I will be emphasizing substance or theme, but will also be organizing this material in a quasi-historical manner to help us see how we have moved along to where we are now.

DEATH IS NEITHER WRONG NOR RIGHT

This is a remarkable idea. Today's psychologist does not appreciate the brilliant and radical nature of this idea because it was passed along unobtrusively as part of both undergraduate and graduate education. It must also be said that today's psychologist is becoming somewhat uncomfortable with this idea, but has not yet figured out what to do about it. Now, just why is this idea so brilliant and radical? Through much of known human history, death itself had been accepted as one of the prime facts of life. *Attitudes* toward death, however, were encased within moral codes. Here is a generic synopsis.

I kill

"It is good for me to kill this tasty creature. Its death is my life. My killing it proves that I am good at being who I am."

"It is good for me to kill you. It feels good to take revenge. It feels good to protect my people. It feels good to kill!"

I am killed

"It is right that I should die in this way. I have done what I knew was the right thing to do, and so my death is honorable."

I mourn

"I am doing what I know I must do for you. It would be wrong, and it would be dangerous if I neglected the sacrifices and rituals that will help you in the perilous passage from this life to the next."

I elude death

"It is good to live. It is right to do what I must do to stay alive. A painful ritual is good if it saves my life. Tricking a demon or deceiving a stranger is good if it saves my life. Almost anything that keeps me alive is good, because being alive is sacred and being alive is the root of all treasures."

I refuse to elude death

"But, no, I will choose death over this disgrace. I will not dishonor my name or the name of my people. I will not deny what is most precious to me. I will not accept this humiliation. Death becomes the good if the alternative is to wrong my life."

I think of death

"There is a right way to think of death and many wrong ways. I choose to think of my death only in the right way (although sometimes wrong thoughts trouble me). I am at peace with myself when I think of death in the right way, and I trust and value those who know how to do this. I feel either scorn or pity for those who think of death foolishly, or who foolishly do not think of death at all."

All these attitudes were tutored by world views and guided by moral principles. (The same was true of the variant attitudes that we would need to consider if this were the place to excavate ancestral ideas in a thorough and systematic manner.) The particular attitude is not as important here as the fact that value-laden attitudes toward death have been the rule throughout history. I might think your gods monsters, and you might think my gods fools; however, we would understand each other nevertheless. We would both be stunned to come on somebody who had *no* set of moral rules that governed killing, being killed, dying, and mourning. We would know ourselves to be in the presence of a madman or madwoman if we were told that "right or wrong" are notions that do not apply to death.

The situation became more complex as the Judeo-Christian world views became articulated and recruited their faithful. The Psalmist of the Old Testament was elegant in affirming a bleak view of death that had already made its deep impression.

Death ends all

"What man is he that liveth, and shall not see death? Shall he deliver his soul from the hand of the grave?"

"As for man, his days are as grass . . ."

"Man is like to vanity: His days are as a shadow that passeth away."

"His breath goeth forth, he returneth to his earth; in that very day his thoughts perish."

These representative Old Testament utterances construct death as a sort of cancellation stamp on all human endeavor. In this sense, death could be regarded as an evil. The Old Testament Psychologist (if this term may be invoked) was taking aim at our *attitudes*, however, not simply at death itself. There are right and wrong ways to think of ourselves, right and wrong ways to chart our course of actions through life. Let us face our common mortality, then, and not dissipate our lives in blinkered vanity and self-deception.

The new-made Christian, of course, did not lose all the feelings and dispositions that dominated in the previous era. Instead, a powerful set of (relatively) novel ideas entered the mix. The believer would now take the following propositions as being central to his or her attitude toward the self and the world.

Death is my deserved punishment

"Then when lust hath conceived, it bringeth forth sin; and sin, when it is finished, bringeth forth death" (James 1:15).

"Wherefore, as by one man sin entered into the world, and death by sin; and so death passed upon all men, for that all have sinned" (Rom. 5:12).

I may pass through death to salvation

"Verily, verily, I say unto you, The hour is coming and now is when the dead shall hear the voice of the Son of God: and they that hear shall live" (John 5:25).

"Behold, I shew you a mystery; We shall not all sleep, but we shall all be changed. In a moment, in the twinkling of an eye, at the last trump: for the trumpet shall sound, and the dead shall be raised incorruptible, and we shall be changed" (Cor. 15:51–52).

These beliefs or constructs have served as tremendous intensifiers of the moral perspective on death. Old Testament death is nature's way of showing us that we are subject to the same laws as the grass and the ox. The psychologist and the moralist—still one person at this point—confronts the challenge of how we are to live with this prospect in mind. New Tesatment death is quite a different proposition. Death is more than the inevitable cessation of life. Anybody can see that flowers eventually wither and die. Christian belief incorporates this concrete and realistic view, but reframes the construct of death and its moral associations. Original sin, personal sin, guilt, hope, faith, resurrection in the flesh, and salvation are among the ideas that become intertwined with the death construct.

Consider, for example, just two implications of the Christian reconstruction of death.

Alienation from realm of nature

"Yes, the grass withers, the blossom falls, and my ox grows old and dies. But I have an immortal soul. My true life is not here on earth among mortal creatures. I claim dominion over the beasts of the field and sky and sea. I take my orders from God, but everybody else takes their orders from me. My life and death are in a class of their own."

Risk-all game of salvation

"What happens during my life is of little consequence when compared with the fate of my soul after death. I am tempted by the pleasures of life; these seem good to me. But I must subdue these cravings. I must keep my eyes fixed on eternity. Give me courage to risk all for salvation. (I mean, there *is* salvation, isn't there? If not, then I'm playing the wrong game.)"

The actual interplay of dynamics that operate within the Christian death construct zone is much more complex and subject to variations. Even when limiting ourselves to the two facets summarized previously, however, we can appreciate the special intensity of the Christian moral psychology. Death has become a salient construct. It is not just something that happens. We might even describe Christianized death as an *electrified construct*. Not only does it occupy a superordinate place in the hierarchy of constructs, but it requires the caution and respect one takes in dealing with a live wire. At any moment and in any situation the death construct can deliver a bolt of stinging energy to any other construct. It would not be accurate to say that death reigns as the supreme construct, however, because it is inextricably connected with other powerful ideas such as guilt, destination, and salvation. A Christian as pious as Cotton Mather doubted and despaired on his deathbed. Had he really held firm to the faith? Would his mortal move bring him eternal blessing or damnation? The personal stakes are enormous in the risk-decision game of salvation: There is more than all the world to gain or lose—there is the fate of one's soul. ("Game" is not used in a derisive sense here; social psychologists have made fruitful use of the game model in approaching many significant questions.)

One cannot venture any distance within the Christian construct zone without encountering that tingling live wire construction of death. Paradoxically, perhaps, death is one of the primary sources of psychological energy here, and this can also be described as a kind of moral energy. If food seems the supreme good to a starving person, then safe passage *from* this imperfect life *through* death and *into* endless blessing is the supreme good for those who accept the Christian message. Along the journey to this destination, the Christian contends with the conflicting (I almost said, *sibling*) constructs of punishment and salvation. The essential points for us here are the consequentiality and moral urgency of the Christian death construct. We will see in a moment how much this differs from the psychologist's version.

Enter the Psychologist

Psychology as an identifiable and independent field of study has been with us for about a century (add another half-century to pioneering beginnings, if you like). A great many people had developed psychological insights long before that time, of course, and elements of psychology frequently appeared in works of medicine, natural science, rhetoric, and so on. The firm beginnings of modern psychology, however, were made in a world that had already transformed itself. The Psalmist of the Old Testament never observed the slums of a great industrial city or felt the hot breath of a steam locomotive. The authors of Corinthians and Revelation did not measure their hours by mechanical timepieces nor read penny-dreadful novels. Mighty empires had risen and fallen—and these included the secular power of the now jarringly diversified Christian church.

The psychologist was part of the new breed. For a few rather enchanted years psychology was led by creative scholars who had the rare ability both to appreciate the past and help to bring the future into being. (William James and Wilhelm Wundt are among the names that come to mind, although one man's work scarcely resembles the other's.) Soon, however, American academic psychology would settle into the functionalist, pragmatic, behavioristic pattern that has contributed so much both to its triumphs and failures. The academic bastion would eventually be tested and tempted by depth psychology from Vienna and Zurich. The emergence of clinical psychology and a host of other applied fields has also had some impact. Nevertheless, American psychology continues to display its profile as a kind of hard-nosed factory that turns out empirical studies in great profusion as well as an annual crop of well-ordealed graduates.

So where was death in all of this? Up in the attic and down in the dungeon. American behaviorism had little use for theory in the old-fashioned sense of this term. In fact, it had little use for anything that looked, felt, or smelled like the baggage of the past. One has the impression that behaviorists of the founding generation took as much pleasure in thumbing their noses at established traditions as they did in creating their own new establishment. This gritty, feisty, let-us-start-the-world-over-again attitude lead to the discard of virtually every scholarly context within which death might have embedded itself. Philosophy was pretty much ashcanned. (Years later, there would be some willingness to be scolded by the new philosophers of science.) Socrates once asked, "for is not philosophy the study of death?" The victors in the competition to establish American academic psychology deftly removed the pug-nosed bust of Socrates from the premises and, by so doing, spared their students the pain of having to face philosophical questions about their own mortality. Needless to say, if the great philosophers and their concerns were not to be allowed within the corridors of the new psychology, then there would certainly be no place for the theologians. Rather quietly, then, some of history's most challenging minds and passionate advocates were barred at the door.

The weeding out process was vigorous within psychology as well. Introspectionism and phenomenology were big losers. Holistic thinking in general was regarded with suspicion, although later the Gestalt movement made some contributions that just could not be rejected. All of this was bad news for death. Looking within our own minds was not to be the method of choice for the new psychology. This was not entirely an arbitrary judgment. The methodological problems inherent in introspective studies were acutely dissected by behaviorists. Furthermore, there was a bright new world of objectivistic research to be done.

The psychology of the public, observable, and countable was not devised as a clever way to dispose of death. It did the trick, nevertheless. Students learned that examining the content of minds was not the business of the modern psychologist. Our thoughts and feelings about death, then, were safe from inquisitive students of psychology (and, as it turned out, from the students of their students as well).

At least two other influences also converged to make psychology a death-free zone. From the exciting scientific ferment of the times, psychology took hold of the concept of objectivity. It was not just that psychologists recognized the value of objective measurement and analysis. Objectivity became virtually an end in itself. This approach has had a mixed effect. The design, execution, and evaluation of psychological studies became more sophisticated; some frequent errors of the past became less frequent. It has gradually become apparent, however, that "objectivity" is also an attitude; it also represents a highly unusual if not artificial relationship between the observer and the observed. Psychology had therefore maneuvered itself into a position in which death could either be (a) ignored, because it is too subjective and too embedded in moral passions; or (b) reframed to meet objectivistic specifications.

From the general American scene at the time, psychology took the cue that death was not a popular topic. There was really no call for it. Hospices were not asking for psychological knowledge to help dying patients and their families: There were no hospices. Suicide prevention centers were not knocking on the doors of academia for data-based techniques to reduce the probabilities of self-destruction: there were no suicide prevention centers. And so on. The idea of teaching a course on the psychology of death was considered peculiar in the mid-1960s when the first such offerings were made; a journal devoted to publishing scientific and professional contributions would not begin until 1970. There was little to prompt American behavioralists to include death among their studies, and there was the prevailing sociocultural attitude ("Don't talk about it, and it may go away") to discourage such thoughts if they did happen to arise.

Today's psychologist, then, has inherited (in modified form) an objectivistic, utilitarian, atheoretical perspective whose many strengths do not include either the conceptualization or the study of death. What happens when a psychologist with this background does encounter death? There will first be the recognition that his or her education as a psychologist has not been an adequate preparation for this encounter.

Next will be the realization that the mainstream journals, texts, and reference books have little to say about death from a psychological perspective. Left to his or her own devices, the psychologist is likely to try out the objectivistic orientation on death. It is then almost a foregone conclusion that the psychologist's death will be one that fits comfortably into his or her existing frame of reference. This means that the passions and the moral urgencies that most men and women have attached to death will be stripped away before the study itself has started.

At one brilliant stroke, the academic psychologist disposes of those facets of death that most thrill or distress us. Should we fear death? Should we long for death? Should we live our lives in the prospect of death? Should we keep the dead alive in our minds? Is death itself a good or an evil? Questions such as these have not won a place in mainstream psychology. The questions themselves are perceived as invalid. *Looked at objectively, death is neither wrong nor right.* We try to look at all things objectively.

Up to this point we have allowed the psychologist to define death only in terms of one of its primary nonattributes (no moral quality). This one negative specification is of some importance, however. It represents a radical break with humanity's long love-hate relationship with death. There is even a prescriptive implication here. The psychologist is all but telling us: "Do as I have done. Put aside the temptation to be ego involved with death, to construct mortality in terms of your subjective needs, hopes, and desires. Instead, make use of the same outlook that has proved so effective in technology and science. Be objective. Observe the stimuli. Determine the response alternatives that are available to you. Behave in the manner that will maximize the probabilities of an effective outcome. In other words: Cool it."

Death Is Irrelevant

This is another significant aspect of the psychologist's death construct that can be most directly expressed in terms of a nonattribute. Death is irrelevant to the systematic study of psychology and irrelevant to most of what psychologists do in the applied sphere. Perhaps we can educate ourselves most readily about this phenomenon by looking first at some of the exceptions. When the Arizona temperature tops 115 degrees, I sometimes stay indoor, sipping ice tea, listening to Haydn or Nielsen, and looking through the subject indexes of the most weighty resource books that I dare place on my shelves. The word death does appear in some indexes. Most commonly, the complete entry is "death rate" (or "mortality, rate of"). In methodology-intensive books, this citation almost always refers to the loss of "subjects" through death. This is a problem that researchers face when conducting follow-up or longitudinal studies. Some people (or gerbils) who were tested at Time A will not be available for retest at Time B because their mortality has asserted itself.

Death (rate) is a nuisance for the researcher who uses time-sensitive designs. It is also a potential source of error. One cannot assume that the deaths have occurred in a random manner. Perceptive psychologists have contributed to knowledge by taking the possibility of a differential death rate as a topic of investigation itself. For example, Klaus Riegel and his colleagues discovered that the aging adults who died in the course of their longitudinal studies usually had shown a greater decline in their cognitive performances, as compared with the survivors. This phenomenon has become known as "terminal drop." (Not all subsequent studies have found results that are consistent with the original findings; it is far from a simple issue.) There are often several significant implications whenever a differential death rate can be detected in a research population. In testing the psychological functioning of octogenerians, for example, we may be dealing with a relatively elite set of people; those whose intellectual functionings had been subjected to more age-related changes are less likely to be in the sample. For every observant and resourceful Riegel, however, there are many other researchers who continue to regard death rate as just one more obstacle to their very important work. Needless to say, how their "subjects" died and what their deaths meant to them is never considered of sufficient interest to deserve comment.

As far as I can tell, the other commonest acknowledgments of death in the general psychology literature are in the areas of parental bereavement and suicide. These topics are most likely to be found in texts or resource books in the fields of personality-clinical, social, or developmental psychology. The discussions are usually brief but informative. Parental bereavement is the aspect of death that seems to be most nearly integrated into general theory and practice. Psychologists have become increasingly aware of the effects of loss experiences on human development, and several theories give some attention to parental bereavement.

Suicide is most typically introduced in connection with adolescence, old age, or substance abuse. Again, the coverage is pertinent and useful, although seldom extensive. More integrated into the core sociological literature than it is in psychology, suicide is treated as one of the many problems with which we must contend. The major theoretical approaches in psychology do not regard suicide either as a core issue or as a clue to the basic understanding of human nature.

Why are parental bereavement and suicide somewhat less irrelevant to the psychologist's construction of death? Both are errors. Both are deviations. Both upset the regular order of things. Parents of young children should not die. People should not throw their lives away through acts of self-destruction. The domesticated (if not entirely docile) mainstream psychology of today is interested in the preservation of social order. This does not imply that psychologists are either uncritical of social institutions or closed to innovation. It does mean that psychologists hope for enough stability and continuity in social institutions to provide a protective framework for their work, and also hope to confirm at least a few enduring laws, principles, or regularities within their work. Death that comes at the wrong time to the wrong people is a threat to this vision of an orderly world (e.g., the death of young parents, the death of a young child). Death that comes in the wrong way is also a threat (e.g., the suicide of a talented teenager or the messy suicide of a family breadwinner).

When death does not violate the implicit rules or otherwise force itself on the psychologist's attention, then death barely exists as a topic for psychological inquiry, education, or application. Specialists in areas such as gerontology, health psychology, and military psychology tend to see death as a more relevant variable than do most of their colleagues throughout the broad spectrum of the sociobehavioral sciences.

There is probably a connection between the psychologist's perceived irrelevance of death and his or her separation, and two other variables: (a) the psychologist's separation from phenomenological and natural time; and (b) the preference for aggregated rather than individual (nomothetic) types of quantitative analysis. Experimental psychology is strong on establishing its own designer time frameworks—reinforcement schedules are one familiar example. Statistical psychology is strong on analyzing data on the basis of techniques and assumptions that have an underlying spatial or other atemporal foundation. This tendency expressed itself in the early days of statistical treatment of behavioral data when research designs were borrowed from agricultural experimentation. (The "hort" in cohort bears witness to its horticultural roots.) Investigators became adept at studying the effects of Treatment A, Treatment B and Control conditions on "crops" of rats or undergraduates who had been assigned to these various conditions, much like sweet peas to Mendellian garden patches. The results are analyzed by aggregated clumps (Groups A to C). We are not really much interested in what happened to this particular sweet pea. Furthermore, natural time (in this case, the growing season) is replaced by quantitative outcome. True, there is the appearance that time has really been taken into consideration. The statistical analysis, however, merely compares two sets of numbers based on aggregated performance. The growing season might have been a month or an hour. The process might have been linear or geometric, smooth or discontinuous. We will never know.

Natural time is seldom treated as natural time in psychological research. It is replaced by outcome measures that are indifferent to the actual temporal course. Similarly, the typical research program concentrates on aggregated numbers. Individuals disappear as individuals almost as soon as they are fed into the computers. Combined, the tendency to dispose of both the individual and of natural time comprises a splendid way to make death appear irrelevant. Without individuals and the actual passage of time, how is this unpleasant topic to intrude itself? Furthermore, the already mentioned dislike of introspective studies has pretty much taken care of phenomenological time as well. Psychologists may not have any extraordinary ways to maintain social stability and continuity, but they can create little time- and death-free worlds in their studies and theoretical models.

It is not surprising that clinical psychologists and others who relate to people on an individual and intimate basis have had more difficulty in regarding death as irrelevant. The psychotherapy client does introspect and has been known to speak of both time and death. On these occasions, the psychologist is not likely to find much to draw on from the general body of academic theory and data that has attended so little to individuality and time, as well as death. I am surely not the only psychologist who has discovered through compelling encounters that it is psychology that tends to be irrelevant—not dying, death, and grief.

Death Responses Destabilize

Death is neither right nor wrong, and it is not all that relevant to psychology as a science. Yet psychology has created somewhat more substantial constructions that are related to death. Psychology has shown some interest in death as a shadowy sort of background stimulus that elicits destabilizing responses. We must shift our thinking now to consider not death but responses to death. Most psychological activity in the area that some call "thanatology" has centered around cognitive, affective, and behavioral responses to the construct of death. This gives rise to implicit replacement constructions: (a) "Death is that which elicits destabilizing responses"; and (b) "Death is that which serves as an alarm function to indicate a destabilizing situation."

If we are careless it might seem to us that the psychologist is really talking about death. In fact, however, the death construct has been replaced by the responses-to-death construct. This cannot be a completely satisfactory solution. Responses to death remain in a conceptual vacuum if we have no clear conception of what these responses are in response to! Most psychologists do not seem to worry about this conundrum, but I will vex you with it from time to time.

The alternative constructions given earlier have both an important commonality and a consequential divergence. (A third construction is associated with a more specific orientation within psychology and will be described in the next section.) The assertion of destabilization is the obvious commonality. The explanations offered for destabilization are about as different as can be, however.

Each construction has its favorite or most convenient source of data, as the following examples are intended to illustrate.

Brooke's mirror presents her with unassailable evidence of a white hair among her raven locks. "I am old!" she laments. "Nobody will love me. Young twerps will call me Ma'm! And—oh, my God—this must mean that I'm mortal after all! Why me?"

The realization of our personal mortality can come about in many ways. Acknowledging signs of physical aging is one of the commoner reminders that if youth is but a temporary gift, then life itself may also not be ours to hoard forever. The death of an old friend ("But he wasn't really old—why, he was my age!") is another frequent *memento mori*. These are examples of private encounters with death. There is also the "brush with death." A reckless driver roars through the intersection and nearly broadsides your car. Angry and relieved at the same time, you realize afresh how vulnerable we all are, how quickly a life can end.

The implicit construction, "Death is that which elicits destabilizing responses" applies to all these situations and many more. Any perceived encounter with death will disturb our equanimity. We no longer feel safe in the world. We dread. Precisely how we respond to mortality's tickle will differ according to our personality and circumstances. We might become so disorganized with anxiety that we cannot act effectively in our own self-interests. Some activities of everyday life may become so aversive to us that we fall into a pattern of functional disability (e.g., afraid to travel, afraid even to answer the telephone). We might also take quite the opposite approach, however. Nothing scares us. We double-dare death to catch us. There are, of course, many variations between these extremes.

Some of psychology and psychiatry's most useful contributions have come in this sphere: recognizing that disturbed or distorted behavior patterns can be interpreted as responses to mortal fears. There is no doubt that some people develop either temporary or enduring disturbances that can be linked to death-related anxieties. But does everybody suffer from a basic anxiety that has fear of death at its root? This question is examined at some length in our chapter on death anxiety. It is not the answer to this question that most concerns us here. What interests us is the plain fact that psychologists often conceptualize death primarily as a stimulus for destabilizing responses. In other words, we "read" death from the way the individual recoils. For the psychologist, death is that-which-we-recoil-from. Death does not have its own direct symbolic construction. What would psychologists do with death-as-death anyway? We feel more comfortable in observing and cataloging the ways in which people respond to this shadowy stimulus. Psychotherapists, counselors, and teachers find that they can sometimes help to reduce the intensity of this fear and to guide people toward more effective response patterns. Death itself remains untouched.

The idea that death always, or naturally, or automatically upsets us has been elevated into a major explanatory principle for human thought and behavior by some scholars with an existentialist orientation. Ernest Becker presented this view eloquently in *Denial of Death* (1973). He criticized Sigmund Freud's earlier position on death anxiety, and this takes us back to the alternative construction: "Death is that which serves as an alarm function to indicate a destabilizing situation." Freud's thoughts about both death and anxiety did not remain constant throughout his long career. Societal, personal, and clinical experiences prompted him to reconsider his views several times, and one may derive different impressions from reading his later conversations and correspondence than from his earlier publications.

The Freud that Becker disputes was inclined to regard death anxiety as a signal that something was amiss—but not because of mortal fear. Suppose that one of your friends has just had a series of terrifying nightmares. They are just full of death or impending death. A Freudian of the old school might well discover that the death dreams represented your friend's anxiety about an upcoming examination or job interview. This career-oriented anxiety was disguised as fear of death. (It is almost a foregone conclusion that the Freudian analyst would have also found a lot more in your friend's associations to his or her dreams. Daddy, authority figures, and fear of sticking one's "neck" out might figure prominently.)

Or suppose that you overhear a very young woman discussing her plans for the evening, "If he kisses me, I'll just die!" Chances are you would not conclude that she is in imminent danger of death. It would not even seem likely that her thoughts and feelings have much to do with death at all. "I'll just die!" expresses a sense of excitement taken almost to the bursting point. This statement does convey information: a mixture of alarm and delight. It would be naïve to insist that people always mean death when they say death. This is one of the major points of difference between Freud and Becker (see chapter 5). Death represents something else. Agitation that *seems* to be related to death should be given attention because it signifies that a destabilizing situation is in process. The knowing person, however, would not assume that death is the underlying issue.

Having noticed the differences between these two constructions of death, let us remind ourselves of the foundation assumption that both share. Each associates death with a destabilizing psychological condition. Each emphasizes cognitive, affective, or behavioral responses rather than death per se. Do you recall that Danny Kaye song in which he informs us that "Water is Nature's way of telling you that you're drowning?" This could be the theme song for either theoretical camp. Death thought, death talk, and death actions tell the world that we are struggling with a force that threatens to overwhelm us.

Death Is a Task

This is perhaps the strangest psychological construction of death that we have yet considered. It is also the most popular view within the vigorous new area of life-span developmental psychology. Few people think of this view as being strange, and that may be the strangest thing of all.

Developmental psychology was once almost synonymous with child psychology. The study of infant and child development continues today as an active and productive field. A growing number of psychologists, however, have taken the entire life-span as their framework. On the whole, these psychologists show a relatively strong interest in processes that unfold in real or natural time. They are also sensitive to variations in the sociocultural contexts of development. For example, the passage from childhood to adolescence is not quite the same in the Navajo nation as it is on the sidewalks of New York. The people who are reaching their 80th or 90th birthdays today are different in many respects from all past and future generations because their life experiences have been so distinctive in a nonrepeatable way. There are many intellectual and personal rewards to be discovered in the textured, culturally aware, and time-conscious world of life-span developmental research.

The death constructions that have already been described on these pages are less likely to claim the allegiances of the life-span developmental psychologist. This is especially true for those who primarily study or provide services for elderly adults. Some years ago I was starting to perform both clinical and research activities in a hospital for the aged.

The morgue was two doors down from my office. Any inclination I might have had to consider death as an irrelevant variable was quickly overcome by the quiet but unrelenting force of reality. Gerontologists (including psychologists but not excluding physicians, social workers, nurses, anthropologists, sociologists, etc.) are too conversant with time, age, and death to find much value in this construction.

It is also somewhat more difficult for life-span psychologists to subscribe to the view that death is neither right nor wrong. Again, the obstacle is their own experience and their tendency to have formed personal relationships with many people whose deaths were in close prospect. As I write these words I think of some of the old men and women I have known as their lives approached the end, and I also think of other psychologists and health care providers who have had similar experiences. "Harriet died just as she had determined to, and just how she lived." "Allan was terrified that he would die alone. And he did. That was not a good death." "Thelma was always dying in her mind. When death actually came, it was so swift and smooth that she probably felt very little at all. I wonder if that's the easy death she earned by rehearsing harder deaths so often?"

It would take some effort on my part to regard these deaths as neither right nor wrong, and I have not even mentioned those that stir up the strongest feelings. This involved and judgmental attitude is common among those who have come to know many lives and deaths. We cannot help but feel that some people died too soon or too late, too painfully or too clouded by drugs, and so forth. We are also aware that some of our clients, research participants, and friends were convinced that they were passing through death to a better life. Others were equally convinced that "dust unto dust" is the way the story must be told. Whatever we felt, it was not as highly objective and distanced observers.

Perhaps our method compromised our philosophy and science. We had to become close to the individuals we were studying or helping, and so we also became close to their deaths. The insidious logic went something like this: "I care about this person. This person is dying. This person soon will be dead. How this person dies matters to me and so does the meaning of his or her death. So death 'itself' must be something that it is natural for us to have strong opinions about; death must be that which can be either very right or very wrong." This contamination of the death construct through our own relationship to the subject matter is certainly open to criticism. (The behaviorist's death construct is no less vulnerable to criticism; the preference for a more remote and manipulative relationship to human thought and feeling eases the way for the construction that death is both irrelevant and devoid of moral qualities.)

Life-span developmental psychologists may agree with their colleagues that death-related responses are often associated with a destabilizing psychic condition. They are perhaps less inclined to conclude that this constitutes an adequate psychological construction of death. They observe that some people seem remarkably at peace with the idea of personal death. These same people often have a view of life in which death is seen as part of the totality rather than as an unexpected and unfair intrusion. Even as their health deteriorates, there is little or no concern about death as such. (They may have a variety of concerns about various aspects of *life* including their ability to engage in self-care activities, the status of insurance policies, etc.)

Having made observations of this type, the life-span developmentalist (and some others) may feel the need for a death construct that is more encompassing and less captivated by the association with destabilizing responses. Although there has been no official contest to select such a construct, there has been an uncrowned winner for at least three decades. Life-span developmentalists know what death is. Death is a task.

Where did this idea come from? Straight from the heartland. The life-span developmental vision emerged a few years after the end of World War II. Some farsighted people recognized that industrial nations would be accumulating ever-greater numbers of elderly adults. Psychological theory and social planning both would require greater attention to old age as a part of the total life-course. This also happened to be a time when the "can-do" spirit was still vital in the United States. Anybody could become successful by working hard and demonstrating some courage and ingenuity along the way. The Vietnam War and the protest movement, Watergate, the loss of U.S. dominance in several major fields of manufacturing, escalating drug problems, and other "downers" had not yet enveloped us.

This conjunction of influences gave us the irresistible concept of the *developmental task*. Life's journey is not for the dawdler or idle wanderer. We are to pause at each of life's work stations just long enough to perform the task that awaits us. Early childhood, late childhood, early adolescence, late adolescence, and so on were conceptualized as work places. The work was primarily "psychosocial" (another term that was in full bloom). We needed to make ourselves physically, mentally, and socially competent to take our places as decent, well-adjusted, and productive citizens.

There was rapid acceptance of the theory that our life is a series of tasks to be accomplished, all strung out across the time dimension from infancy through old age. It was quite an attractive proposition at the time. The "task" image accorded well with the work ethic that had contributed much to this nation's rise to power. Moreover, this seemed to be a much more positive alternative to conceptualizing the human life-span than anything else that was readily available. Psychoanalytic theory was still influential, although fighting for every inch of (temporary) gain in the halls of academe. The newly hatched life-span developmental psychology did not want to attach itself too closely to a pessimistic Old World theory that gave more attention to neurosis than to health. Soon there were many variations on the theme of developmental tasks. Help also arrived from mildly renegade psychoanalysts such as Erik Erickson. Psychological textbooks swarmed with lists of developmental tasks, and the fervor spread as well into social work, nursing, and other adjacent fields. It was not long before death itself had been transformed into a developmental task. I recall hearing the wheels grinding all around me as this process was occurring. The burning task faced by task psychology was to find something for old people to do. The very young had the task of developing trust. Later one had to achieve the task of becoming independent and so on. By the time we reached old age there was not much left on the bottom of the developmentalist's sack. Well, why not death? This would kill the proverbial two birds with the same proverbial stone. Old age and death could be wrapped up together and in a rather philosophical and poetic package. Theorists differed in their terminology and emphases, but the basic view was broadcast with rare unanimity: Old people should be occupied psychologically in preparing themselves for death.

This influential view did not derive from systematic research. In fact, at that time there had been very little research on the ways in which older people orient themselves toward death. Furthermore, the construction of death as a developmental task did not lead to a great deal of hypothesis-testing research either. The theory just sounded good and seemed to meet the needs of life-span developmentalist. What kind of research would have provided an adequate test of this theory? Most life-span developmental studies are descriptive rather than experimental, and the same holds true for most studies of death-related behavior. Although it would be useful—indeed, essential—to describe the ways in which mature adults cope with the prospect of death, this information would not necessarily tell us how they *should* cope. Developmental task theory is about "shoulds" as well as "is's." There are some research strategies that could provide a basis for informed evaluation of death task theory. The need has seldom been felt, however, not even to this day. Although developmental tasks are no longer as dominant in life-span theory as they were a few years ago, the construction of death as a developmental task is still invoked more frequently than any other view. Until further notice, then, preparing one's self for death remains the old person's primary developmental responsibility.

One of the most significant features of death task theory has already been mentioned. It offers a view of our relationship to death that is not couched within a psychopathology model. Although psychoanalytic theory has made contributions to our understanding of healthy as well as disturbed human behavior, it bears many marks of its origins in psychiatric practice. Death-task theory proposes that it is normal (or normative) to confront the prospect of death as our lives draw to an end. There may be stress, challenge, and conflict involved in this confrontation, but coping with difficulty is something that humans are equipped to do. As we grow older, it is normal for us to reflect on the shape our lives have taken and to consider what options remain to us in a foreshortening future. At some later point it would be considered mature rather than neurotic to consider how we can best manage "final things" (living will, disposition of estate, funeral arrangements, etc.). The fact that a person is considering death is seen as a continuing fulfillment of one's responsibility to self and others.

A second distinctive feature is also worth noting. In life-span developmental psychology, the death construct tends to be much more integrated into the overall theoretical structure. Encounters with death are not treated simply as incidents that disturb the peace. We *expect* to have encounters with death. Moreover, developmental task theory is not complete without considering old age and death. We could pare death-related discussions from most other psychological theories and find that we have had little if any impact on their overall structure. By contrast, developmental task theory would miss its final pages without its death construct. This would represent not only an abridgement of the theory but a serious distortion as well. A life-span developmental approach to human behavior and experience cannot be considered complete and credible without attention to death.

This appealing theory will be called on in several contexts throughout this book. It would be wise to temper our enthusiasm, however, with the following thoughts:

1. Developmental task theory is a way of looking at human behavior: It has not been "proved" through systematic testing with rival hypotheses. We can accept or reject this theory on the grounds of usefulness or any other functional criteria we choose. It would be going beyond the established facts, however, to believe that developmental task theory has been proved through systematic research.

2. There is still a residue of assumptions and prescriptions from the earlier days of developmental task theory. In other words, experts are generously telling us things that even they do not know. The advice we are given might be thoughtful and useful, but—again—it is largely opinion. Perhaps we will find some of the death-as-task discussions quite valuable. There is no adequate shared data base for advocating that older people *should* select death as their number one "task," however, or that they should approach this task in the particular way favored by the particular theorist. With the best of intentions, death-task theory has been contributing its share of rigid and premature material to a surprisingly docile readership.

3. Developmental task theory has given its seal of approval to the already impressive link between old age and death. More people do survive into old age; therefore, this is the sector in which deaths occur ever-more frequently. Unfortunately, though, this theory has made it even easier to treat death as though a specialty of the aged, and therefore of only academic interest to the young. Trapping death in the geriatrics department was probably not part of the life-span developmentalist's plan, but the outcome has drifted in that direction. The major theorists themselves have not advocated this denial maneuver; rather the "let-the-old-people-do-all-the-worrying-about-death" implication has been drawn by popularizers and consumers.

4. Conceiving the entire human life-span as a series of developmental tasks is a bourgeois artistic creation that has been "standing in" while the field awaits a more adequate theoretical framework. As already mentioned, the idea of developmental tasks was congenial to American tradition and especially to the historical period in which it emerged. It feels as comfortable as an old pair of bedroom slippers, and, generally speaking, offers about as much precision and predictive power. I do not intend to throw my old slippers away, nor do I urge that the like be done with developmental task theory. What I do urge is that we bear in mind that this is essentially a home-spun image of human development that selects one predominant image—Man the Worker—over all others. There are worse images to be sure. There are also a variety of other images that might be enshrined in their own theories of development. These include theories of some antiquity and demonstrated appeal such as the Hindu, Buddhist, and preindustrialization Judeo-Christian conceptions. Send out for pizza and we will create two or three new theories before it arrives. The crucial point here is that the life-span developmentalist's construction of death as a task to be completed flows from our sociocultural dispositions, not from any compelling scienfitic perspective. I have

yet to hear anybody ask, "But why is death a *task*?" Perhaps we should start asking this question. This might be preferable to the docile acceptance of a comfortable image that continues to take the place that might be occupied by a more rigorous and productive theory.

Pop Psych and the Death Meld

There is at least one other contemporary psychological construction of death that should be mentioned. It expresses a powerful urge that we cannot afford to neglect if we are serious about exploring the psychology of death. "Pop Psych and the Death Meld" does sound like the kind of rock group one might expect to be playing for private parties when the band one originally hired cancels out at the last moment. A vivid descriptive term seems appropriate for this vivid approach to constructing death.

Many people receive their psychology through the popular media. Prominent among these are the talking heads of television, and the numerous books and tracts that propose to liberate us from the disappointments and cares of everyday life through a heightened (or deepened) spiritual experience. Even the diligent student of official psychology might turn to these sources after a hard day of being Skinnerized or multivariated.

Death has become a salient topic in pop psychology. It is here, on the fringes, if you will, that a bold construction of death has found its most receptive home. What is death? Death is a kind of life. Death is the other side of life. Death is the ecstatic fulfillment of life. Death is everything life should be but is not. The pop psychologist's construction of death includes some elements that can be found in other views, but seldom in as pure or dramatic a form. The construction seems to have been assembled from selected elements of Eastern and Western thought, rearranged to suit one's own preferences.

Essentially, pop psychology's construction regards death as a phenomenon that is positive in both senses of the term: Death is really "something" (not simply the absence or end of being), and it is something that is desirable. One hopes to attain the degree of spiritual enlightenment that makes possible a kind of meld between life and death. Opposites disappear. Life and death appear as a single, united reality. Rhapsodies on the near-death experience (discussed in detail elsewhere in this book) are often introduced to explicate and support this view.

If we can bear to review all the death constructs that have been identified here, it will be seen that the death meld occupies the furthest extreme from the behaviorist's indirect and minimalistic offering. Melders are very much interested in death, not just in cognitive and behavioral responses to death, and they would not find much satisfaction in the behavioral corollaries that death is pretty much irrelevant and is devoid of moral attributes. The view that death can best be conceived as a source or signal of a destabilization is shared by both academic and clinical behaviorists, and by many others who have intervention on their mind. Life-span developmentalists tend to find more use for the death construct within their overall theoretical structure, and also to see our concern with death as serving an approved, nonpathological purpose (assuming we keep our developmental task schedules in proper sequence). The pop psychology construction of death as the secret and delightful room just a breath away from life is enticing to some people who have found that neither orthodox religion nor orthodox psychology offers them a satisfying image. The death meld construction might be considered too far out by mainstream psychology—but then, some independent-minded spirits might consider the behavioral, clinical, and developmental conceptions to be too far in. (Is it better to die with a worker's satisfied grumble: "There, now that's a good job if I say so myself?" or with an ecstatic tremble and sense of union with the Allness of All?)

Choice of Death Constructions

Psychology offers us a choice of implicit death constructions that I have tried to make a bit more explicit in this chapter. I ask myself: Should I accept the death construction that "comes with the turf" in my own approach to psychology? This would be the most convenient basis for making the selection. All I would have to do is check the identification bracelet on my wrist: Now, what kind of psychologist am I supposed to be these days? A behaviorist? A clinician still under the Freudian or Jungian enchantment? A scruffy existentialist with a far-away look in his eyes? A responsible life-span developmentalist? I have known the joys of all these identities at one time or another, and I cannot be certain that I will be forever indifferent to the allure of pop mysticism. Psychologists who have maintained one steadfast identity could decide in an instant. "I'm a behaviorist, and this is how we behaviorists construct death!"

I wonder, however, if this is the best approach in the long run. Perhaps death should not be treated as a throw-in with whatever psychological package we happen to espouse. Perhaps we should give more attention to our basic assumptions and principles. Perhaps we should even struggle first toward the most adequate (or least inadequate) conception of death that is within our mind's reach—and *then* select our psychology! As matters now stand, psychologists are most likely to call on the implicit construction of death that is most convenient to their overall approach. This construction is not likely to have been rigorously tested, nor is it likely to have received much scrutiny from a logical standpoint either. It will be the death construction that is least disturbing to the psychologist's general stance, the construction that least interferes with his or her routine functioning.

What we can do in this book is to remain sensitive to the influence of implicit psychological constructions of death on the formulation of questions, the choice of methodology, the interpretation of results, and the implications for action. We will not be resolving the differences between the constructions in this way, nor necessarily proving one to be clearly superior. But we will be protecting ourselves from imagining that we have reached fundamental conclusions when all we have done is bumped against one theoretical wall or fallen out of the window of another. This will help us to rejoice quietly when we do occasionally discover something that is not only worth learning but that also happens to be true.

NOTES

1. The anthropological study of death rituals offers many rewarding examples of the points made here. J. G. Frazer's seminal writings, notably *The Fear of the Dead in Primitive Religion* (1933) are still worth reading but have been surpassed by more recent scholarship. Hans Abrahamsson's *The Origin of Death* (1951/1977) is a brilliant and original work that can be recommended without reservation. Theologian J. Zandee's *Death as an Enemy According to Ancient Egyptian Conceptions* (1960/1977) offers a wealth of material about death-related attitudes and practices in the ancient world in general. Jack Goody's *Death, Property and the Ancestors* (1962) provides insights about West African practices well into the 20th century. Ellen Badone's *The Appointed Hour* (1989) describes how social changes continue to affect death attitudes in the Western world today, using Brittany as her example. Current anthropological journals and monographs add new material on death rituals on a fairly regular basis.

2. For a history of psychological contributions before the 20th century, see Brett's monumental, three-volume *History of Psychology*. Standard histories such as Murphy's *An Historical Introduction to Modern Psychology* (1929) provide a great deal of information on the sequence of movements within psychology but do not convey much sense of the psychopolitical struggles involved. The functionalistic, pragmatic, behavioristic triumph did not come easily, and it has never been complete. To capture some of the cool logic and heated passions involved in the debate over the future course of psychology, it

is enjoyable as well as instructive to read primary sources. The writings of Johann Friedrich Herbart (1891/1977), William James (1896), William McDougall (1908/1963), and Wilhelm Wundt (1912/1973), for example, can be more or less pitted against those of John B. Watson (1919; 1924), Clark L. Hull (1943), and B. F. Skinner (1938). Their memoirs and correspondence are even more interesting. The debate is still with us, of course, but has taken different forms.

3. Klaus Riegel and his colleagues did the original research on this topic, drawing primarily on a longitudinal study in Hamburg. Siegler (1975) provides a critical review of subsequent research on this topic. An updated review would be useful.

4. Accidents, murder, and suicide are the three leading causes of death among American youth (ages 15–24). Males are at a particularly high risk. There is no single cause, but it is clear that a tendency toward risk-taking behavior and disregard of safety considerations plays an important role.

5. The developmental tasks proposed by Robert J. Havighurst (1953) were perhaps the most influential. Eric Erikson (1959) and Robert Butler (1963) offered subsequent versions that have also been very popular.

REFERENCES

Abrahamsson, H. (1977). *The origin of death*. New York: Arno Press. (Original work published 1951)

Badone, E. (1989). *The appointed hour*. Berkeley: University of California Press.

Becker, E. (1973). *The denial of death*. New York: Free Press.

Boring, E. G. (1950). *A history of experimental psychology*. New York: Appleton-Century-Crofts.

Brett, G. S. (1914–1921). *A history of psychology*. 3 volumes. London: Unwin.

Butler, R. N. (1963). The life review: An interpretation of reminiscence in the aged. *Psychiatry, 16*, 65–70.

Erikson, E. H. (1959). Identity and the life cycle. *Psychological Issues, 1*, 18–164.

Fraser, J. T. (1977). *The fear of the dead in primitive religion*. New York: Arno Press. (Original work published 1933)

Goody, J. (1962). *Death, property, and the ancestors*. Stanford: Stanford University Press.

Havinghurst, R. J. (1953). *Developmental tasks and education, 3rd edition*. New York: David McKay.

Herbart, J. F. (1977). *A text-book in psychology*. Washington, DC: University Publications of America. (Original work published 1891)

Hull, C. L. (1943). *Principles of behavior*. New York: Appleton-Century-Crofts.

James, W. E. (1896). *The principles of psychology* (2 Vols). New York: Henry Holt.

McDougall, W. (1963). *An introduction to social psychology*. New York: Barnes & Noble. (Original work published 1908)

Murphy, G. (1929). *An historical introduction to modern psychology.* New York: Harcourt, Brace.

Siegler, I. C. (1975). The terminal drop hypothesis: Fact or artifact? *Experimental Aging Research, 1,* 169–185.

Skinner, B. F. (1938). *The behavior of organisms: An experimental analysis.* New York: Appleton-Century.

Watson, J. B. (1919). *Psychology from the standpoint of a behaviorist.* Philadelphia: Lippincott.

Watson, J. B. (1924). *Behaviorism.* New York: Norton.

Wolman, B. B. (Ed.). (1973). *Handbook of general psychology.* New York: Prentice Hall.

Wundt, W. (1973). *An introduction to psychology.* New York: Arno Press. (Original work published 1912)

Zandee, J. (1960/1977). *Death as an enemy according to ancient Egyptian conceptions.* New York: Arno Press.

4

How Do We Construct Death? A Developmental Approach

> I can recall the hour in which I lost my immortality, in which I tried on my shroud for the first time and saw how it became me. . . . The knowledge of my dying came to me when my mother died. There was more than sorrow involved. Her vanished voice echoes in my head and the love she bore me struggled painfully to stay alive around me. But my heart did not claw at the emptied space where she had stood and demand her return. I accepted death for both of us. I went and returned dry-eyed from the burial, but I brought death back with me. I had been to the edge of the world and looked over its last foot of territory into nothingness.
>
> —Ben Hecht, *A Child of the Century*

We have visited a hypothetical world that is free from "natural death," and we have also visited the specialized realm within which psychologists discourse. Now we are ready to explore our own neighborhood. How do real people think about death in their own real lives? We also *construct* death. We search for a way to orient our thoughts and feelings toward a topic that can seem almost unthinkable. These constructions begin very early in our individual development—and, right from the beginning. Our individual constructions of death are influenced by our own unique experiences within our unique physical, interpersonal, and cultural milieu. Even within the same family, no two infants ever have quite the same experience. We will find that developmental level strongly influences a person's conceptions of death, but that marked individual differences can be found among people of comparable age. We will see that our constructions of death are far from idle: They play a role in our interpersonal relationships, decision making, self-image, and overall world view.

It will be tempting for us to pass judgment as we examine thoughts of death from youth to old age. "That's an immature idea!" "That's a ridiculous idea!" "That's an inspiring way to look at death!" The judgment I would like to propose for your consideration at this time, however, is that we suspend judgment as best we can. Later in this chapter we will reward ourselves for this noble behavior by becoming quite opinionated indeed.

"YOU ARE DEAD" AND "I WILL DIE": TWO SIMPLE CONCEPTS THAT ARE VERY DIFFICULT

We begin with two basic concepts that can be stated in so few words that we might be inclined to believe them simple and self-evident. As we come to appreciate the complexity of these ideas, we will also become more sensitive to the challenges the child must overcome in its efforts to comprehend death.

"You Are Dead"

Our constructions of death can be analyzed in many ways. Perhaps the most fundamental distinction is between our conceptions of the death of the other and the death of the self. We will represent the first of these constructions with the simple term, "You are dead." It is more concrete and more within the young child's grasp to begin with "dead" rather than "death." "Hammy the Hamster is dead" literally makes more sense—especially when one is looking at or touching Hammy—than "Death has taken our beloved hamster as it must all mortal beings."

There is reason to believe that "You are dead" develops earlier and more rapidly than the inward-looking, "I will die." What else must the child know, guess, or imagine to arrive at the conclusion: "You are dead"?

1. *You are absent.* What does it mean to be absent? We must appreciate the observer's frame of reference. For a young child, the frame of reference is largely perceptual. Absence means *not* here-and-now. The younger or less developed the child, the more that here-and-now is constructed as a global unit. Spatial and temporal dimensions are not yet treated independently. Suppose that you are "away," in another city. From an adult frame of reference, you have a spatial existence at the present time, even though you are not within my own personal space. The child experiences your total absence, however. You are not in the child's perceptual space at this moment, therefore, you are *not.*

2. *I am abandoned.* This statement is the organismic reciprocal of the first proposition. Your disappearance from my perceptual frame of reference has destroyed my sense of security. As the child, I am not merely aware of your absence but also of the presence of dysphoric feelings within myself. Your absence and my anxiety are intimately related.

3. *Your absence plus my sense of abandonment contributes to the general sense of separation.* I have been isolated from the contact and support that I need to feel safe in the world and good about myself. This separation may also lead me to experience a pervasive sense of having lost contact with the environment, not just with you. I am nowhere. I am anxiety. Furthermore, my distress may have been intensified by the feeling that I was forcibly separated from you, wrenched away. This trauma could intensify the already bleak picture of absence and abandonment.

4. *The separation has no limits.* The young child does not grasp the concept of futurity, nor of time in general. The child lives in a world of what might be called "local time" that is limited to its overall egocentric organization of experience. One of the implications of the child's limited and egocentric organization of time is that the immediate experience of separation cannot be modulated by future expectations. The infant or young child cannot say to himself or herself, "Mother has gone away, but she will return Wednesday and have a nice present for me." The young child cannot distinguish among short-term, long-term, and final, irreversible separations. Once the separation experience has been induced, the child has no dependable way of estimating or anticipating its conclusion. What the outsider may regard as a brief separation may be indistinguishable in the child's mind from the prospect of prolonged separation.

5. *The child's involvement in recurring psychobiological rhythms complicates its relationship to separation and death.* You and I have accepted the existence of "objective" or "external" time that moves unit

by standard unit from the past, through the present, to the future: a clockwork universe that does not much care about our own wishes and priorities.[1] It is different for the child whose time begins afresh each morning when he or she awakens. Midday nap signals a "time out." The child's experience of time is strongly influenced by its internal rhythms of hunger-satiation, sleep-activation, and so forth, as well as the recurring rhythms of night and day.

How does this relationship to time affect the child's construction of death-of-the-other? The vulnerability to separation has already been emphasized. For example, the child cannot distinguish well between the prospects of brief and extended or final separation. Now we must give more attention to an apparent contradiction within the child's experiential world. The sense of limitless separation and the endlessness of any experience conflicts with the recurring rhythms, the periodicity that characterizes infancy and early childhood. As a child who feels abandoned, I have no way of establishing a future limit on my present experience. In fact, the intensity of my distress is related to my fear that this will go on and on without relief. Nevertheless—and this is the more difficult part to grasp—my psychobiological state is always in transition. I am always becoming hungry or sleepy or curious—or something! The environment in which I am embedded is also in transition. The sun is coming up, or it is going down. Various periodic household routines are being started or completed. If the cat has just jumped on the ledge of the living room window, this means that the sound of Daddy's or Mommy's car will soon be heard; those rattling sounds in the kitchen suggest that food is again on the way and so forth.

As a cyclical creature in a cyclical environment, I do not maintain a constant frame of reference over a protracted period of clock or calendar time. There are breaks and interruptions in even my most steadfast thought and behavior patterns. In other words, I do not have a continuous experience. Periodic changes in my inner state and in my relationship with the external environment rest, refresh, and distract me. This means that my experiential world is subject to both rules: (a) the lack of limits or boundaries within which to place a separation experience, but also (b) the inability to maintain a steady frame of reference over an extended period.

As a young child I might misinterpret your temporary departure as being a consequential separation. By this same token, however, I may *under*estimate a consequential separation—even your death. My cyclical pattern of functioning has lead me to anticipate that every end has a fresh beginning, just as every beginning has an end. There is no end to ends, however. You have been away a long time now. I measure "long time" arbitrarily by my own feelings—long enough to make me feel uncomfortable, abandoned. I have deeply rooted within me the expectation that the familiar pattern of separation-reunion will be repeated.

Two opposite responses can testify to the young child's special relationship to time: (a) The child may respond in panic or despair over what is objectively a brief and insignificant separation because to the child this feels like total and unmoderated abandonment; or (b) the child may respond as though expecting a dead parent, sibling, or animal companion to return any minute now.

6. *You do not respond.* This applies to the specific situation in which an infant or young child is in close contact with a dead person or animal. It can also involve a "dead toy" that does not do what it was supposed to do. The most characteristic behavior I have observed in this kind of situation involves the child's attempt to persuade the dead other to respond. Nonresponsiveness, of course, remains an important constituent of the death construct for adults as well. This includes death in the literal sense: "The eyes did not respond to light; there was no response to pressure or pain stimuli, or to words." It also includes death in the figurative sense: "Alas, Percy was dead to my pleas." For the young child, it is clear that the concept of nonresponsiveness arises from an interactive context. "I will make you move. I will make you talk to me. I will make you smile." It is only through the expectation of responsiveness and through failed attempts to elicit responsiveness that the child can generate this facet of the "You are dead" concept. Very early in development, then, an infant or young child will have considerable difficulty in grasping the concept of nonresponsivity. Experience with the world as well as maturational changes in the central nervous system will soon teach the child that it is characteristic of living things to respond, and, therefore, a discomfirmation of expectation when they do not.

For children as well as adults it is much easier to *realize*[2] death when one has had the evidence of one's own senses to support this conclusion. This is a major reason for advocating the somewhat controversial practice of open caskets at memorial services: There really is a body in that casket, and it is the body of our deceased friend. The young child's direct experience of a dead person or animal will differ appreciably from an adult's, but in either instance this kind of contact does provide a firmer reality base for one's response. A 2-year-old does not think of death the way his or her parents do, but the encounter with a cold, still, unresponsive form conveys vital, if still mysterious information.

"I Will Die"

This proposition is even more complex and rigorous in its requirements. We are not in a position to make this statement in a meaningful way until we have mastered several related concepts. These include the following:

1. *I* am a person with a life of my own, a personal existence.
2. I belong to a *class* of beings, one of whose attributes is mortality.
3. Using the intellectual process of logical deduction, I conclude that my personal death is a *certainty*.
4. There are *many possible causes of my death*, and these causes might operate in many different combinations.
5. Although I might overcome or evade one particular cause, *I cannot overcome or evade all causes.*
6. My death will occur in the *future*. By future, I mean a time-to-live that has not yet elapsed, a time that I have not previously experienced.
7. I do not know, however, *when* in the future my death will occur. The event is certain; the timing is uncertain.
8. Death is a *final* event. My life ceases. This means that I will never again experience, think, or act, at least as a human being on this earth.
9. Accordingly, death is the *ultimate separation* of myself from the world.

"I will die" implies self-awareness, logical thought operations, conceptions of probability, necessity, and causation, of personal and physical time, of finality and separation. It also requires the bridging of a tremendous gap: from what I have actually experienced of life to a construction of life's negation. I have not been dead (the state). I have not experienced death (the process of life coming to a final halt).[3] Therefore, the mental operations that I call on in my efforts to fathom death tend to falsify as they proceed. If death implies lack of movement, then my eyes conspire against this fixed image by moving restlessly as I scan the environment (your eyes do the same). If death implies emptiness or silence, my mind again rushes ahead to fill in the void with its own operations, just as people in sensory deprivation experiments manufacture their own stimuli to satisfy our need for cognitive activity. Our mind's own *modus operandi* equips us for interpreting life, not life's negation.

Having seen a dead person, animal, or plant is likely to contribute to my conception of death. Yet these perceptions do not truly bridge the gap. The deadness is perceived from the outside only. *What it feels like not to feel* eludes me. Furthermore, under some circumstance I am liable to misinterpret my perceptions, taking the living for dead, or vice versa. Experiences with the dead, however, must be considered as we attempt to understand the development of death conceptions.

CONSTRUCTION OF DEATH IN INFANCY AND EARLY CHILDHOOD

Developmental psychologists have often told us that the very young children (from birth to about 2 years) have no understanding of death when they happen to mention this topic at all. This opinion is consistent with the contention that young children lack the ability to grasp *any* abstract conception. Jean Piaget, for a prime example, offered a fine-grained analysis of mental development from infancy through adolescence.[4] Within the period of infancy alone, Piaget identified six stages of mental development. Abstract thinking ("formal operations" in Piagetian argot), however, does not emerge until early adolescence. Although the 10-year-old is adept with "concrete operations"—thinking about the actual—it is not until the teen years that a person is able to think about thought and bring to bear the full intellectual powers that seem to be required for a mature comprehension of death. A Piagetian analysis would reach the same basic conclusion as our examination of the proposition, "I will die," although differing in some particulars and emphases.

There is another aspect of Piaget's influential theory that has contributed to a lack of interest in the young child's conception of death. Piaget and his colleagues devoted much attention to clarifying the development of the concept of constancy, conservation, or invariance (three ways of saying pretty much the same thing). Many innovative studies were devised for this purpose. These experiments have contributed much to our understanding of early cognitive development and honed our observational powers. An overriding bias in this approach has gone largely unnoticed and unchallenged, however, Piaget's emphasis on that which does not change has diverted attention away from the significance of actual transience transformation. Yes, it is useful to know when a child has achieved the concept of conservation and can therefore tell us with absolute certainty that pouring water from the long, tall beaker into the short, squat glass has had no effect on the amount of water involved. But reality includes real change as well as real constancy. There is a tendency in developmental theory to treat evanescent or mutable circumstances as a kind of error variance. The developmental psychologist forgets that children cannot truly grasp that which does not change unless they also have an acute appreciation for that which perishes (the goldfish floating at the surface of the water) and that which becomes something else (the ice cream cone on a hot day). It is as though child psychology has decided to create an idealized universe in which constancy and invariance rule supreme: This is not the world we know, however, and children are quick to find this out.

In what follows we will try to stick as close as possible to what has been observed about the infant and young child's experiences with death. Our data base is still limited, although several helpful studies have been conducted in recent years. If these observations do not always fit neatly into existing theories, then perhaps the problem is not entirely with the observations.

Early Exposure to Death of Others

Let us first consider young children's responses to the death of a person who has been important to them. One of the earliest researches into the psychology of death touched on this question. G. Stanley Hall and Colin Scott (reported in Hall, 1922) asked adults to recall their earliest experiences with death. Analyzing the questionnaire responses, Hall tell us that

> the first impression of death often comes from a sensation of coldness in touching the corpse of a relative and the reaction is a nervous start at the contrast with the warmth that the contact of cuddling and hugging was wont to bring. The child's exquisite temperature sense feels a chill where it formerly felt heat. Then comes the immobility of face and body where it used to find prompt movements of response. There is no answering kiss, pat, or smile. . . . Often the half-opened eyes are noticed with awe. The silence and tearfulness of friends are also impressive. . . . Children of from two to five are very prone to fixate certain accessions of death, often remembering the corpse but nothing else of a dead member of the family. But funerals and burials are far more often and more vividly remembered. Such scenes are sometimes the earliest recollections of adults. (pp. 439–440)

Despite Hall's stature as a founder of American psychology, there was no evident follow-up to this study. A few later studies of early memories Costa & Kastenbaum, 1967; [e.g., Tobin, 1972] also found that death experiences are often reported).

We cannot assume that the young child's experience of death is the same today—in this era of violence-drenched television—as it was in the early years of this century. It is worth listening, however, to Hall's further comments on the children of his own time.

> Little children often focus on some minute detail (thanatic fetishism) and ever after remember, for example, the bright pretty handles or the silver nails of the coffin, the plate, the cloth binding, their own or others' articles of apparel, the shroud, flowers and wreaths on or near the coffin or thrown into the grave, countless stray phrases of the preacher, the fear lest the bottom of the coffin should drop out or the straps with which it is lowered into the ground should slip or break, a stone in the first handful or shovelful of earth thrown upon the coffin, etc. The hearse is almost always prominent in such memories and children often want to ride in one. (pp. 440–441)

And Hall even has an explanation to offer. He refers to the "well-known laws of erotic fetishism by which the single item . . . [finds] room in the narrow field of consciousness [and is] over-determined and exaggerated in importance because the affectivity that belongs to items that are repressed and cannot get into consciousness is transferred to those that can do so." This is a remarkable interpretation to come from an academician writing in the twilight of his own life and at a time when the psychoanalytic approach was meeting a mostly hostile response from university-based psychologists. An independent thinker, Hall decided that his data did point in the direction of an intriguing selective memory process. He dared to compare the emotions aroused by exposure to death with erotic sensations—and both in childhood!

Hall's interpretation is not inconsistent with Piaget's later theory. The childhood experiences are of very particular events and sensations, not of well-formed concepts. It is also consistent with psychoanalytic theory's emphasis on the subterranean ways in which our memories are shaped to reduce internal conflict. The emotion-laden experiences at the graveside could not be represented effectively through verbal-conceptual categories that had not yet developed, nor could they be forgotten. It is a reasonable working hypothesis that the recollection of a "minute detail" served as a kind of code for the total experience.

Ernest G. Shactel's (1959) stimulating essay on memory and childhood amnesia would make an excellent starting point for those who are interested in tracing adult memories back to their roots in childhood experience—or to understanding why it is so difficult to recapture our earliest memories. He makes a strong case for the proposition that the processes of memory in adulthood "substitute the conventional cliché for the actual experience." It may well be that our sense of wholeness as adults will elude us unless we can somehow liberate and integrate our early memories into our total being. If this is true, then our earliest exposures to death and other forms of loss may be significant not only for what their role in our development of death constructs and attitudes, but for understanding the entire shape of our lives.

Case histories offer many examples of significant links between early childhood experiences with death and subsequent adult behavior. Here is an example provided by psychiatrist David M. Moriarty (1967).

> Mrs. Q had undergone severe depressive episodes for over a decade. She made three suicidal attempts and twice was treated (unsuccessfully) with electroconvulsive therapy. When Mrs. Q was 3 years old, her mother had died of appendicitis. She recalled standing beside her uncle at the graveside, her arm around his leg. This memory was recovered during psychotherapy after she had several panic episodes in which she reported in great alarm that "the world is coming in on me." Moriarty notes that "The thought behind this fear was traced to this graveyard scene when they threw a shovel full of dirt on the lowered coffin. . . . She (Mrs. Q) felt dead, non-existent, wanted to die, and feared dying. . . . The most impressive fact was that she talked and thought about the death of her mother as much as if it had just happened. This tragic event of forty years ago was still uppermost in her mind" (p. 88).

The sense of time described here seems more appropriate to the young child's experiential world rather than the adult's. Objective time (the passage of 40 years) was not nearly as significant psychologically as the still fresh, painful feeling of losing her mother. It is not that unusual for highly anxious people to distort or compress time into idiosyncratic patterns that conform to their emotional states rather than to standard, consensual time. We should not overgeneralize from case histories, however. There is no direct and automatic connection between death of a parent in early childhood and subsequent depression and suicidality. This is a major life event, but the outcome depends on many factors including the type of interpersonal support available to the bereaved child and the arrangements made for the child's subsequent well-being.

The rapidly increasing literature on childhood bereavement is a valuable source of information on human development in general, as well as on the effects of loss.[5] Here is just one example that might stimulate interest in further reading: "From Wellington to Chamberlain, Britain had twenty-four Prime Ministers, of whom fifteen, or 62.5 percent, were orphans. It is estimated that in general in the British population the proportion of orphans is 1 to 1 percent maximum" (Rentchnick, 1989, p. 64). As this excerpt illustrates, the literature includes data suggestive of positive as well as negative sequelae to the death of a parent. It is important, however, for us to distinguish two very different aspects of parental death: (a) *the death itself*, which may or may not be experienced closely by the child; and (b) the *consequences* of the death (e.g., reduced family income, a new stepparent, etc.). Both aspects are likely to have powerful but differing types of influence on the child's development. It is probable that the child's formulation of a death construct will be most affected by seeing (or not seeing) the person move from health through terminal illness to death, attending (or not attending) memorial services, and so on.

Many studies have relied partially or exclusively on retrospective accounts. This was true, for example, of Hall's survey and Moriarty's case report. But it is also possible to observe the death-related behaviors of infants and young children more directly. Consider the "death-exposure" responses of these two very young boys, David and Michael.

David

David, at 18 months, was toddling around the back yard. He pointed to something on the ground. Daddy looked. It was a dead bird. The boy labeled what he saw, "buh, buh" (his approximation, at the time, for bird). But he appeared uncertain and puzzled. Furthermore, he made no effort to touch the bird. This was unusual for a child who characteristically tried to touch and handle everything he could reach. David then crouched over and moved slightly closer to the bird. His face changed expression. From its initial expression of excited discovery it had moved to puzzlement, and now it took on the aspect of a grief mask. To his father's surprise, David's face was set in a froze, ritualized expression that resembled nothing so much as the stylized Greek dramatic mask for tragedy. Daddy only said, "Yes, bird . . . a dead bird." In typically adult conflict, he thought of adding, "Don't touch," but then decided to say nothing more. In any event, David made no effort to touch.

Every morning for the next few days, David would begin his morning explorations by toddling over to the dead-bird place. He no longer assumed the ritual mask expression, but he still showed no inclination to touch the bird. The small feathered body was allowed to remain in place until greatly reduced by decomposition. The parents reasoned that he might as well have the opportunity to see the natural processes at work. This had been, to the best of the parents' knowledge, David's first exposure to death. No general change in his behavior had been noted at that time, nor had any been expected. This concluded David's first brief experience with death. But a few weeks later there was a second dead bird to be discovered. (This fatality was clearly the work of a well-known local cat whose name need not be mentioned here.) David showed quite a different orientation toward the second death. He picked up the bird and gestured with it. What was on his mind? Something—because he was also "speaking" with insistence. When his parents did not seem to comprehend his wishes, the boy reached up toward a tree, holding the bird above his head. He repeated the gesture several times. Finally comprehending, Daddy tried to explain that being placed back on the tree would not help the bird. David continued to insist, accompanying his command now with gestures mimicking the flight of a bird.

All too predictability, the bird did not fly when returned to the tree. David insisted that the effort be repeated. And again! And still again! Abruptly, he then lose interest altogether in this project.

There was to be a sequel, however, a few weeks later. It was now a New England autumn. David and Daddy were strolling in the woods. There were many small discoveries to be made. After a while, though, the boy's attention became thoroughly engaged by a single fallen leaf. He tried to place it back on the tree himself. Failure. He gave the leaf to his father with "instructions" that it be restored to its rightful place. Failure again. When Daddy started to try once more, David shook his head, "No." Although leaves repeatedly were seen to fall, and other dead animals were encountered every now and then, little David made no further efforts to reverse their fortunes.

This exposure to death seems to have called forth behavior that was unusual and unprecedented for this very young child. Whatever responses were touched off in him by the sight of the dead bird, these represented something new and consequential. The "mask of tragedy" expression suggests the possibility of an almost instinctual and archaic response to death, but this is a question raised, not a theory proved. Perhaps the most impressive feature of this experience was David's persistence in working with the dead-bird image over a period of time. He already had enough experience with the world to know that birds were supposed to rest in trees or fly about, and that leaves also belonged on their branches. Some connection was made in his mind between the dead birds and the fallen leaf, and in all these instances he expressed the desire to see things set to right. In effect, David was testing the principle of commutability in the biosphere—and finding that it doesn't hold up very well.

I find it difficult to escape the conclusion that David formed some connections and concepts through this set of experiences. He could not express his new-made death construct in words, but it seems obvious that he entertained, tested, then rejected the idea that the dead bird can be returned to life. Since this incident, I have collected many others from friends, colleagues, and students who welcomed the opportunity to talk about their own children, grandchildren, students, or patients. It is clear that other—probably very many other—very young boys and girls have made their own personal discoveries about death. It may seem foolish to suggest that a child barely 2 years of age can sometimes grasp the essence of death, but the testimony I have heard and the several examples I have seen for myself make it seem perhaps more foolish to insist that we do not comprehend the central facts of death until adolescence.

Michael

Michael had not drunk from a bottle in more than a year. As a big boy who was almost 3 months past his second birthday, he was a competent and articulate member of the family (Brent, 1977–1978). Now there was a problem, however. For the past several weeks, Michael had been waking up several times during the night—screaming hysterically for a bottle. He could not be satisfied unless the ingredients included both warm water and sugar. Attempts to talk him out of it were useless. He would tearfully insist, "But I *have* to have it!"

One night Michael had been especially upset—so desperate sounding that his father took him out of his crib and sat with him in the rocking chair. The boy relaxed a little but was still tense. His father asked what would happen if he did not get his bottle. "'Then I won't (or can't) make contact!' he replied through his tears." But what did that mean—'make contact'? "If I run out of gas, I can't make contact—my engine won't go. You know!"

Within a few minutes of further discussion the mystery had been solved. Michael had been with his father on three separate recent occasions when their vehicle ran out of gas (twice in the family car, once in a speedboat in the center of a large lake). These situations had confused and disturbed Michael (and did not exactly please his father, either). Michael feared that "My motor won't run, and then I'll die." His father then recalled still another episode in which the engine of their old car refused to start while they were trying to sell it. The conversation at that time had included the key phrases, "Maybe it's not making contact," "the motor died," and "I guess the battery's dead." Michael had listened to this discussion and had drawn his own conclusions.

There was a happy ending to this part of the story. His father reminded Michael that a car was very different from a boy. "Let me see. Can I turn your motor on and off?" Michael laughed. Soon Michael was reassured that he did not have to be filled up with "gas" every night: His motor would keep running very nicely anyhow. Michael kissed his father goodnight and never again awakened to ask hysterically for a bottle of warm sugar water.

The total story was more complex. Gradually Michael's parents pieced together a picture of what had happened as background to the nocturnal anxieties. This story is a little too involved to retell here, but it is instructive to note that another dead bird had figured prominently. This was the family parakeet who was found one day lying motionless at the bottom of its cage. Michael was very upset and persisted in asking what had happened to it. His father had explained: "Every animal has a kind of motor inside that keeps it going. When a thing dies it is like when a motor stops running. It's motor just won't run any more." Michael's father had not been satisfied with this explanation, but it was the only thing he could think of at the moment. There had also been other elements in the family's recent life-and-death adventures, and all of these had been observed by Michael and contributed both to the need to develop a death construct and to the particular form it had taken. This set of related incidents is useful in reminding us that parent–child communication has a telling influence on the development of death-related thoughts and feelings, just as it does in other aspects of life.

These two excerpts from the early biographies of David and Michael suggest that exposure to death can contribute to emotional and behavioral disturbances in early childhood, but also stimulate intellectual curiosity. Furthermore, there was a strong sense of caring, of involvement on the part of both David and Michael for the dead birds they encountered. The death of another creature touches something within the young child. We also see that ambiguities in adult language and thought are apt to confuse young children as they attempt to make sense out of death.

Intimations of Self-Mortality: Does It Start in the Crib?

These two boys were already up and about when they had their observed encounters with death. There is an even more extreme view that asserts that intimations of self-mortality start even earlier. This provocative idea is based on direct observation of infant and child behavior, although not in a systematic manner. Adah Maurer (1966) begins with a premise we have already explored: that the world of the newborn is dominated by periodic awakenings and snoozings sensitizes the infant to the dichotomy between being and nonbeing. This leads to the additional proposition that the infant is capable of experimentation with the states of being and nonbeing:

> By the time he is three months old, the healthy baby is secure enough in his self feelings to be ready to experiment with these contrasting states. In the game of peek-a-boo, he replays in safe circumstances the alternate terror and delight, confirming his sense of self by risking and regaining complete consciousness. A light cloth spread over his face and body will elicit an immediate and forceful reaction. Short, sharp intakes of breath, vigorous thrashing of arms and legs removes the erstwhile shroud to reveal widely staring eyes that scan the scene with frantic alertness until they lock glances with the smiling mother, whereupon he will wriggle and laugh with joy. . . .
> To the empathic observer, it is obvious that he enjoyed the temporary dimming of the light, the blotting out of the reassuring face and the suggestion of a lack of air which his own efforts enabled him to restore, his aliveness additionally confirmed by the glad greeting implicit in the eye-to-eye oneness with another human. (p. 36)

Maurer finds that the term "peek-a-boo" derives from an Old English phrase meaning "alive or dead?" In her view, the infant and toddler's first games are not to be dismissed as inconsequential. She believes these activities should be regarded as an integral part of the long-term process of developing a self identity. Beyond "peek-a-boo," the very young child is likely to engage in a variety of other disappearance-and-return games. These, suggests Maurer, are little experiments with nonbeing or death.

> During the high-chair age, babies persist in tossing away a toy and fretting for someone to return it. If one has patience to replace the toy on the tray a dozen or twenty times, the reward is a child in ecstacy. (p. 37)

Gradually, the child learns that some things do not return. "All-gone" becomes one of the child's most popular expressions. In fact, the child may become a diligent researcher of the all-goneness phenomenon. Maurer cites three examples:

> Offer a two-year-old a lighted match and watch his face light up with demonic glee as he blows it up. Notice the willingness with which he helps his mother if the errand is to step on the pedal and bury his banana peel in the covered garbage can. The toilet makes a still better sarcophagus until he

must watch in awed dismay while the plumber fishes out the Tinkertoy from the overflowing bowl. (p. 37)

Is Maurer reading too much into the behavior of infants and toddlers? Perhaps so. She has identified some actual and common types of early behavior, however, that do pertain to the phenomena of presence versus absence, return versus loss, and so forth. The concepts of constancy-conservation-invariance that are so heavily emphasized in the child development literature would not have much meaning without the contrasting concepts of inconstancy-change-loss and the mediating concepts of return-restoration-revival. A key characteristic observed by Maurer is the motivational and emotional connection between the very young child and loss-related phenomena. It is not just a cognitive task: The child expresses terror, fascination, delight.

This pattern of highly involved, affect-laden behavior is most readily comprehensible within organismic-type theories of human development such as those introduced by Kurt Goldstein (1939), Kurt Lewin (1936), and Heinz Werner (1957). Learning, interacting, and experiencing are not fragmentary activities: These occur as expressions of the total organism ("Short, sharp intakes of breath, vigorous thrashing of arms and legs"). On this view, what eventually emerges as a set of verbal and conceptual formulations about life and death may begin as a highly involved participation in the wonders of immediate experience.

Death perceptions are probably the forerunners of death conceptions. Perhaps this long developmental sequence originates in the infant's experiences of the periodic alternations in its own internal states. Then, if Maurer is correct, the infant actively seeks out the experiences of coming and going, appearing and disappearing. This is a stage marked by intensive organismic participation. Later in childhood, he or she is able to stand a little apart from the immediate experience. The child now perceives changes, losses, disappearances that have "deathish" resonance (e.g., David and Michael with their dead birds). After some years of additional psychobiological maturation and life experience, the individual develops the type of cognitive structures to which such terms as "conceptual thinking" or "formal operations" can be applied.

This is a scenario. It has not really been tested, let alone proved. It is worth our attention, however, because it does use relevant behavioral observations that we can check out and extend if we so choose. It also makes some intuitive sense—that our quest for understanding life and death begins with a lively curiosity based on our own immediate experience of the world, and that this curiosity is charged with strong affect. The infant may not yet be a logician, but it has an excellent reason to be interested in the phenomena of loss, disappearance, separation, and return. For what is the infant, but itself a newcomer on the scene, whose hold on life is still precarious, and whose security in intimately linked with supportive human contact? "Peek-a-boo!" What an odd little theory! Do we have a better one?

Construction of Death Through Childhood

We will now look at the continuing development of death constructs throughout childhood. Research in this area has been much more prolific than with infants and toddlers. Several studies take all of pretoddler childhood as their span (approximately from age 3 to 12), whereas a few concentrate on a particular age level. First let us try, however, to capture the tone of a young child's view of death by listening into this conversation, which I did in fact eavesdrop on in a geriatric hospital ward. A 4-year-old girl is visiting with her 84-year-old great-grandmother. "You are old! That means you will die. I am young, so I won't die, you know. . . . But it's all right, Gran'mother. Just make sure you wear your *white* dress. Then, after you die, you can marry Nomo [great-grandfather] again, and have babies."

This 4-year-old obviously has caught on to something about death. There is a connection with age. It is comforting to believe that she herself will not die, because that is something that only old people do. For a moment or so, the girl seems to be on track—but then she reveals her belief that death is only a temporary state of affairs, an ending that is followed by another beginning. (Developmental psychologists consider this kind of idea to be "immature" when it occurs in young children. It would perhaps be unkind as well as uncomfortable to remind ourselves that this concept has its close parallels in more than one religious doctrine held by millions of adults.) Essentially, we will find in children's thoughts about death an interesting and ever-shifting mixture of solid fact, wishful thinking, guesswork, and the occasional riveting insight.

Pioneering Studies

Psychological studies of death did not start appearing with any frequency until the 1960s, mostly through the activities of American researchers. Two important investigations of children's concepts of death, however, were conducted in Europe during the 1930s. Maria Nagy's study (1948/1959) has gained deserved recognition as a landmark investigation on which many subsequent studies and much of our knowledge has been based. Sylvia Anthony's study (1940) often has been noted in passing, but has received little detailed attention.

British psychologist Sylvia Anthony made a series of inquiries into the child's discovery of death during the 1937 to 1939 period under the guidance of J. C. Flugel, an eminent psychoanalyst. She interviewed and tested 117 children herself, and also arranged for home records to be kept over an extended period by 13 families with children (Anthony, 1940; 1972). Her most basic finding came as a surprise to some people: Normal children *do* think of death. It had previously been supposed that only emotionally disturbed or traumatized children would think of death. This view was often associated with the strong inclination to protect the child from any contact with death. Most parents seemed to believe that they could and should insulate children from awareness of death, and this was the usual advice they received from psychologists and teachers (not that the topic of children's death experiences received all that much attention from parents or professionals). Anthony's study provided one of the first clear indications that children are quite capable of discovering death for themselves and of generating some ideas about it.

Usually, the child's conception of death was associated either with the theme of loss, separation, and abandonment, or with the theme of violence and aggression. The children did not have to experience these catastrophes themselves to offer them as fantasies: The little girl who is very sad because her father is dead, or the little boy who was killed by a burglar who broke into their house. Children could regard death with fear, curiosity, and wonder even if they do not comprehend exactly what it meant to *be* dead. It was enough to know that loved ones had been separated from each other, or that a person had fallen victim to an act of violent aggression.

Anthony interpreted many of her findings in terms of psychoanalytic theory. She gave particular attention to universal themes that may have been expressed throughout human history and are recreated anew by each child. For example, one of the girls in her study told a story in which a child was "paddling in the water, and a great big fish came up and ate her." In another response, the girl's mother was said to have "heard someone crying in the bedroom, and it was a lovely new baby for her, and the same name as the other little girl." Anthony suggests that this thought process reveals the child's association of death with life before birth, as well as the compelling tendency to continue the cycle with rebirth. Drowning fantasies were fairly common in her responses, and she often interpreted them as representing womb symbolism (e.g., Freddie feared that the burglar who killed him would put his body in a sack and throw it into the river.)

Another common fantasy centered around the "bird's-nesting theme." In one typical example, the child fantasied that a boy had "accidentally" broken eggs that he discovered in a nest. Later he felt guilt about this, and feared that he would be punished. He might be taken away and destroyed by a giant. The boy solves his fantasy predicament by turning to his mother for protection, wishing to remain snug and safe in his own nest. According to Anthony, the bird's-nest theme is intimately associated with the oedipal complex. The boy wanted mother all for himself. This led him to destroy sibling eggs and take on the characteristics of a powerful father who can destroy competitors. This daring act, however, exposes him to the wrath of the real father-giant. The boy scurries back to his uncompetitive role as a baby bird under mother's wing.

As we can see from these examples, Anthony did not limit her analysis to the face value of a child's discussion of death. She sought an underlying structure in which the manifest content (e.g., the egg-breaking story) represents an inner conflict that is related to the child's relationship to significant others. She also attempted to discover the basic principles that guide the child's construction of death-related concepts. One of these, she believes, is the *law of the talion*. This is the famous principle of "an eye for an eye." If the child commits—or even thinks of—an aggressive action, there will be equally severe retaliation.

It is worth following this line of conjecture a little further. The talion dynamics involve a kind of psychological *oscillation* on the part of the child. One is the aggressor—then one is the aggressee. Aggression is a constant: The nature of one's own participation in the aggression alternates between perpetrator and victim. Anthony sees an even more primitive cognitive mechanism beneath this phenomenon: "the idea of retaliation itself, primitive as it is, develops from a manner of thought still more general and primitive. This manner of thought is an oscillation of attention, by which a whole fantasy of thought-complex is alternately seen in primary and then in reversed aspect, and then again in primary. Thus, a mother loses her child by death, and then the mother herself dies; and then the child (or a substitute) is alive again; and then the mother comes back, too" (1940, p. 46).

Anthony further suggested that the oscillation tendency can be traced back to very early infancy, specifically to the feeding situation. First in fantasy, then in overt behavior, the infant may exchange places (oscillate) with the mother with respect to who is feeding and who is being fed. "Infants barely weaned, long before they can walk or talk, may be seen spontaneously to offer their biscuit to their mother to eat" (p. 48). Still another factor bears even more directly on the development of the death concept. The tendency for the child's cognitive pendulum to swing back and forth makes it natural to replace, "He is dead" with "I am dead"—and vice versa. This implies that the child does not go through two independent lines of development for personal mortality and death of the other. Whenever the thought of death enters the mind of children, they are likely to put this idea through both passive and active orientations. Furthermore, the continuing alternations between self and other do not end where they started. The child's thoughts and feelings become increasingly enriched and refined. For example, the primitive idea of retaliation tends to be replaced by fantasies of reparation, which is a more complex and sophisticated concept.

The child's inclination to use "magical thinking" (thinking about something can make it happen) leads to emotional vulnerability when bad things do happen. The death of a person or pet may lead to guilt feelings because the child has occasionally had some mean thoughts about them. By appreciating the child's back-and-forth processing of death-related events, adults may be in a better position to share their concerns and relieve their anxieties.

Anthony, like Maurer, also found that children can sometimes take pleasure in their dealings with death or all-goneness. This is most likely to occur when the child is playing out the role of the aggressor rather than the victim. I remember an incident in which delight burned in the eyes of a little girl who approached a family guest (by far the grouchiest of the adults) with a plump woolly caterpillar in hand. She displayed her find directly in front of Auntie Rosanne's eyes—and then pulled the unfortunate little creature apart. "Oooh! It's *juicy!*" the little killer squealed with undisguised satisfaction. Auntie's response was somewhat lacking in delight. Encounters of this sort may alarm some adults. If, however, we accept Anthony's frame of reference, it is natural and instructive for children to imagine themselves as both "producers" and "consumers" of death. Through a variety of experiments, some in their minds and some out in the world, the child continues to test and extend its emerging constructions of death.

Valuable if circumstantial evidence in support of Anthony's observations was provided several decades later when Opie and Opie (1969) published *Children's Games in Street and Playground*. One of their major findings was that children have delighted in playing death-related games for centuries—from ancient Rome to the present time. They demonstrate, for example, that hide-and-seek has many variations throughout the world (e.g., "Dead Man Arise") in which it is clear that

"*It*" is the death-person who pursues the other children with a fatal tag to bestow. "Ring-around-the Rosie" became an elaborate and popular children's game during the plague years as "Ashes, ashes, all fall down" was an all too accurate representation of what was taking place about them. This line of research suggests strongly that children are, and probably always have been, fascinated by death and have attempted both to control their anxieties and improve their grasp of this mystery by incorporating death into their everyday thoughts, games, and rituals.

Despite—or because of—its wealth of observations and suggestions, Anthony's work has not fared very well. Perhaps her psychoanalytical approach has seemed too speculative for the tastes of later psychologists, or perhaps they have been discouraged by the discursive way in which her findings were presented. Nevertheless, there is much in Anthony's contributions that are still worth attention and that have yet to be tested systematically.

The pioneering study conducted by Maria Nagy (1948/1959) has had a much more productive afterlife. This project deserves close attention because it set the pattern for much of what has followed—and also because many of her findings have held up fairly well. She conducted this study in Budapest in the 1930s, although it did not enter the research literature until 1948 and then became more accessible when reprinted a decade later. Nagy met individually with each of the 378 children (ages 3 to 10) who participated. The interview method was supplemented by asking the older children (ages 6 to 10) to make drawings that represented their ideas of death and to explain these drawings. Furthermore, children aged 7 and older were asked to "Write down everything that comes to your mind about death." Her sample was almost equally divided between girls and boys, and she made an effort to include children with various social and religious backgrounds as well as with a broad spectrum of intellectual functioning.

Nagy found that her results could be categorized into three major developmental phases, although there was some overlapping.

1. *First stage: up to about age 5*. The preschool child usually *does not recognize that death is final*. This is probably the most significant characteristic of the first stage. The child, however, also looks on death as being continuous with life—that is, *deadness is a dimunution of aliveness*. A close relationship is seen between death and departure. The person who has gone away is sort of dead, and the dead person has sort of gone away. "To die . . . means the same as living on but under changed circumstances. If someone dies no change takes place in him, but rather our lives change since we can no longer see the dead person as he no

longer lives with us" (Anthony, p. 83). Given this interpretation, the child is mostly likely to be distressed by *death's most palpable aspect: separation.*

> Most children, however, are not satisfied when someone dies, that he should merely disappear, but want to know where and how he continues to live. Most of the children connected the facts and absence and funerals. In the cemetery one lives on. Movement is to a certain degree limited by the coffin, but for all that the dead are still capable of growth. They take nourishment, they breathe. They know what is happening on earth. They feel it if someone thinks of them and they even feel sorry for themselves. Thus the dead lie in the grave. However, the children realize—with a resulting aversion for death—that this life is limited, not so complete as our life. Some of them consider this diminished life exclusively restricted to sleep. (Anthony, p. 83)

In this first stage, the children often begin their remarks with the description of a death perception. The perception itself appears authentic and accurate enough. It is the mental elaboration that goes astray (according to adult standards). This characteristic of Nagy's protocols is consistent with the view that the young child can notice the essential facets of death-related phenomena, but does not yet possess a mature framework within which to interpret and contain them.

2. *Second stage: between ages 5 and 9.* The distinguishing characteristic of this stage is that the child now tends to *personify* death. Although images of death in the form of a person were reported at all ages in the Nagy study, this was the dominant view for the 5- to 9-year range. Two forms of the personification were found: death seen as a separate person, and death as being a dead person (the personifications were usually masculine when a gender was indicated). Several children spoke about a "death-man" who goes about at night. He is difficult to see, although one might get a glimpse of him just before he carries you away. Death, however, might also be a skeleton-man, an angel, or someone who looks like a circus clown, among other variations.

There is a protective feature here: The death-man can be avoided by an alert and clever person. Run faster than the death-man, lock the door, trick him. Find a way to elude Mr. Death and you will not die. As Nagy puts it, "Death is still outside us and is also not general."

The child now does seem to comprehend that *death is final* (although these data are not reported fully). What is not yet fully comprehended is that death is certain and universal.

3. *Third stage: ages 9 and 10 (and, presumably, thereafter).* The oldest children in Nagy's study usually recognized that *death is inevitable*

and universal as well as final. There is no escape, no matter how clever or fast we are. The 10-year-old knows that everybody in the world will die. "It is a thing from which our bodies cannot be resurrected. It is like the withering of flowers," as a 10-year-old-girl explained to Nagy.

What Has Been Learned from More Recent Contributions?

The personifications that were reported so frequently by Hungarian children in the late 1940s have turned up only occasionally in subsequent studies. Why personifications have become less popular has not been clearly established. There is, however, an obvious time and place differential. The follow-up studies were done with children who were born anywhere from one to three decades later, and most were growing up in the United States. It is possible that the Nagy's respondents were more influenced by folk traditions than subsequent generations of children, especially in the United States, who were far more likely to absorb their stories from television than from storytellers and books who were still mining the old traditions. We also appear to live in a media-saturated world in which technology appears more powerful and attractive than the magic and mystery of "fairy tales." Perhaps children have decided to ally themselves with the power of technology and, as a consequence, have found less place in their imagination for personifications of the old-fashioned sort. Supernatural explanations no longer seem to be popular among children—although perhaps of renewed appeal to adults!

The curious dropout in personifications is the major difference between Nagy's original findings and those of subsequent studies. In her valuable review of the literature, Wass (1989) notes "the striking similarity from studies carried out over 30 years apart." This comment applied specifically to children aged 9 and older, but it also characterizes the entire range. Nagy was on the right track when she reported that death concepts undergo a decisive development from early through later childhood.[6] It takes some time for the child to recognize that death is final (not reversible), inevitable, and universal. One particularly useful study (Koocher, 1973) provided empirical evidence for a viewpoint that is held by many developmental psychologists: The chronological age of a child is not as important as its level of maturation. When an independent measure of developmental level is included, this offers a more adequate basis than chronological age for predicting the nature of a child's conceptions of death. The same is true in other areas of cognitive development as well.

Attention has shifted to determining the relative influence of maturational and environmental factors. I do not know any psychologist who denies that both sets of factors must be considered. Both Anthony and Nagy, the pioneers of developmentally oriented research on this topic, were aware of sociohistorical influences and believed that death constructs were generated as part of an ongoing interaction with the environment. Piaget, perhaps still the most impressive contributor to the understanding of cognitive growth, often made it clear that we develop our powers through transactions with other people and the world in general. Nevertheless, there has been a pattern of continuing controversy in which those who emphasize environmental influence seem to be most active.

The available research has been pretty much limited to efforts to establish whether maturational or environmental-experiential factors have the greater effect. It would be far more useful to identify the specific processes that are involved and observe them in action. Whether a particular child or group of children seems to be more influenced by developmental or environmental factors may be less important than our ability to understand the processes that are involved—how the children make use of their own skills, needs, and experiences to create death constructions.

The most convincing indications that life experiences affect the child's cognitions of death has been provided by clinical and field observations. Myra Bluebond-Langner (1978) did an intensive ethnographic study of 40 leukemic children whose ages ranged between 18 months and 14 years. She found that all the children who were 3 years of age or older became aware that they were dying before death was close. The following sequence usually appeared: "the children moved from a view of themselves as 'seriously ill' to 'seriously ill but likely to get better,' and then to 'always ill but likely to get better.' This was followed by a perception of self as 'always ill and not likely to get better' and, finally, to a view of themselves as dying" (Bluebond-Langner, 1989a, p. 47).

This sequence of cognitive formulations depended on the child's opportunity to make certain kinds of observation. For example, children would notice that parents and other adults had started to treat them differently after the diagnosis was made. At first the diagnosis itself did not mean much to the children, but the change in adult behavior did convey a message that they needed to decode. They did not draw the conclusion that they were dying until they had undergone a sequence of experiences including awareness of the death of another sick child they had known. Basically, they seemed to learn a series of events that can happen to children with leukemia and then figure out where they fit into that sequence. Clearly, the endangered children's thoughts about death had been influenced by their circumstances. It is also clear that the children had been working hard at trying to understand their situation; after some time and experience they "take all of these isolated bits and pieces of information and put them into a larger perspective, the cycle of relapses and remissions" (p. 49).

At various times the same child might express several different views of death

> as separation, mutilation, loss of identity, the result of a biological process that is inevitable and irreversible. Death comes across as many things, even contradictory things at once. For example, one 5-year-old concerned about separation who talked about worms eating him and refused to play with toys from deceased children was the same 5-year-old who knew that the drugs had run out and demanded that time not be wasted. . . . We find views of death that one would expect for children their age as well as ones we would not. . . . When a child is dying, his or her experiences are very different from other children of the same age, and hence the accepted developmental model of children's view of death is not as applicable for the dying child as it would be for healthy children. (Bluebond-Langner, 1989b, p. 9)

The siblings of dying children also face special challenges, as studies by Bluebond-Langner and others have found. Both dying children and their siblings are under intense pressure to understand what is happening and what it means to them. Bluebond-Langner is justified in noting that traditional models of psychological development do not provide an adequate basis for comprehending the world of dying children and their siblings. We might add that most theories of personality do not adequately predict or explain how adults cope with dying, death, and grief. This does not necessarily mean, however, that existing developmental and personality theories are useless in the sphere of death-related behavior. What it does demonstrate is the need to enrich the scope and effectiveness of existing theories by including the encounter with death as a significant issue. Weak and brittle theories are not likely to survive this challenge, but the most viable theories are likely to become stronger and more useful. Returning to the child's construction of death, it would be a seriously flawed developmental theory that could not incorporate such vital situational dynamics as life-threatening illness into its scope. Eventually we might be forced to conclude that all current theories are inadequate—as tested by the encounter with death. It cannot be said, however, that either developmental or personality theories have been given much of an opportunity to determine their value in this sphere.

Let us take one example in which knowledge, theory, and practice might be expected to come together. What should be done—if any-thing—when one of the 3-year-olds participating in the activities of a children's center becomes terminally ill? This was the question faced by the instructors in a Pittsburgh preschool program. We are fortunate to have a report published by Joanne Pohlman (1984) that documents the attempt to provide a helpful response by caring adults who have some familiarity with the literature on children and death.

Marjorie was one of 16 3-year-olds enrolled in this preschool program. She had already been under treatment for cancer. The two instructors experienced "dismay and fear with a touch of anger" when they first saw Marjorie: She had lost her hair as a result of chemotherapy, and the tumor had caused the loss of one eye, which had been replaced by a prosthesis. At this very early point in the process, the instructors faced the challenge of coping with their own personal anxieties as well as the effects on the other children if Marjorie was accepted into the class. They decided to accept Marjorie and to integrate her into the group "as normally as possible and . . . deal with her differences as they came up in the normal context of the program" (Pohlman, p. 125).

It is obvious that death education and research played a significant role even before Marjorie's first day in the preschool program. In reading Pohlman's report we can see that (a) the instructors knew that children did think about death, and in a distinctive way that intertwined reality and fantasy; (b) it was normal for them to have some personal anxieties; this did not have to be denied but could be worked through; (c) the children would probably have a variety of concerns that would be expressed over time and in many different ways; and (d) the teachers would need to be good listeners and observers who were able to respond to subtle meanings as well as to the surface communications. In finding the courage to accept this challenge, the instructors drew not only on their personal resources but also upon readings they had encountered in the dying and death literature. Perhaps the most essential fact was simply that the topic of children and death had been legitimatized. In the past, the implicit message had been that one should pretend children are unaware of death and that adults can really protect them from all death encounters. Now it was not only acceptable to face death together with children but a potential growth experience for everyone involved. Furthermore, the prevailing philosophy in the new death-related literature asserted the rights of the dying person. People who are facing death should not be isolated and rejected because of society's own anxieties: This is one of the times when people most need each other. "Do something—face the challenge—try to help!" was the message they received from the death-related literature. The instructors apparently found little guidance within the traditional child developmental literature as such.

The instructors integrated Marjorie's wig into the category of the different types of clothing that the children wore (red shirt, green shirt, blond wig). The discussion eventually expanded to include illness and medicine. It turned out that many of the other children had their own concerns about doctors, hospitals, injections, and so forth. Had Marjorie not been in the program, the other children probably would not have had the opportunity to express their own health-related concerns and have some of their questions answered.

The children became especially concerned about Marjorie when she came to class with a patch over one socket. Her prosthetic had been removed to be enlarged. This led to discussion about "pretend eyes."

> The children were given bandages, gauze, cottonballs, old syringes, and stethoscopes as part of their free play equipment. The intensity of their play indicated the impact of our discussion. There was not a sound in the room as the children administered medicine and cared for their babies. Many of the babies' eyes were covered with bandages, and during the play several children, including Marjorie, tested the problems of eye loss by covering first one and then the other of their own eyes. This play continued for several days. When we held back the materials thinking it was time to move on, the children asked for them. Children most often played the roles of parent, nurse, or doctor. . . . The doctors always were able to make these babies better. . . . Soon the children's interest in the hospital play waned, and they returned to the usual preschool activities. (Pohlman, 1984, p. 127)

We can see in this description some evidence of the oscillation phenomena that was first reported by Anthony: The children first chose to play the role of the patient, then became competent adult caregivers. We also see the value of allowing the children themselves to decide how much time they need to experiment with loss before moving on to something else. Furthermore, through the group activity and the instructors' approval, the children had the opportunity to learn that it was acceptable to notice and respond to loss: They did not have to keep all their fears to themselves or their curiosity under wraps. It is important to add that adults were available to the children throughout their school hours for individual interactions as needed.

Marjorie died rather suddenly during the seventh week of school. She was one of several children who had been ill, apparently with the flu. The class had been acknowledging the absence of the sick children during each day's "sharing time." During the next day's sharing time, the instructors introduced the topic by talking about Marjorie's eye. Some of the children hoped that she would be able to see again. When the instructors said that this was not so, the class began to come apart. The children showed a high level of anxiety and started to talk to each other about other things—anything but Marjorie and her pretend eye. "We had to insist on quiet and attention, assuring the children they would have their turn to talk later." The instructors explained that the doctors had done everything they could, but that Marjorie had died. They described cancer as "being inside of you where no one can see; so we had not known how sick Marjorie was." They also emphasized that many people with cancer do get better, and then they spoke of their sadness that Marjorie would not come back to school and that they would not see her again.

During the next several days the children expressed curiosity and concern about many aspects of Marjorie's illness and death. The teachers attempted to answer the questions simply and specifically; they also tried to help the children differentiate between her illness and other illnesses that they or their family members had experienced. Some questions were asked over and over again (e.g., "Is cancer like a cold in your eye?"). The children seemed to be checking the instructors out to see if the answers were still the same. Some information the teachers had previously given to the children now made it more difficult for them to integrate the facts associated with Marjorie's death. For example, they had learned that shots and medication and doctors help to keep you from getting sick—but look what happened to Marjorie!

The pattern of response to Marjorie's death extended over time and took many forms. Hospital play resumed, but now the doctors could not always make the babies well. In other games, such as cops and robbers, people also died sometimes. Some sad-looking children seemed to wait for others to express the feelings they could not put into words themselves. Returning to the same preschool program a year later, the children spoke occasionally of Marjorie and raised further questions about her. Throughout all this time, the teachers and the program director had remained in frequent contact with the parents and kept them informed of what was occurring.

To an appreciable extent, this set of experiences demonstrate that the academic and clinical literature can help adults to help children cope with death-related issues as they arise in real life. The instructors were fairly well aware of the nature of children's constructions of death and prepared for the likelihood that the 3-year-olds would be actively "processing" Marjorie's death during an extended period. Yet this courageous venture also demonstrated some of the difficulties inherent in sharing death with children. Pohlman retrospects that she and the other adults involved had not allowed themselves to anticipate Marjorie's death. It was just too painful to think about that possibility. Obviously, the instructors and their assistants knew that Marjorie had a life-threatening condition and that she might die during the school year. They had stopped short of drawing this inference, however.

I have found this type of thinking to be highly prevalent in death-related situations. We do not "deny" most of the facts. We do not deny the situation is serious. We cope with many of the changes and challenges. We allow ourselves, however, the secret comfort of holding back that further concession to reality, that chilling conclusion, "Yes, it is so: death." The preschool instructors were just being normal human beings in leaving themselves the hidden mental escape hatch, the thought that "Marjorie is not really going to die—not now, not soon, not while I'm teaching this class." This was not only a private arrangement within the mind of each participating adult but also seemed to be the group's strategy. It is useful to remind ourselves here that although the focus in this chapter is on the individual's construction of death, there are also interpersonal and social constructions that need to be identified.

Pohlman remarks that their own anxiety-motivated evasion of Marjorie's impending death interfered with opportunities to offer preparatory experiences for the children. "For example, when a gerbil died . . . we did not talk with the children about it. Talking about death at this point would have given them an experience to build upon later" (p. 129). She also felt they might have had more open communication with the parents in advance of Marjorie's death, thereby perhaps reducing subsequent anxieties.

We have looked at this sequence of experiences in some detail because it illustrates what has been accomplished and what has yet to be accomplished in sharing death-related experiences with children. There is an adequate data base available to indicate that even very young children are sensitive to absence, separation, disfiguring changes, loss, and other phenomena associated with death. It is also evident that children hone their minds on death-related phenomena as part of their general grasp of the world: Curiosity and concern are engaged when they observe disappearances, decay, nonresponsiveness, and so forth. As adults we will not succeed in protecting them from all such experiences—and, as adults, we will be modeling attitudes toward death that are either open or closed, consistent or inconsistent, anxious or comforting.

Marjorie's peers in the preschool program probably experienced some anxieties that would not have entered their lives at that moment if she had been excluded from the class or if the instructors had worked diligently to deceive them. Nevertheless, they probably also drew some valuable lessons about life and death, including the feeling that people have the strength to cope with sad and frightening things; we do not have to keep all these bad feelings and confused thoughts to ourselves. The instructors were handicapped to some extent, however, by the relative lack of attention to death-related issues in teacher education. The major theoretical orientations and data bases that are influential in schools of education still resemble Marjorie's "pretend eye" when it come to death-related phenomena. The instructors had come across some relevant literature, and this proved useful. They had not been given much opportunity to explore their own thoughts and feelings about death, however, and to develop skills specific to the challenging situation that confronted them here. Realistically, it is difficult to expect teachers and other human service providers to be expert in helping children cope with death when their own educational background has given meager attention if any attention at all to constructions of death.

Constructing Death From Adolescence Through Adulthood

What happens to our death-related thoughts after childhood? There has been a strong presumption that we comprehend what there is to comprehend about death by late childhood or early adolescence. The continuing passage of years is assumed to have no significant effect on our basic concepts of death, although our attitudes may alter with age and circumstance. By our 16th birthdays, for example, we know that death is inevitable, final, nonreversible, and universal. We have passed through all the preliminary stages of cognitive development observed by Nagy and others. However, we still have a choice of attitudes toward death. I might shave my head, create my own black T-shirt adorned with a nasty luminescent skull, and cruise along to the Walkman beat of the latest violent death-obsessed hip-hop song.[7] You might choose instead to devote yourself to preparing for a career in nursing, social work, or environmental sciences, motivated by the urge to protect lives. Although we would have selected very different pathways (for the moment, at least), we would both be cognizant of the basic facts of death, and we would both feel the need to respond in some wholehearted way.

Years later, both of us may appear indistinguishable from most other people who are also in their midlives. We do not seem to have *any* particular orientation toward death. We are engrossed in the routines and details of our daily lives and show little or no obvious concern for death. (Although on closer inspection, we might wonder about your exercise program and my purchase of a red sports car: Could we be jogging and racing away from that grim old figure with the scythe?) Attitudes and actions influenced by death-related thoughts are apt to be more obvious in youth and to be more disguised in middle age. In both situations, however, we are presumed to share a basic comprehension of death even though our attitudes and actions may vary considerably.

Beyond the Standard Story

This is pretty much the standard story. It is implicit in much of the research and pedagogical materials we find in the children-and-death literature. It is also consistent with the general accounts of human cognitive development that have been offered by Piaget and several other writers. The standard story does have much to recommend itself. Nagy in her one study and Piagetians as well as counterPiagetians in a prodigious number of studies have demonstrated that childhood is a period of intense cognitive activity from which people of normal mental endowment emerge with the basic constructs that are required to comprehend our relationship to the world. Many questions and controversies remain, but there is no reason to doubt that death-related thoughts undergo a vigorous sequence of maturational and experiential changes before they reach their mature configuration.

Can we really be so sure, however, about what constitutes "mature" thoughts of death? There are three major difficulties with the prevailing assumption that our death constructs have reached maturity in late childhood adolescence.

1. "Maturity" can be a culturally biased concept.
2. The preservation and application of mature death concepts throughout adulthood has not been systematically established.
3. The possibility that additional types of death constructs may develop during adulthood has not been systematically investigated.

Let us begin by looking at the construct of "maturity" with something other than rapt adoration. This concept has proved useful, perhaps even indispensable, in the biological sciences where it can be anchored to well-specified referents. We are not left wondering what the difference is between a mature and an immature lemur, or a mature and an immature nerve fiber. There is no ideological or political advantage to be had through arguing that this lemur is mature or that nerve fiber is not.

We are in trouble, however, as soon as we try to array human thought, feeling, and action along the immaturity-maturity dimension. Our biophysical characteristics are not especially problematic. For example, we have reached our mature skeletal growth; our children have not. But have we attained the height and depth of cognitive maturity? Psychological and biophysical statements about maturity can be framed within identical propositional forms. Of course, "maturity" itself or some equivalent term can be featured in either a biophysical or a psychological formulation. This similarity of propositional form, however, conceals a world of difference—literally, different universes of discourse. There is potential for misunderstanding if we assume that the psychologist and the bioscientist share the same definition of "maturity." Usually, the bioscientist works with a definition that is closely grounded in empirical observations and relatively free from value bias. By contrast, the psychologist tends to think of maturity as a favorable or positive condition, and the definition itself is likely to be vague around the edges. This confusion and its resultant mischief is not limited to the domain of death-related constructs. We can detect it throughout a broad spectrum of psychosocial writings. But the loose and value-inflected use of "maturity" does extend to our death constructs, and that is what concerns us here.

Cultural differences in the construction of death can offer us a perspective on our own inclination to array concepts along a single dimension of maturity. I am thinking, for example, of several adults who have repeatedly demonstrated their ability to comprehend and cope with the challenges of modern life. One young man, in particular, has managed to support his wife, children, and grandmother while working his way through graduate school. Several of his positions have been with governmental or quasi-governmental agencies and have required a high degree of tact, judgment, and sophistication. The fact that he has always had more employment offers than he can accept attests to his competence, as does the successful completion of his master's degree and the warmth of his family life. A "mature" person? Definitely—if this term has any meaning at all.

But it is frustrating and almost pointless to "talk death" with this young man if we insist on remaining within the standard Euro-American universe of discourse. He is Navajo, and Navajos have their own ways of thinking (and not thinking) about death. *Can* he think about death in the manner described by Nagy and others? Yes, of course. Does he *choose* to think of death as a "mature" mainstream American would? Not when he really has a choice about it. His heritage equips him with a view of death that does not just differ from the Euro-American mainstream in some details, but also in its overall conception that cannot be separated from the Navajo view of life and the universe.

A point-by-point academic comparison of the Navajo with the mainstream construction of death would hold some interest—but it would introduce a significant distortion. It would be the imposition of a non-Navajo framework for analyzing and evaluating Navajo thought. So where does this leave us? We might continue to insist that there is only one mature way to think of death (and it happens to be ours). Or we might allow ourselves to consider an untraditional and perhaps alarming alternative: There are as many kinds of "mature" constructions of death as there are ethnophilosophical orientations toward life. Then again, we just might decide that "maturity" is a term to be used with great caution when applied to a topic that so challenges the limits of human thought and knowledge. Do we really know death so well that we can say that somebody else's construction is "immature?"

We will consider the second and third points together. It is usually assumed that the basic concepts we develop during childhood and adolescence stay with us forever. An exception is sometimes made for the adverse effects of life events (e.g., head trauma, abuse of alcohol, or drugs) or disease (e.g., dementia of the Alzheimer type). This is a reasonable enough assumption. In many fields of science, however, "reasonable enough assumptions" have often failed to meet the test. There has been an encouraging recent trend (perhaps "trend" is too optimistic a term) in developmental psychology to explore the ability of adults to use some of the concepts that emerge in late childhood and adolescence (e.g., causality, conservation of mass). There has been practically no research to determine whether or not "mature" death-related constructs are consistently and appropriately employed by adults.

At present, then, one might as well offer an alternative hypothesis: *The mature construction of death is achieved by adolescence, but remains dominant and effective for only those adults whose cognitive style and activity is receptive to this view.* (In this context, by "mature construction of death" I mean the related ideas that death is inevitable, certain, nonreversible, final, and universal.) Perhaps most of us do acquire or develop this configuration of death-related concepts in our youth. Perhaps we also "deselect" this array in favor of more congenial ideas, however, as we move from the adventuring of adolescence into the obligations and repetitions of middle age.

Maturity may be only a passing phase—something we get over, if we are lucky or clever enough!

The other side of this proposition is also worth attention, if only to keep us from settling into our assumptions too comfortably. Perhaps through childhood and youth we develop constructions of death that are adequate as far as they go, but that are only the foundations for what will eventually become a more impressive edifice of thought. Favoring this view is the recent revival of interest in the "wisdom of old age."[8] Life-span developmentalists and some others are at least considering the possibility that we may continue to enrich our thinking throughout life; this is also a view that Piaget expressed as he himself aged.

It is a reasonable enough proposition that with advancing age and experience we do—at least some of us—become more adept in the interpretation of life's more challenging contingencies. Many of us can think of elderly people who do seem to have a superior understanding of life, death, and baseball. Yet, again, a "reasonable enough proposition" should not be (mis)taken for established fact. Note, for example, that research on cognitive functioning across the life-span still finds a pattern of age-related deficit, despite some more encouraging results (e.g., Schaie, 1987). Furthermore, the heightened wish to discover wisdom in old age may be father, mother, or press agent to the deed. For now, the point is that Nagy-type "maturity" of death construction could be only the foundation on which some people (but who? and how? and why?) develop a richer and more encompassing conception.

I suggest that we keep our minds open on this topic. Systematic research into the expression and use of death constructs throughout the entire adult age range might lead to significant revisions in our understanding. We might "unpack" the concept of maturity so that it does not introduce a variety of ideological and ethnophilosophical prejudices under the guise of a neutral scientific term.

MENTAL GYMNASIUM: WORKING AND PLAYING WITH THE THOUGHT OF DEATH FROM YOUTH THROUGH OLD AGE

There is no well-documented later-life equivalent for the stages of death comprehension observed in children by Nagy (1948/1959) and others. We do continue to modify our constructions of death, however, and we do use them in quaint, resourceful, and fantastical ways. I have selected a few examples that have received little or no previous attention and hope these will be useful as a guide to your own observations. I have also noticed several types of cognitive operation that we often call on when we either work or play with our constructions of death. Four of these operations—let us call them the mental gymnastics required for advance performances—are worth identifying at the outset.

1. *Awareness versus habituation or denial.* This represents a complex set of perceptual and cognitive operations, but it comes down to the choice between accepting or dismissing a signal. When reading the newspaper tomorrow morning my well-practiced information-processing system and my usually vigorous anxiety-reduction system may collaborate to shield me from responding to the days' crop of murder, accident, suicide, AIDS fatalities, and so on. Perhaps just one of these signals will get through to me, however. I lose my distance. I feel something.

2. *Activation versus inactivation of a death construct.* There will be no need to draw on particular concepts of death if I have succeeded in dismissing the morning's death signals as irrelevant, redundant, or just too destabilizing to consider. If I have become "alive to death," however, then I must do something with this signal. My basic choice here is to activate or deactivate the various death constructs that are featured in my repertory. Most theories assume that if we have concepts we will use them. I don't think so. I think we have several linking operations that give us the flexibility to apply or to exclude the concepts that are available to us, depending on our interpretation of the total situation. Perhaps, then, tomorrow morning I will allow myself to be pierced by a death signal but will not go so far as to think through its implications. If I caught myself thinking, why that could be serious! So I may have almost patched over my fairly intense but momentary exposure to death by the time I have finished with the newspaper. I did not act on this signal with my death construct system; therefore, I did not let it make a lasting impact on me.

3. *Reframing of signal.* This is a technique that can be used in an almost infinite variety of ways. I become aware of a death-related signal, and I accept it as such. I now make a set of perceptual, cognitive, and symbolic arrangements, however, that will have the effect of transforming the original meaning to something else—usually something less threatening. Perhaps I substitute professional or ideological jargon for the earthy emotional words that first rush to mind. I witnessed many examples of this legerdemain while I was a hospital director who met frequently with other health officials. Almost never was there discussion of real people really dying—but there were frequent bureaucratic rhapsodies that surrounded this theme (bolstered by references to "the bottom

line"). I soon learned it would be a violation of the participating officials' tender sensitivities if I dared to speak of dying, death, and grief as the actual perils these posed for the actual (aged) patients in my charge. If I would join in the reframing game, then I might accomplish something now and again by exchanging coded messages. Reframing can also accomplish its mission by making the urgent seem routine, the preventable seem out of our hands, or the tragic seem quaint and humorous. Unlike habituation or denial, reframing acknowledges the existence of a death signal, but, mostly through symbolic manipulations, it transforms the original encounter to something that appears less threatening, more controllable.

4. *Interpretation of death signals as special or as integrated phenomena.* People sometimes are able to cope with death signals in a highly focused and effective way. This efficiency, however, may be purchased at the cost of excluding the event from one's overall view of self and world. Paramedics repeatedly find themselves in the kind of situation that encourages this approach. Unlike most other people, the paramedic has been well trained to respond to life-and-death emergencies in the community. The paramedic is not likely to shy away from a death-relevant situation: He or she will not deny what meets the eye; on the contrary, close and attentive observations will be made. Basic death constructs will be activated as part of the recognition that this is a consequential situation. Although the paramedic will frame this situation in a distinctive manner, this will not represent an evasion of reality, but, rather, will prepare him or her to function effectively and with a minimum of wasted effort. The one "luxury" the paramedic has at this moment is to focus all attention on the job to be done. In fact, paramedics may experience emotional suffering if their thoughts are invaded by the broader implications of the situation. By contrast, a person who has the time to reflect may interpret a particular death (even his or her own) as only one aspect of a larger pattern. Death is given its place, but it is not allowed to dominate one's entire thoughts and values.

Some Death Thought Games in Youth and Early Adulthood

The following examples of thought operations involving death are usually found more often in youth and early adulthood, but they are not practiced by all young people nor are they entirely neglected by their seniors.

"I die, therefore, I am."

This game, like all the others, is serious—that is why it is such a good game. During adolescence we reconstruct the ideas and attitudes that served us through most of childhood. It is during this process that some young men and women write poetry for the first and only time in their lives, and even characteristically unreflective people wonder why we are born to die and why girls (or boys) are so difficult to understand. Equipped with the ability to think more abstractly and flexibly than before, the adolescent and young adult also has a more vivid awareness of the dialectic between being and nonbeing (Kastenbaum, 1986). This is intensified by interest in futurity. "I might be this, or I might be that—or, I might not *be*!" The child's earlier oscillation of thought has reached a new level with the realization that the future holds both everything and nothing.

It is at this developmental moment that the young person is most endangered by the perceived polarities of being and nonbeing—*and* simultaneously faced with the question of self-identity. "Who am I becoming?" A transitional, fragile, but very intense sense of selfhood may emerge at this time, formed around the dialectics of being and nonbeing. "This is who I am. I am the one who is torn by conflict. I am the one who wants to go back and go forward and not move at all. I am the one who has everything, I mean nothing, I mean everything to live for. I am the one who will live forever but who may die tomorrow."

The solution to both challenges may be found—temporarily—by drawing on the power of metaphor. Dying is an especially potent metaphor during transitional situations and when one must cope with extremes of stimulus overload and deprivation. The same person may feel "bored to death" and slain by excitement ("I just died!") in passing from one unmodulated experience to another. Furthermore, one may also feel he or she is dying from the past of childhood without having yet reached the relatively secure ground of adulthood. In short, "I am the dying person" or "I die; therefore, I am (still alive)." The adolescent, in this sense, needs the thought of death. It provides an image that resonates to some of his or her core experiences. In a paradoxical way, the sense of dying is enlivening, and the uncertain destination offers direction.

The rules that distinguish metaphorical from literal meaning may not be firmly enough established to resist pressure. For example, "If my life is like dying, then maybe dying is like my life. And if sleep is like death, then death should be like sleep. And if sex is so exciting I could just die, then death might be even more exciting than sex." Often adolescents have little opportunity to try out their more lavish death-related thoughts on more experienced minds. A feeling may therefore spark an image that enlists a thought and encourages a course of action that actually threatens life. The three leading causes of death in adolescence—accident, homicide, suicide—are closely related to the victims' own behavior; it is probable they are also related to the intense, imaginative, but "unseasoned" mix of death-related constructs at this time of life.

"The future can wait."

This mind game becomes appealing when one feels rushed—unprepared—toward an uncertain or alarming destination. It has been suggested that the catatonic form of schizophrenia is a strategy for controlling annihilation anxiety by controlling time and motion. "I do not act. I do not change. Therefore, time is suspended, and death must wait." Adolescence is not catatonia. Many teenagers, however, do feel themselves accelerating toward the future, hurtling rapidly from the known to the unknown. These were among my findings when I studied future time perspective and orientations toward death in high school students (Kastenbaum, 1959; 1961).

1. Typically, the teenagers directed their thoughts to the future—but only to the near future. Almost everything important in life was just about to happen. By contrast, the second half of their projected life-span was almost barren. Seldom did anybody mention even the fourth or fifth decade of their own lives, let alone the seventh, eighth, or ninth.

2. Much of the past was neglected or blanked out as well. They expressed a sense of uneasiness when asked to turn their thoughts toward their own childhood. "I wasn't anything!" is the way one high school senior put it, and he seemed to be speaking for most of his peers.

3. The sense of rapid movement from the present to the future has already been mentioned. There was not a strong relationship between the sense of forward motion, however, and the extent to which the individual was thinking ahead into the future. In reading the responses I could not avoid the impression of a person at the wheel of a hot sports car, tearing along a road without knowing—without *wanting* to know—what might lie beyond the next curve.

All these adolescents could conceive of futurity. They also had the intellectual ability to think about their lives as a whole: who they had been, who they were now, who they might become. Nevertheless, most seemed to have erected psychological barriers between their momentary selves, and both their past and their adult selves. Subjectively, they existed in an intense, narrow chamber or tunnel that, despite its hectic pace, did not actually take them anywhere.

Two other studies may help us to put these findings into perspective. College students (males only) were asked a set of direct questions about death, (e.g., "I think about my own death . . . more than once a week, once a week, once a month, every few months"). They were also given a time perspective task and the Picture Arrangement subtest of the Wechsler Adult Intelligence Scale, which some clinical psychologists regard as a measure of the capacity to anticipate future events. Dickstein and Blatt (1966) found that those who reported the most "thinking about death" showed a more limited tendency to project into the future. This finding is based on correlational techniques and, like my studies, cannot demonstrate causality. Nevertheless, it does suggest that apprehension about death may be a major factor in the tendency of adolescents to allow themselves relatively little attention to their extended future. Perhaps one does not care to gaze too far down the road because he or she just might see something (i.e., *nothing*) there.

If death concern does restrain one's view of the future, then it may also impair the ability to plan ahead, to anticipate both hazards and opportunities. A teenager might appear to be impulsive or shortsighted when in fact he or she is a highly intelligent person who has averted attention from all but the near future because the feared annihilation of self is "out there, someplace." The fact that the adolescent has had a relatively limited opportunity to learn how to schedule and organize events in time may also make it difficult to "finesse" the future. Midlife adults are more likely to protect themselves from naked encounters with the thought of death by arranging their minds and schedules so that the "plannedness of time" serves as a subjective shield against the pricklers of mortality.

In a sense, then, the adolescent has

- More to lose from death because so much of his or her desires and identity depend on the future for fulfillment
- Less experience in shaping and scheduling subjective time
- A sense of rushing (being rushed) without a strong sense of destination
- Often little opportunity to discuss life-and-death issues with mature adults who might serve as guides or models (because many adults are busy in being busy (i.e., avoiding thoughts of death)

Given these circumstances, it might be comforting to let the future wait. Keep the excitement, the sense of motion and acceleration, but not actually venture out too far into that murky place where annihilation is but one of the terrors. In reporting my earliest study on this topic (1959), I tried to make sense of the pattern of findings by suggesting that there may be a close link between the adolescents' rejection of their childhood past and their avoidance of their extended adult futurity. So similar were the statements they made about past and remote future that they seemed to come from the same psychological source. It was as though the dysphoric who-I-was-is-not-who-I-want-to-be past was hurled as far away as possible—into the formless future. This sets the individual up for more difficulty. Eventually, the comforting sense that time is holding fairly constant will be destablized and the future become more real (e.g., parents die or move to Florida, the first gray hair is discovered on one's own head). When forced to recognize the reality of change and futurity, one may encounter the anxious, dysphoric feelings that had been projected from childhood to the remote-seeming zone of middle and later adulthood.

The other study that may help some in understanding the adolescents' thoughts of death requested college students (all women) to write a set of six personal essays. These were to describe pleasant and unpleasant future events, pleasant and unpleasant past events, the earliest memory, and the day of one's death (McLaughlin & Kastenbaum, 1966). They were also asked to rate each of their essays on a scale of engrossment or self-involvement. Those who felt objective and detached, as though they had been writing about somebody else, would have low engrossment scores.

The findings most relevant for us here begin with the tendency of these young women to describe their own deaths in a rather tranquil—and distant—manner. This unruffled emotional tone and the omission of symptomatology had much in common with the imagined deathbed scenes I have collected during the last several years and reported in another chapter. These young women placed their days of death well off into the future, usually into the "unimaginable age of 60!" as one commented, or beyond. Not much emotional conflict was expressed—in fact, not much emotion at all. Graceful, peaceful acceptance and resignation were the general themes. The self-engrossment scores were lower than for any of the other essays they were asked to write.

It would appear that these young women were not nearly as concerned with death as we might have expected from the preceding discussion. Furthermore, they did project ahead into the remote future (the modal death was seen as occurring in their sixth decade). The study did not end with the procedure that has been described, however. After completing all the essays, the respondents were asked to imagine the day of their death in a *different* way. This unexpected request was intended to determine what subthreshold image, if any, might be available for sampling after they had offered the portrait of their personal death that had come most readily to mind. We did not specify what was meant by "different."

The second projected day of death was markedly different from the first. Death was now much closer. Many of the young women described deaths that would occur within the next few years. For the total group, the distance between one's present situation and death decreased by more than 20 years. The specific form taken by death also changed. Accidents and acts of violence became much more frequent. Furthermore, the death situations were described more vividly, in greater detail, and with more use of emotion-laden words. The writing style became less restrained and "proper." The young women seemed to be expressing themselves more spontaneously and idiosyncratically as they portrayed an alternative version of their demise. Emotional conflicts—almost completely absent from the first stories—were abundant in the second set. Judges who read both sets of stories ("blind") rated the second set as conveying more emotional impact and a greater sense of involvement on the part of the authors.

Yet the respondents themselves reported, through their self-ratings, that they were even *less* engrossed in these essays than they had been in the first version! The self-ratings and the judges' ratings were contradictory. At the same time that these young women were depicting their deaths as being closer to them in time, more vivid, disturbing, and emotional, they were reporting that they had felt very little involvement. Methodologically, this study underscores the importance of going beyond the respondent's first or most accessible response.

What does this study suggest about the relationship between concepts of death and futurity in young adults? Futurity is rolled out, and insulation buffers one's present self from the self that eventually must die. The success of this insulation may be judged by the fact that the other aspects of the personal death essay were neutral and tranquil. The respondent could rely on readily available stereotyped expressions—a sort of greeting card view of one's own death.

The requirement to deal twice with the same question forced the respondents to find an alternative organization of thought and feeling within themselves. It was especially interesting to see the compensatory dynamics at work: As one's death was moved closer in time, it was moved further away in psychological (self-involvement) distance. Yes, the day of death was now much closer at hand, and the events surrounding death were also a lot more disturbing. But who was dying? Not me. Only that paper-and-pencil character who happens to have my name.

"*The future can wait*" strategy seems to involved an intense sense of one's present self, but a derealization of the past and a nonrealization of the future self. Because it is only the future self that can die, one can trick death into leaving Real-Me-Right-Now in safety. The Somebody-I-Don't-Identify-With that death takes in the future is not of much concern. Should death be brought forward in time, then I can adjust (up to a point) by reducing my emotional involvement with death's prey. Death may then be part of a violent and scary story, but is not really about me.

"*The future is dead—so why live for it?*"

This way of thinking about death was often attributed to young people during the long period of tension between the United States and the Soviet Union. A leading spokesperson for this view is psychiatrist Robert Jay Lifton (1979; 1982), who has been a perceptive observer of the human response to 20th century war and terror. Lifton believes that the fear of nuclear holocaust has become the major psychological concern of our times and is especially influential on the minds of young people. He reminds us that "end of the world" fears have been expressed numerous times in human history. The contemporary version, however, is rooted in the reality of the megadeath threat.

Why should anybody do anything—or do anything that counts on the future—if the world could be destroyed at any moment? This is the obverse of the scenario we asked our respondents to consider in the World Without Death exploration. None of our respondents reported having previously considered this possibility; many spontaneously commented on what a strange thought it was and how, at first, it was difficult to imagine. Lifton felt that almost all young people were aware of the nuclear menace and profoundly concerned about it. If adolescents seemed to be alienated from society, rejecting conventional moralities and career lines, seeking pleasure restlessly without concern for consequences, and engaging in risk-taking or suicidal behaviors—why, what else would we expect from the post-Hiroshima/Nagasaki generation? Isn't this quite an understandable way to attempt to cope with the vision of a futureless future?

This conceptualization was valuable, I think, in attacking our characteristic unwillingness to take the possibility of catastrophe with the seriousness it deserves. Devastating fires in 17th-century London, and 19th-century Chicago and Boston are but a few past catastrophes that were recognized as definite risks by a few people but resolutely ignored by most. The extent of the AIDS epidemic is a current example in which the most determined efforts have been made to pierce society's shield of indifference and denial. The hypothesis advanced by Lifton and some others helped to focus some attention on the world situation on the part of behavioral and social scientists and allied health professionals who might otherwise have attended only to the challenges they saw directly in front of them every day.

This powerful and plausible idea was often treated as though established fact (neither the first nor the last time that the death awareness movement has substituted enthusiasm for critical analysis). I don't think we will ever know how this theory fit the facts. The world situation itself has changed significantly with the break-up of the Soviet bloc and the welcome reduction in the prospect of nuclear confrontation between antagonistic Euro-American powers. From a psychological standpoint, however, it would be useful to know if the nuclear threat did exert such influence over the thought, feelings, and actions of young men and women. There is no reason to doubt that thoughts of death can be influenced by many situational factors, including but by no means limited to war, crop failure, disease, and economic upheaval. Perhaps an entire generation can be dominated by one particular death-related theme, such as the threat of nuclear disaster.

The available information points in both directions. It depends on who is pointing and with what type of measure. Surveys taken over a period of more than four decades indicate that American children as well as adolescents rated nuclear war as one of their greatest concerns. Attitudes of American and Russian youth were compared in a rare collaborative study while the international tensions still existed (Chevien, Robinson, Tudge, Popov, & Andreynekov, 1988). A curious finding emerged: Almost all the Russian adolescents reported themselves to be intensely concerned about the possibility of nuclear war, but few expected this catastrophe to actually happen. By contrast, many more Americans— about half the respondents—did expect the world to be destroyed in a nuclear holocaust within their lifetime. *But that did not much worry them*! This odd set of findings suggests that complex relationships exist between concepts of time and death in adolescence. In this example, it is possible that when the prospect of death is perceived as becoming too close or intense, the resourceful youth may compensate by "withdrawing cathexis," as the psychoanalysts say.

Tolstoi gives us a splendid example in *The Death of Ivan Ilych*. (1886/1960). Peter Ivanovich, a friend of the deceased, is confused and ill at ease as he sits with the widow in the presence of very dead-looking Ivan Ilych. After a few minutes of mental gymnastics, however, Peter persuades himself that *he* is not the sort of person who dies—after all, the fact that Ivan is dead and that Peter is alive *proves* that it is natural for *that* sort of man to die. Immediately, Peter is released from his anxiety. He climbs back into his social facade and now happily feigns compassionate concern for Ivan's most disagreeable widow. This sort of trick—withdrawing self-involvement at the same time that one seems to be facing a death threat realistically—may well have permeated the results of nuclear war surveys.

Another problem: The available data is almost completely survey dependent. We simply do not know how much concern about nuclear war had actually influenced the thoughts, feelings, decisions, and actions of adolescents and young adults. A person might respond to a survey as though concerned because that seemed the mature or expected thing to do, but never really give a thought to megadeath in his or her everyday life.

The conditions for a natural experiment occurred concerning the futurity-and-death thoughts of American adolescents when the nuclear threat dissolved so rapidly and unexpectedly in late 1989 and thereafter. If young men and women had been living under the shadow of nuclear anxiety, then one might have expected a tremendous sense of release. "The show will go on! We will live out our lives! We will be able to achieve our desires and play with our grandchildren!" This explosion of joy and relief simply did not occur. I saw hundreds of college undergraduates during that period, and they barely seemed to notice that the end of the world had been postponed until further notice. Establishing telephone contact with several other "deathniks" across the nation, I heard similar observations: the sharp reduction of the nuclear threat was pretty much a nonevent as far as college students were concerned. In taking up this topic with a large general studies lecture section and with several individual students, the first impression was confirmed: They did not think much about the escape from nuclear war because they had not thought much about it before.

Not surprising. A year previously I had surveyed more than a thousand college students on a variety of experiential and attitudinal questions that included but were not limited to death-related issues. Given a "menu" of various possible concerns, the students had clearly indicated that they were most worried about their grades (and not an idle worry, I am sure). At the very bottom of the worry list was concern about a nuclear war that might take their lives and destroy all forms of life on earth. It was not even close.

There are reasons. Perhaps the most obvious is the pragmatic. Most of us—not just adolescents—may give more attention to goals we can achieve and problems we can influence through our own efforts. The international nuclear confrontation was not something that we could solve as individuals, but trying to get a decent grade on the next examination was at least within the realm of the possible. It may also be, however, that future terrors and existential concerns in general were the specialty of a relatively small number of sensitive and articulate people. The same young men or women who did not really believe that the time would come when they would actually have to take the final examination in Communication 100 may have had even more difficulty in realizing that they were just one button push away from universal holocaust.

Because the world was in peril and because this was a horrifying thought, it was natural to assume that most people were going around in fear and trembling. Young people seemed to be the best candidates for high anxiety because they had the most to lose. But there is little direct evidence for these propositions. Some people did embrace a powerful construction of death that has been neglected by traditional developmental research: humankind destroyed by humankind. Many other people, though, found challenge and pleasure enough in their immediate daily lives and *refused*—a more appropriate word here than *denied*—to "heed the thunder of distant drums." Talking to each other, psychologists, psychiatrists, "deathniks" and people of that sort may have been troubling themselves about the psychic response to nuclear annihilation, whereas most other people just went about their lives as usual.

Beyond Adolescence

We have explored—far from exhaustively—some of the processes and some of the outcomes involved in the development of death concepts from infancy through adolescence. The further we move away from the early years of life, the more difficult it is to say that development occurs—in any strict sense of this term. We do change in many ways, some of us more than others. The case can be made, however, that most modifications in our thought, behavior, and relationships in the adult years are products of our idiosyncratic experiences and personality styles rather than the continued unfolding of a universal maturational process. For example, did Ben Hecht take a basic step of continued growth when he ventured to "the edge of the world and looked over its last foot of territory into nothingness?" Or was that just a modification in Ben Hechtedness? Is there, in fact, a "mature view of death" toward which we should all aspire? This question is one of several that await us as we pursue the construction of death beyond adolescence in the next chapter.

NOTES

1. The conceptions of time that prevail in Euro-American society today are less "natural" than those held by most other people before the rise of industry and technology. By this, I mean that diurnal and seasonal rhythms, although still important, no longer provide our primary orientation toward time. Some earlier conceptions of time could become complicated in their details (e.g., auspicious and inauspicious days), but the general pattern could be more easily grasped and entered into by a young child. To the extent that time made more sense to the child in preindustrial society, so the course of life and the role of death also made more sense. For insight into the way that political, economic, industrial, and other forces have shaped our prevailing conceptions of time, one can do no better than Michael O'Malley's informative *Keeping Watch: A History of American Time* (1990). Cultural, literary, psychological, and philosophical dimensions are well set forth in such basic resources as J. T. Fraser's *The Voices of Time* (1966) and *The Study of Time* (1972; 1975), Eugene Freeman and Wilfrid Sellars *Basic Issues in The Philosophy of Time* (1971), my review article on time perspective across the life-span (1982) and Hans Reichenbach's seminal *The Direction of Time* (1956). It is doubtful that the overall relationship between time and death is well understood in scientific and philosophical circles today; in fact, few systematic efforts have been made to achieve a new synthesis. Our children face the daunting challenge of moving from their natural experiential worlds to a tangle of superimposed, nonintuitive, and occasionally contradictory time frameworks.

2. It is well known that a person may be exposed to a death-related situation and yet behave as though nothing has really happened. Playwright Ben Hecht, quoted at the beginning of this chapter, recalled that in his days as a young journalist in Chicago he had numerous encounters with death in many forms. Often he wrote about them. Yet it was not until his mother died that Hecht could *realize* death. Many other people also float away from their death encounters without a sense of personal involvement. In Avery D. Weisman's useful term, realization refers to establishing the personal and feeling reality of death. As Weisman (1974) observes: "we are always haunted by awareness of our time-limited existence. Nevertheless, we readily, gladly postpone, put aside, disavow, and deny its relevance for us. Consequently, death as a personal experience is extruded from our field of reality and realization until, of course, sooner or later, it thrusts back upon our consciousness" (p. 1). One especially relevant implication for us here is that when a person exhibits a pattern of behavior that implies a lack of death awareness, the underlying cause may be either developmental immaturity, or the motivation-driven lack of realization.

3. Reports of NDE in recent years have provided an apparent alternative to the conclusion that we do not experience death until we die. The NDE is considered in more detail elsewhere in this book. It is clear that some people now draw on NDE reports for their personal constructions of death. This is an

interesting phenomenon in itself and adds to the spectrum of death-related cognitions on the current scene. The fact that NDE-type episodes also have been reported frequently when the person's life is *not* in jeopardy is one of several reasons for using caution in concluding that the NDE proves that a person has actually visited death and returned. Perhaps an even better reason for caution is that NDEs are reported *only* by those who did survive: "What death is like" for people who die and stay dead cannot be assumed to be identical with the round-trip implicit in NDE reports.

4. Useful presentations and discussions of this schemata can be found in *The Construction of Reality in the Child* (Piaget, 1954); *The Growth of Logical Thinking From Childhood to Adolescence* (Piaget & Inhelder, 1959); and the retrospective *The Psychology of the Child* (Piaget & Inhelder, 1969). Not all of Piaget's findings and conclusions have been accepted by subsequent researchers, but there is no doubt that his work has made a deep, enduring, and enriching contribution to the study of human development.

5. Useful resources include *Childhood Bereavement and Its Aftermath* (Altschul, 1988); *Attachment and Loss* (Bowlby, 1980), a concise literature review; *Parental Death and Psychological Development* (Berlinsky & Biller, 1982); and a National Research Council (1984) monograph *Bereavement: Reactions, Consequences, and Care*. Articles on this topic also are published with some frequency in *Death Studies* and *Omega: Journal of Death and Dying*.

6. Among the studies that have confirmed at least some of Nagy's findings and supported the general thesis that cognitions of death undergo major development from early childhood through adolescence are those of Childers & Wimmer (1971); Gartley & Benasconi (1967); Hoffman & Strauss (1985); Kane (1979); Menig-Peterson & McCabe (1977–1978); Safier (1964); Wass, Guenther, & Towry (1979); and Wenestam & Wass (1987). See also Lonetto's (1980) review *Children's Conceptions of Death*. It should be remembered that these studies have varied considerably in methodology, although most included and some relied entirely on direct questioning. Here are a few questions from the recent Hoffman-Strauss (1985) study: "What could cause a person to die? Must every person die at some point? Can a dead person see? Can a dead person speak? Can a dead person move? Can a dead person dream?" By contrast, the Koocher study includes a deliberately misleading question, "How do you make dead things come back to life?" Again, by contrast, Menig-Peterson & McCabe (1977–1978) told brief life experience stories and asked children if they had ever had anything like that happen to them. Although none of the researchers' stories included any references to serious injury or death, many of the older children did offer death-related narratives of their own.

7. Themes of violence and death are expressed in the lyrics of many rock songs. In fact, some high school students prefer music that explicitly advocates murder or suicide (Wass, 1989). The heavy beat and high volume of the music itself might also intensify the textual message. With the collaboration of students in my Introduction to Human Communication course, it was possible

to analyze more than 200 rap (or "hip hop") songs. Not surprisingly, sex was the most prevalent theme (pushing 90%), but death-violence also proved to be common (about 40% on a conservative rating basis). Some students, however, expressed surprise when they actually stopped to listen to the texts. "I've always just danced to it. I never thought what it was about!" We should be cautious in concluding that today's youth are any more death engrossed than those of past generations. There are no strictly comparable data, and it might be that the current expressions of fascination with death imagery are just a little more explicit (and noisier) than what was enjoyed by the degenerate youth of my own generation.

8. Wisdom has become a sufficiently recognized concept in gerontology to win a brief but informative entry in the *Encyclopedia of Aging* (Clayton, 1987). Hayslip and Panek (1989) also observe that might be called "the wisdom factor" probably contributes to survival. This, however, is a laboratory-bred definition of wisdom. It is based upon the ability to perform well on a battery of verbal, perceptual, and motor tasks. We do not know if this definition bears any resemblance to the wisdom that is imparted by the hypothetical guru on the mountaintop.

REFERENCES

Altschul, S. (Ed.) (1988). *Childhood bereavement and its aftermath.* Madison, CT: International Universities Press.

Anthony, S. (1940). The child's discovery of death. London: Routledge & Kegan Paul.

Anthony, S. (1972). *The discovery of death in childhood and after.* New York: Basic Books.

Berlinsky, I., & Biller, E. (1982). *Parental death and psychological development.* Lexington, MA: Lexington Books.

Bluebond-Langner, M. (1978). *The private worlds of dying children.* Princeton, NJ: Princeton University Press.

Bluebond-Langner, M. (1989a). Children, dying. In R. Kastenbaum & B. K. Kastenbaum (Eds.), *Encyclopedia of Death* (pp. 46–48). Phoenix: Oryx Press.

Bluebond-Langner, M. (1989b). Worlds of dying children and their well siblings. *Death Studies, 13,* 1–16.

Bowlby, J. (1980). *Attachment and loss.* New York: Basic Books.

Brent, S. B. (1977–1978). Puns, metaphors, and misunderstandings in a two year-old's conception of death. *Omega: Journal of Death and Dying, 8,* 285–294.

Chevian, E., Robinson, J. P., Tudge, J. R. H., Popov, N. P., & Andreynekov, V. G. (1988). American and Soviet teenagers' concerns about nuclear war and the future. *New England Journal of Medicine, 319,* 407–413.

Childers, P., & Wimmer, M. (1971). The concept of death in early childhood. *Child Development, 42,* 705–715.

Clayton, V. (1987). Wisdom. In G. L. Maddox (Ed.), *The encyclopedia of aging* (p. 696). New York: Springer Publishing.

Costa, P. T., Jr., & Kastenbaum, R. (1967). Some aspects of memories and ambitions in centenarians. *Journal of Genetic Psychology, 110,* 3–16.

Dickstein, L., & Blatt, S. (1966). Death concern, futurity, and anticipation. *Journal of Counseling Psychology, 31,* 11–17.

Fraser, J. T. (1966). *The voices of time.* New York: George Braziller.

Fraser, J. T. (1972). *The study of time* (Vol. 1). New York: Springer-Verlag.

Fraser, J. T. (1975). *The study of time* (Vol. 2). New York: Springer-Verlag.

Freeman, E., & Sellars, W. (Eds.). (1971). *Basic issues in the philosophy of time.* Lasalle, IL: Open Court.

Gartley, W., & Benasconi, A. (1967). A concept of death in children. *Journal of Genetic Psychology, 110,* 71–85.

Goldstein, K. (1939). *The organism.* New York: American Book.

Hall, G. S. (1922). *Senescence.* New York: Appleton.

Hayslip, B., Jr., & Panek, P. E. (1989). *Adult development and aging.* New York: Harper & Row.

Hecht, B. (1970). *A child of the century.* New York: Ballantine Books. (Original work published 1954)

Hoffman, S. I., & Strauss, S. (1985). The development of children's concepts of death. Death Studies, *9,* 469–482.

Kane, B. (1979). Children's concepts of death. *Journal of Genetic Psychology, 134,* 141–153.

Kastenbaum, R. (1959). Time and death in adolescence. In H. Feifel (Ed.), *The meaning of death* (pp. 99–113). New York: McGraw-Hill.

Kastenbaum, R. (1961). The dimensions of future time perspective: An experimental analysis. *Journal of Genetic Psychology, 65,* 203–218.

Kastenbaum, R. (1982). Time course and time perspective in later life. In C. Eisdorfer (Ed.), *Annual review of gerontology and geriatrics* (Vol. 3, pp. 80–101). New York: Springer Publishing.

Kastenbaum, R. (1986). Death in the world of adolescence. In C. A. Carr & J. N. McNeil (Eds.), *Adolescence and death.* New York: Springer.

Koocher, D. (1973). Childhood, death, and cognitive development. *Developmental Psychology, 9,* 369–375.

Lewin, K. (1936). *Principles of topological psychology.* New York: McGraw-Hill.

Lifton, R. J. (1979). *The broken connection: On death and the continuity of life.* New York: Simon & Schuster.

Lifton, R. J., & Falk, R. (1982). *Indefensible weapons: The political and psychological case against nuclearism.* New York: Basic Books.

Lonetto, R. (1980). *Children's conceptions of death.* New York: Springer Publishing.

Maurer, A. (1966). Maturation of concepts of death. *British Journal of Medicine and Psychology, 39,* 35–41.

McLaughlin, N., & Kastenbaum, R. (1966). Engrossment in personal past, future, and death. Paper presented at the annual meeting of the American Psychological Association, New York.

Menig-Peterson, C., & McCabe, A. (1977–1978). Children talk about death. *Omega: Journal of Death and Dying, 8,* 305–318.

Moriarty, D. M. (1967). *The loss of loved ones.* Springfield, IL: Charles C Thomas.

Nagy, M. (1959). The child's view of death. In H. Feifel (Ed.), *The meaning of death* (pp. 79–98). New York: McGraw-Hill. (Original work published 1948)

National Research Council. (1984). *Bereavement: Reactions, consequences, and care.* Washington, DC: National Academy Press.

O'Malley, M. (1990). *Keeping watch: A history of American time.* New York: Viking.

Opie, I., & Opie, R. (1969). *Children's games in street and playground.* London: Oxford University Press.

Piaget, J. (1954). *The construction of reality in the child.* New York: Basic Books.

Piaget, J., & Inhelder, B. (1959). *The growth of logical thinking from childhood to adolescence.* New York: Basic Books.

Piaget, J., & Inhelder, B. (1969). *The psychology of the child.* New York: Basic Books.

Pohlman, J. C. (1984). Illness and death of a peer in a group of three-year-olds. *Death Studies, 8,* 123–136.

Reichenbach, H. (1956). *The direction of time.* Berkeley: University of California Press.

Rentchnick, P. (1989). Orphans and the will for power. In M. Eisenstadt, A. Haynal, P. Rentchnick, & P. de Senarclens (Eds.), *Parental loss and achievement.* Madison, CT: International Universities Press.

Safier, G. (1964). A study in relationships between the life and death concepts. *Journal of Genetic Psychology, 105,* 283–294.

Schactel, E. G. (1959). *Metamorphosis.* New York: Basic Books.

Schaie, K. W. (1987). Intelligence. In G. L. Maddox (Ed.), *The encyclopedia of aging* (pp. 357–358). New York: Springer Publishing.

Tobin, S. (1972). The earliest memory as data for research in aging. In D. P. Kent, R. Kastenbaum, & S. Sherwood (Eds.), *Research, planning, and action for the elderly* (pp. 252–278). New York: Behavioral Publications.

Tolstoi, L. (1886/1960). *The death of Ivan Illich.* New York: The New American Library.

Wass, H. (1989). Children and death. In R. Kastenbaum & B. K. Kastenbaum (Eds.), *Encyclopedia of death* (pp. 49–54). Phoenix: Oryx Press.

Wass, H., Guenther, Z. C., & Towry, B. J. (1979). United States and Brazilian children's concepts of death. *Death Education, 3,* 41–55.

Weisman, A. D. (1974). *The realization of death.* New York: Jason Aronson.

Wenestam, C-G., & Wass, H. (1987). Swedish and U.S. children's thinking about death: A qualitative study and cross-cultural comparison. *Death Studies, 11,* 99–122.

Werner, H. (1957). *Comparative psychology of mental development.* New York: International University Press.

5

Death Anxiety in the Midst of Life

I find myself standing in my bedroom at home in New York
. . . something has awakened me from my sleep. I look out
through the bedroom window. Suddenly I am overcome with
intense feelings of fear and at that instant there is a white flash
from outside my window. I then realize that someone has just
shot me in the face. Slowly I begin to fall to the floor, realizing
that I have just been killed. The sensation of dying is very
pleasant and I begin to enjoy the experience. The dream ends.

—D. Barrett, *Dreams of Death*

I met him when I was the admitting doctor in a busy general
hospital. . . . He was an ordinary labouring type, in his early
forties, who had been picked up wandering in the town. . . .
He was literally terrified—I have never seen anybody so afraid,
so much so that we were unable to converse with him at all. He
would answer none of our questions, but kept shouting, "Im
going to die. Please don't let me die, please don't let me die."

—J. C. Barker, *Scared to Death*

Some therapists state that death concerns are simply not
voiced by their patients. I believe, however, that the real issue
is that the therapist is not prepared to hear them. A therapist
who is receptive, who inquires deeply into a patient's concerns
will encounter death continuously in his or her everyday work.

—Yalom, *Existential Psychotherapy*

One person fears that the tests will prove positive for AIDS. Another person's fears have already been confirmed. Still another person prepares to leap from a plane as part of a sky-diving exhibition. Thousands of miles away, a civilian enters a combat zone—simply by opening the door and heading for work. Each of these people lives with death in salient prospect. We would not be surprised to find that this risk affects their thoughts, feelings, and actions. Furthermore, we might also find that their orientations toward death are far from identical. Perhaps suspenseful waiting arouses thoughts and feelings that are quite different from certain knowledge, even when the same life-threatening disease is involved. Perhaps the sense of personal choice and control is another critical dimension. The sky diver elected to take this risk; the civilian caught in the middle of hostile factions did not ask for this menace.

How people orient themselves to death when there is a salient and objective threat is a significant question. This chapter, however, examines an equally provocative matter: How do we think about death in the midst of daily life, when there is *no* obvious, pressing, extraordinary threat to our existence?

The distinction between contemplating death in danger situations and in ordinary life is not without its difficulties. Nevertheless, we improve our opportunity to understand the perceptions and meanings of death if we respect the differences between these two frameworks. It would be naïve to assume that our cognitive and emotional orientation to death is unaffected by circumstances. It would also be naïve, however, to assume that we have certain fixed responses when in life-threatening and in ordinary circumstances. Perhaps the most obvious assumption would be that the fear of death varies directly with the prospect of death. Interestingly, a study of reported death fear in parachute jumpers found no significant differences between experienced sky divers and matched respondents who had never engaged in this activity (Alexander & Lester, 1972). This isolated study does not close the subject, but it does help to caution us against premature acceptance of even the most tempting generalizations. Do people *necessarily* become more anxious as the objective threat of death increases? This is but one of many assumptions that need to be examined in light of the available evidence.

It is the evidence that will mostly concern us here. Much of this chapter focuses on the questions raised, methods employed, and findings obtained by those who have studied "death anxiety" or "fear of death" in adults who were not at obvious risk at the time of their participation. ("Fear" and "anxiety" will be used interchangeably at this point in the discussion, although later these terms will be reexamined.)

SOME BASIC QUESTIONS AND THEORIES

How *should* we contemplate death in the midst of life? This could be considered the most pressing question. Is there a "normal," "proper," "useful," or "ideal" way to regard our own mortality? Psychology and the social sciences may be better equipped, however, to examine a simpler question: How do people *actually* think and feel about death? Even this more circumspect question leads us into challenging problems. How much do people think about death as they go through life? What is it we actually fear when we "fear death"? What role does our orientation toward death play in our personality and life-style? How does this orientation develop from youth to old age? How is it influenced by situations and events? Pursuing questions such as these might be expected to contribute to self-knowledge. In turn, enhanced self-knowledge might illuminate the choices we make in our orientations toward death.

Several broad answers have been proposed for the "should" question. These theoretical positions make several assertions and assumptions about the contemplation of death in everyday life. We will see that there is a large gap between the Big Theories and the Little Studies in this area. This gap is disconcerting. One might expect a close link between theory and research. With some exceptions, however, we find instead a few competing and ambitious conceptual positions on one hand, and a myriad of modest and atheoretical empirical investigations on the other.

Most studies convert the broader question of "how do we contemplate mortality?" to the more limited "How anxious are we about death?" We begin, then, with a brief examination of the Big Theories. This is followed by an inspection of the empirical methodologies and findings. Attention is then given to some of the major conceptual and applied issues, taking both theories and data into account.

Never Say Die?

The best-hated Big Theory in this area is the one attributed to Sigmund Freud. To the question: "How should we contemplate death?" Freud would be expected to respond, "Never say die!" What Freud actually did suggest is a little more complicated. He was well aware that people had many concerns about death. It was not unusual to find death fears prominent in an anxiety reaction or expressed through dream reports. Freud even shared some of his own death-associated fears.[1] He refrained from drawing the most obvious conclusion, however. Just because an anxious person spoke of death did not necessarily mean that death was at the root of the problem. This was not an unusual proposition within the psychoanalytic approach that attempted to see "under" the presentation layer of words and behavior. But Freud later ventured the opinion that death was *never* at the root. *Thanatophobia* (fear of death) was the symbolic expression for some other unresolved conflict.

In a passage that has become rather famous, Freud (1913/1953) wrote:

> Our own death is indeed quite unimaginable, and whenever we make the attempt to imagine it we can perceive that we really survive as spectators. Hence the psychoanalytic school could venture on the assertion that at bottom nobody believes in his own death, or to put the same thing in a different way, in the unconscious every one of us is convinced of his own immortality.

There is a fundamental basis for the inability to comprehend our own mortality.

> What we call our "unconscious" (the deepest strata of our minds, made up of instinctual impulses) knows nothing whatever of negatives or of denials—contradictions coincide in it—and so it knows nothing whatever of our own death, for to that we can give only a negative purport. It follows that no instinct we possess is ready for a belief in death. (pp. 304–305)

This view is consistent with Freud's overall conception of the "unconscious system" in which there is "no negation, no dubiety, no varying degree of certainty." Unconscious processes are not responsive to the passage of time, "in fact, bear no relation to time at all." By inference, then, death as the end point of personal time would have no meaning to the unconscious. There is still another Freudian argument against thanatophobia as a deep and authentic orientation: We have not actually experienced death—so how can we fear it?

Death-related fears must therefore be formulated at the more superficial levels of mental functioning. The terror arises from instinctual conflicts that are well within our experience. These relatively prosaic conflicts may cloak themselves in death imagery. Castration anxiety, for example, was thought by Freud to present a normative challenge in childhood development. The adult who is beset by death fears may be representing unresolved castration anxiety through this subterfuge.

Perhaps the most obvious implication is that we should not yield to fears of death. The presence of these fears is a signal that we are having difficulties with our basic instinctual life. It is not "wrong" or "bad" to have such fears, but they point to hidden problems that should receive therapeutic attention.

Freud was clear enough about the inability of the unconscious to believe in its own death. Nevertheless, this is but one facet of his overall view of mortality and the human condition. Proponents and critics alike have tended to overlook the underlying purpose of the essay *Thoughts for the Times on War and Death* (1913/1953) in which Freud presented the "never say die" theory. The essay was Freud's powerful response to World War I and its aftermath. It is a death-haunted quest to examine "a world grown strange," a world in which civilized peoples had attacked each other with brutal violence. War had stripped the trappings of civilization from us, revealing the primal being in all its blood-red emotions. If civilization—if humankind—were to survive, we would have to face some difficult truths about ourselves. In particular, we must recognize our unstable mixture of loving and hating tendencies, our potential for evil and destruction, and our own vulnerability. "Would it not be better to give death the place in actuality and in our thoughts which properly belongs to it . . . ?"

Freud's view is more complex and poignant than many advocates and critics have acknowleged. Yes, superficial fears of death are hints of deeper instinctual conflicts, and our unconscious in its stubborn, magnificent, and childish way cannot be persuaded to conceive of its own demise. But, no, this does not mean that we would be wise to put death out of our minds. It is, in fact, our capacity for murder as well as for love—linked to increasingly more devastasting means of killing—that is the central problem for humankind. The wise person will indeed contemplate death in the midst of life—and live in a more enlightened and responsible manner for so doing so.

It is a mixed message that Freud has given us, and he may be faulted for not troubling to reconcile and integrate the two strands of thought more satisfactorily. Many of us may also be faulted, however, for fastening on the "never say die" aspect, and neglecting the survival warning that was at the heart of his message.

We Cannot Help but Fear Death

The fear of death is not to be explained away as a superficial and disguised representation of a "deeper" conflict. Quite the opposite! Anxiety—all anxiety—is rooted in the awareness of our mortality. The consequences are enormous, and reveal themselves in virtually every aspect of individual and cultural life. The late Ernest Becker (1973) was a leading proponent of this view. (Soren Kierkegaard, William James, and Gregory Zilboorg may be counted among his predecessors.[2]) The schizophrenic and the person suffering from a psychotic depression are driven to these extreme states by the terror of death. Becker recalls William James's thought that psychosis was the most realistic response to the horrors of organismic life on this planet.

We buffer ourselves in many ways from the acute realization of helplessness, hopelessness, and death. Some people, however, are naked against this threat. In particular, the schizophrenic lacks the insulation provided by the ability to identify with or lose one's self in the activities and relationships of everyday life. "He cannot make available to himself the natural organismic expansion that others use to buffer and absorb the fear of life and death" (Becker, 1973, p. 219). Poorly integrated into the supportive cultural structure, the schizophrenic must face death alone. "He relies instead on a hypermagnification of mental processes to try to be a hero almost entirely ideationally, from within a bad body-seating, and in a very personal way." The sad, contrived, and failed heroism of the schizophrenic reveals in its distinctive way the strenuous efforts of the "normal" person to combat what is at root the same sense of impending loss by death.

Ordinary life in today's society is marked by heavy repression of death-related anxiety (which is to say, *all* anxiety), according to Becker and others. This takes a toll on us. This is why we become conformists. We seek the security that is promised by tying into a system that will meet our dependency needs and help us deny our intrinsic vulnerability. Certain events and experiences may disrupt this "let's pretend" arrangement. We are then faced with the challenge of either restoring the tenuous system of mutual (illusionary) support, or confronting death as aware and vulnerable individuals.

What does Becker's position imply for the "should" question? This might be answered in two different ways, depending on the framework we choose to use. Guardians of the status quo might urge that fear of death is a negative and asocial attitude. It bespeaks a weak personality or an undeveloped mind. A flourishing society requires active participants who work, breed, interact, and believe in shared values. Fear of death intensifies self-preoccupation, and thereby reduces the attention and energies necessary for group endeavors. If too many people become preoccupied and dysfunctional because of their indulgence in death anxiety, then the viability of the society itself may become imperiled.

A focus on individual development, however, might encourage a very different position. We should acknowledge our anxieties and contemplate death if we intend to live as enlightened and self-actualized persons. The repression of death-related thoughts and feelings requires too much effort and drains too much energy. We cannot be whole and mature adults unless we live with the full realization of our mortality.

Interestingly, this interpretation is as much at home in Freud's conception as it is in Becker's. One asserted that, fundamentally, we cannot believe in our own death and that thanatophobia must represents other, more basic conflicts. The other asserted that the terror of death motivates much of individual and social functioning. Yet both urge that we give death its due. Becker argues that we must retain a keen sense of death threat to protect ourselves from threats to our lives. The late Walter Kaufmann (1976) proposed that it is the awareness of death that enriches life with much of its joys and meanings: "Those who have loved with all their heart and might have always thought of death, and those who knew the endless nights of harrowing concern for others might have longed for it" (p. 214). Freud argues that the fate of civilization as well as the maturation of the individual requires a greater willingness to contemplate death (the reluctant unconscious notwithstanding).

A very obvious point is worth remembering: Overwhelming, disruptive, crippling anxiety is not what has been recommended by Freud, Becker, Kaufmann, or any other psychologist writing on this subject. We are urged to bring out highest intellectual and emotional resources to bear on the problem of death, even though this may expose us to "live anxiety" on occasion. Spinning through our lives in panic, however, is quite a different matter. The trick is to be aware of the fullness of life—including our mortal vulnerability—without giving way to despair.

Welcome Dread Death

This peculiar phrase draws on the mixed message offered by Christianity. Strictly speaking, theology perhaps should not be included in an examination of psychological theories. It is obvious, however, that the thoughts, feelings, and actions of a great many people have been influenced by religious doctrines. There have also been many treatises on the influence of psychological factors on the development, spread, and use of religious doctrines. We will limit attention here to the core Christian conception as it is related to death anxiety.[3]

The fact that death concern is at the core of Christian doctrine is not in doubt. Believers hold that the tormented death of Jesus holds the promise of salvation and eternal life. What does this imply for the way that Christians *should* orient themselves to death? One vital tradition urges the believer to think of death with wonder and gratitude. This corrupt and imperfect life is exchanged for everlasting bliss. There is little reason, then, for either fear or sorrow.

> Our aged father is now conveyed
> To his long home in silence laid
> Hast burst his cage and winged his way
> To realms of bliss in endless day. (Wallis, 1973, p. 79)

This "endless bliss" more than compensates for the pains and disappointments of earthly life as well as the ordeal of "passing on." The believer loses only the shell, not the substance of being.

> Under the sod
> Under these trees
> Lies the body of Jonathan Pease
> He is not here
> But only his pod
> He has shelled out his peas
> And gone to his God. (Wallis, p. 79)

Yet Christian doctrine has often been presented in a much more fearsome guise. Death is a punishment. "In Adam's fall, we sinned all." The believer faces judgment, rejection, and torment for personal shortcomings as well as original sin. "Hell and brimstone" sermons once were commonplace. How could the believer *not* fear "the wages of sin"? How could the individual undergoing a crisis of faith *not* fear that failure to believe wholeheartedly could result in eternal damnation?

Should the Christian believer, then, fear death because it might be followed by judgment, damnation, and punishment? Or should a believer contemplate death with serenity—even with longing and impatience—because the best is yet to come? Every believer must somehow reconcile these two aspects of Christian tradition, as well as personal thoughts and experiences with death. It is possible that both anxiety and serenity are intensified by Christian doctrine. A naturalistic, matter-of-fact attitude might be developed by particular individuals, but the doctrine as such encourages the extremes of anxiety and serenity-joy-transcendence. The intense Christian orientation toward death stands in marked contrast to academic psychology's objectivistic stance as we have seen in the chapter on The Psychologist's Death.

There Is No Point in Thinking of Death

We should not think of death because this is a stupid waste of time and effort. All we would accomplish is to depress ourselves and others. We cannot change the facts, so, in the words of one of the best known philosophers of our time, Alfred E. Neumann: "What, me worry?"

This familiar attitude is often associated with a fatalistic view of life. Among the elements in this (usually implicit) theory is the reduction of cognitive dissonance by avoiding thoughts that reveal a painful discrepancy between wish and efficacy. The odds are not very favorable when we challenge the fates directly. By studiously ignoring death on an overt level, we can continue to play covert fantasy games:

> I don't know how many times I did it. I'd jump in the car, peel away, and not know where I was going or much care. Really brilliant! I would live forever, if I didn't kill myself around the next corner! . . . Great logic, you know. You die when your number's up, so there's no point to thinking about it, but, at the same time, you try to get yourself killed so [that] if you don't, hell, then your number wasn't up and the Big Guy doesn't want you for a while. Made perfect sense. As long as I was bombed out of my mind.

This young man was reflecting on a recent period in his life that he could now see as dominated by death anxiety. He attempted to cope with this anxiety by convincing himself that he had no control over his fate and, therefore, no need to think about death. Nevertheless, he also "tempted the fates" in a dangerous fantasy attempt to persuade "the Big Guy" not to call up his number. One does not have to go to this extreme to conduct a series of covert operations to forestall (or invite) death while at the same time resisting conscious thought and open discussion on the subject. This double-pronged attitude toward death is far from uncommon, especially among young men. Risking death through macho exploits may actually hold one's fears in abeyance; however, the same person may become highly agitated when the situation requires personal thought and feeling about death.

Learn not to Fear—Too Much

This position has not had as much currency as the others. It has been suggested, however, that death-related concerns develop as part of the general interaction between a person's level of maturation and his or her distinctive life experiences (Kastenbaum, 1987–1988). One does not require special assumptions such as a Freudian unconscious that cannot handle endings and negations, a Beckerian primary terror that must be restrained by all the resources of the individual and society, or the sacrificial death of the Son of God. Instead, one can study the development and function of death-related concerns as part of the total course of human growth.

This approach lends itself more readily to controlled observation; therefore, the "should" question can be converted into a set of specific contingencies. We would be in a position to learn under what circumstances, what type, and what level of death concern is related to what outcomes. Lacking the appeal of grand theories, this is nevertheless an alternative approach that may be more congruent with the skills and limitations of contemporary psychology.

This brings us to some methodological considerations that influence the type of findings obtained and the type of conclusions reached by empirical studies.

Sources of Information

There are several ways in which we might learn how people contemplate death in the midst of life. Each approach has its advantages and limitations.

Self-report: Structured

We might ask people to convey their orientations toward death through a direct and highly structured technique. The commonest example is the fixed-choice questionnaire.

Among the advantages:

1. This questionnaire is easy for the researcher to administer, score, and analyze.
2. It requires little time from the respondent and does not require a deep "opening up."
3. This format makes it possible to build up a standardized data base to compare populations, examine time trends, and so on.

Among the disadvantages:

1. Qualitative and individual facets of death orientations are not given the opportunity to express themselves.

2. The fixed-response format also constricts what can be learned about the processes involved in trying to cope with death. Because the format is limited to a "T" (true) or "F" (false) response alternative, the participant can tell us very little (which seems to be just fine with some researchers).

3. A direct and highly structured format is subject to falsification and evasion. This would be less of a problem—in fact, it could even become a source of useful information—if it were possible to distinguish between forthright and less forthright responses. There is no way to do so with the self-report questionnaires currently in use in this area.

The fixed-choice type of instrument accords is an operationalization of the first type of psychological construction that was described in an earlier chapter. The psychologist does not conceptualize death per se, but instead collects objectivistic and quantitative data on destabilizing responses to death. There is a streak of genius in this approach: Exclusive reliance on fixed-choice death anxiety scales will never find evidence for any psychological response to death other than anxiety!

Self-Report: Freely Structured

We might provide respondents with more natural, flexible, and spontaneous ways of sharing their death orientations. A variety of techniques could be employed. The possibilities include, for example, diaries and semistructured interviews. Each technique has its own particular values and limitations. As a set, however, the more freely structured procedures have methodological characteristics such as the following:

Among the advantages:

1. Respondents can use their own words and express their own feelings and views without being confined by preset categories.

2. There is more opportunity to learn about the thought processes used as well as the feelings and ideas that have emerged.

3. There is more opportunity to discover nuances, contradictions, conflicts, leading themes, and the overall texture of the respondents' ways of contemplating death.

Among the disadvantages:

1. These techniques require more time and effort from the researcher in all phases of investigation.

2. Respondents are also asked to give more time and thought, and to open themselves up to an inquisitive stranger.

3. It is more difficult to accumulate comparable and easily reducible data.

Indirect and In-Depth Methods

Orientations toward death also might be explored through dreams, fantasies, and projective techniques (such as the Thematic Apperception Test).

Among the advantages:

1. The respondent is given an opportunity to express thoughts and feelings beyond those that can be neatly packaged in response to direct questions.

2. Death-related fantasies and conflicts may come to the fore.

3. Individual patterns of thought and feeling are more likely to be expressed than with more structured techniques.

4. Counseling, psychotherapy, and other possible interventions might be guided to some extent by the responses.

Among the disadvantages:

1. The scoring, reliability, and interpretation of these responses may be subject to question.

2. The relationship between fantasy-projective responses and actual behavior may be tenuous and obscure.

3. Again, this approach is time intensive for both the respondent and the investigator.

Behavioral Observations

Instead of limiting our information to what the respondent tells us, we might focus on what he or she actually does. Behavioral observations have contributed significantly to many areas of psychological research (infant and child development, for example). Documenting how people actually behave in death-related situations might also be productive.

Among the advantages:

1. Behavior in a situation could be regarded as the most appropriate outcome measure for the various theories of death attitudes. So unless actual behavioral observations are made, then, the theories might always remain just that.

2. Behavioral observations can lend themselves to objective assessment and quantification.

3. Prevention and intervention efforts might best be guided by observing behavior rather than attempting to interpret verbal statements.

Among the disadvantages:

1. Observations of behavior in "real-life" situations poses many difficulties (such as the role and influence of the observer), and these intensify in sensitive and emotionally charged circumstances.

2. Questions can be raised about the unit and level of measurement. (Should we study "microunits" of individual response or "macrounits" of complex interpersonal actions?)

3. Generalizing across situations (as well as establishing "reliability" within the same type of situation) can be as difficult as drawing conclusions from studies of verbal behavior. (Does anxiety in one death-related situation predict that this person will also show anxiety in all other death-related situations?)

Experimentation

The experimental method has been responsible for many breakthroughs in science. Few investigators would limit themselves to descriptive studies if they could find a way to subject their material to experimental manipulation. It might be argued that we will know very little about the process and consequences of contemplating death until we have identified and manipulated the relevant variables within a thoroughly controlled research design.

Among the advantages:

1. There is probably no better way to test a hypothesis than to manipulate the relevant variables in a controlled experiment.

2. Experimentation tends to demand a higher quality of thought and effort on the part of the investigators, so even the planning process may advance the field.

3. Prevention and intervention efforts—on both a personal and

sociocultural level—might be developed and tested most effectively through a true experimental approach.

Among the disadvantages:

1. The sensitive nature and complexity of many death-related situations makes experimental manipulation a risky, problematic, and, at times, ethically questionable enterprise.
2. Experimental simulations can significantly reduce the problems noted earlier, but a new difficulty is created: The question of generalizing from the simulation to the real-life situation.
3. Good experiments in this area are difficult both to design and to complete. They are subject to failure at many points.

AVAILABLE RESEARCH: CHARACTERISTICS AND LIMITATIONS

The findings that will be reviewed subsequently are based primarily on self-report questionnaires. These procedures have proved the most popular with those who have chosen to study orientations toward death. Durlak and Kass (1981–1982) reviewed 15 procedures, and more have appeared since this report. The Death Anxiety Scale (DAS) developed by Donald Templer (1970) and his colleagues is the instrument most frequently employed, a 15-item inventory with true-false response options. The DAS is the first self-report questionnaire to have gone through the mill of psychometric evaluation, and therefore has an advantage over the "home-made" instruments and scales that some investigators introduce for their own studies. By now, the relatively widespread use of the DAS has led to the buildup of the most diverse data base for a self-report instrument in this area.[4]

Because so much of the available information does come from the DAS and similar procedures, it is important to keep the limitations of this approach in mind (Kastenbaum, 1987–1988). The typical study restricts its attention to "anxiety." Other kinds of response have no opportunity to reveal themselves. An individual's total orientation toward death might include sorrow and rage, for example. These feelings might contribute indirectly to the anxiety score because there is no other way to express them on the scale. This would lead to an artificially inflated "anxiety" score. The other-than-anxiety attitudes might not show up at all. Moreover, there is no opportunity for respondents to express positive orientations toward death. Even an anxious person might also have such other attitudes as relief or transcendence. The death-anxiety concept tends to perpetuate itself and to command almost all of the attention because the typical study does not identify and assess other responses.

The typical study also has many other limitations. Usually, the respondents are studied on only one occasion. Furthermore, the respondents are often selected on the basis of easy availability. Captive populations such as college students are rounded up frequently, as is also true in some other areas of psychological research. There is some value in using opportunistic samples—these are real people, too, of course. This preference for easily available samples, however, has resulted in a narrow band of data. Non-Anglo and ethnically diverse populations have received relatively little attention.

The problem is intensified by a frequent lack of theoretical direction. College students and other captive populations are on hand, and so is a simple death-anxiety instrument—let's do a study! If you would like to waste a few precious hours of life, scan through several dozen death-anxiety studies with these questions in mind: "What is this study really about? What issues are at stake? What could it possibly illuminate or prove?" There are exceptions, to be sure, but the typical study has essentially been an exercise in raw empiricism, animated by the availability of an instrument and a docile sample.

Other limitations? Few studies employ experimental or quasi-experimental procedures. Even fewer studies attempt to relate death-anxiety scores to behavior and decision making. It is also typical to ignore the respondent's overall attitude structure and belief system. The population samples are usually described in minimal fashion. Curiously, studies often fail to report the basic data they have obtained! This is most likely to happen when the investigator attemps to justify the existence of the study by testing for possible differences in death-anxiety level between two samples.

A fictitious example will serve our purpose and yet protect the innocent and guilty alike. Dudley Deathnik has access to a population of sale representatives for a widget dealership and also to summer students in a remedial backgammon course. Both groups complete a self-report instrument. The computer obligingly runs through a set of packaged statistical tests. The printout reveals that there is not a significant difference between widgeters and backgammonites. The author's brief report (not published in my journal!) offers a paragraph of discussion that suggests there may be "real" differences in death anxiety between the groups, despite the lack of clear-cut statistical findings. A popular way of sliding past such a nonfinding is to assert that one of the samples indulged in *denial*. The widgeters, let us say, are the chief suspects. They are really more anxious about death than the backgammonites, and this is shown by their artificially lowered scores. Please understand that I am not spinning a fantasy here; only the particular samples have been invented. You will find in the empirical literature a recurrent effort to explain lower-than-anticipated scores as manifestations of denial, thereby implying much higher "real death anxiety."

These gratuitous interpretations are the more repellent because the studies involved have not bothered to include a *measure* of "denial." At the same time, the report fails to describe the *actual* death-anxiety scores obtained by each group. It reports only the (non)differences. After reading the study we do not know anything more about the actual self-reported level of death anxiety among widgeters and backgammonites than we did before. This is not a particularly effective way to build up a data base for the field.

Enough! It should be clear by now that studies too often have contributed their own inadequacies to the intrinsic limitations of death-anxiety scales. Fortunately, there are exceptions, and these positive exceptions are now becoming more numerous. The DAS and other self-report scales can be useful when combined with additional sources of data, and when used in more sophisticated research designs. Moreover, several other instruments have appeared that have some of the advantages of the usual death-anxiety scale yet that provide different kinds of information. The following survey of research findings will include descriptions of some studies that have gone beyond the usual "cookie-cutter" format. When no methodological comments are offered, however, the reader can safely assume that we are dealing with self-report questionnaires.

One more general thought might be remembered, however. The recent spate of interest in death anxiety has not stimulated much attention to the *contemplation* of mortality. The focus has been more on feelings than cognitions, with very little exploration of the way in which the human mind interprets death as part of personal life and cosmic existence. Interestingly, it is in the study of children's views of death that psychology has come closest to this topic. Is it not paradoxical that we should delve with some enthusiasm into the development of children's ideas and show so little curiosity about the conceptual structures and processes achieved by adults?

WHAT HAS BEEN LEARNED FROM STUDIES OF DEATH ANXIETY?

We begin with the questions and topics that have attracted the most research attention. Some attempt will be made to evaluate and interpret the results.

How Much Do We Fear Death?

If "death anxiety" is what most of the instruments do measure, then we should be able to answer this question by looking at the scores obtained by normal adults in their normal life circumstances. The DAS offers the best opportunity to do so because it has been employed in more studies than any other single measure. Fortunately, Templer and some other pioneering investigators have published their basic data, although many subsequent researchers have not.

How much, then, do we fear death? *Not very much at all.* Most normal respondent samples have produced mean scores that are slightly *below* the scale midpoint, as previous literature reviews have also found (Kastenbaum & Costa, 1977; Lester, 1967) and more recent studies continue to demonstrate (e.g., Schell & Zinger, 1984). The general population reports a moderately low level of death anxiety.[5]

Several interpretations compete for our endorsement. Perhaps the direct self-report technique allows people to understate their "real" anxiety. The normal person, then, could be seen as "well defended" against death anxiety. With this interpretation one could continue to favor the assumption that we are all fighting death anxiety but succeeding in keeping it under conscious control. It is consistent with two rather different views: (a) "We cannot help but fear death" position (e.g., Becker, 1973); and (b) industrialized technosocieties such as the United States are dedicated to the denial of death (e.g., Wahl, 1959).

A simpler alternative is that most people really do not concern themselves much about death! This conclusion has the advantage of sticking closely to the facts and invoking no additional assumptions. It has the disadvantage of failing to please any of the theoretical camps, and of calling into question one of the principal tenets of the death awareness movement: Is it necessary—all this death education, all this preaching, all this advocacy? Perhaps most people have come to reasonable terms with death and do not need to be enlightened, uplifted, desensitized, or therapized!

The methodologist could propose still another alternative. Perhaps the obtained levels of death anxiety are essentially artifacts of the scale. A score of 6, for example, does happen to fall somewhat below the midpoint. The midpoint itself might not mean anything in particular, however. In nature, there is no Death Anxiety 6, 12, or 15. Because the scale numbers are merely functions of the psychometric mill, perhaps the relatively low scores obtained actually do represent a high level of anxiety. This might seem a splendid position to assert. We can have both our low scores and our high anxiety! Unfortunately, it invites some equally dubious rejoinders. For example, a person with a much higher DAS score could be regarded as actually having relatively low death anxiety—and for the same reason. If the scores yielded by psychometric measures are not anchored in a firm external reality base (and they are not), then one is free to give them almost any interpretation. How low is low? How high is high? One has only the framework provided by the scales themselves; the relationship with "real anxiety in the real world" remains to be determined (a question to which we will later return).

Both these interpretations might be rejected, however, in favor of a more critical perspective. Perhaps the self-report instruments really have very little to do with death anxiety. Perhaps we can draw *no* conclusions about the level of death anxiety in the general population from these measures. One might arrive at this critical view either by finding debilitating flaws in the instruments that are most often employed, or by maintaining that death anxiety cannot be realistically assessed by *any* psychometric technique. This tool will never get the job done—but we keep using it because it is so handy!

More skeptical still is the last interpretation we will identify here. Perhaps these studies fail to assess death anxiety adequately because they are pursuing a chimera. "Death anxiety" is not a solid and distinctive entity. At best, it is a loose designation that has some value in calling attention to death-related themes that might occur in association with emotional arousal. Conduct a thorough examination of anxiety and stress responses across a broad spectrum of respondents and situations. Include psychophysiological and environmental as well as cognitive and affective dimensions. What do we learn? Perhaps we learn that anxiety does not come in several different flavors. Perhaps the anxious state of being is fundamentally the same, although it may appear in a variety of contexts and be cued off by a variety of threats. There is no pure and distinct psychological function or entity that answers to the term "death anxiety."

Not everybody will agree with this position. Nevertheless, one must consider the possibility that death anxiety is a seriously flawed conception that has been invoked by naïve investigators employing dubious measures.

Of course, a new question peers at us if we decide that all these studies have been studying something other than death anxiety—what *have* they been studying? These alternative lines of interpretation will be reconsidered after examination of other topics and findings in this area. (We will continue to speak of "death anxiety" because this is still the commonest term in use.)

Are There Sex Differences in Death Anxiety?

This has been one of the most popular research questions. It does not owe this popularity to any compelling hypotheses. There has been little discussion of what difference it should make if one gender expresses a higher level of death anxiety. My impression is that analysis of sex differences is simply one of the most obvious and convenient types of analysis to perform. What else would you do with a hundred or so scores and no hypotheses?

Hypotheses or no hypotheses, a clear pattern has emerged. In general, women answer more self-report items in the "death anxious" direction. The first adequate study in this area was conducted by Templer, Ruff, & Franks (1971), an important contribution because it provided a beginning set of normative data on the DAS. (The results are summarized by Lonetto and Templer [1986] in a book that also covers many other studies of death anxiety—a valuable resource.) In this first study, four diverse samples were drawn from the community, as well as a sample of psychiatric patients. In all these samples, the female respondents produced significantly higher DAS scores than the males. (This study also established the precedent for DAS mean scores to prove lower than the theoretical midpoint of the scale, for women as well as men.)

The relatively higher scores obtained by women must be regarded with caution. As we will see subsequently, these differences are most apt to appear when death anxiety is treated as though a single, unitary variable. Caution is also required in drawing conclusions from the studies that do find this difference, however, Perhaps the most tempting conclusion is that women are more anxious about death than men. This would seem to be the most direct inference. It is not a conclusion to draw lightly, however, because a series of possible consequences could follow. Are women "too anxious" about death? If so, we should find out why. Then we should do something about it—right?

This approach would play into traditional assumptions about "the weaker sex" and lead to some unfortunate outcomes. Notice that quite the opposite conclusion could also be drawn from the differential responses. *Perhaps men are not anxious enough!* Perhaps women are closer to their feelings or less inhibited about sharing them honestly. Taking this tack, we might then try to make men *more* anxious about death—or, at least, more aware of their own feelings.

The fact that such conflicting conclusions can be drawn with equal ease from the same data should caution us against indulging too quickly in either adventure. We must have more adequate answers to several questions. One of the most relevant questions has already been touched on: What do these scores really mean? The available data do not license us to conclude either that women are too anxious, or men not anxious enough. Not only do we lack sufficient external (validating) evidence on "how high is high," but there is also much to learn about the sociobehavioral consequences of a particular level of anxiety.

Nevertheless, I suggest that one of these interpretations is more likely to hold true than the other. Consider, if you will, one of the most obvious facts about care for the dying and the bereaved. Who are the caregivers? Who are the people most likely to provide intimate, hands-on, everyday help? *Women!* Whether one steps into a "death education" course, by the bedside of a hospice patient, or the home of a recently bereaved spouse, one is much more likely to see a woman seeking knowledge or providing a personal service. The higher level of self-reported death anxiety, then, is also somehow associated with sensitivity to the needs of others and a willingness to provide care and comfort. John Wayne and Rambo are seldom on the scene.

Another study suggests that the macho stance has something to do with the relatively low expressed death anxiety among men. DaSilva and Schork (1984–1985) drew several questions from a questionnaire developed for *Psychology Today* by Shneidman (1970). The respondents were graduate students in public health at a major midwestern university. Summarizing their findings, the investigators state:

> The typical male respondent . . . recalls that death was not only not talked about openly in his family during his childhood, but when it was mentioned it was with some sense of discomfort. Although he thinks occasionally of his own death, he would be quite comfortable avoiding such thoughts and thinking about death not more than once a year. . . . He does not believe that religion had a very significant role in the development of his attitude to death. Possibly as a consequence he tends to doubt life after death and would rather believe in death as the end. . . . He feels motivated to achieve more in life when he thinks of his own mortality. The profile of the typical female respondent is quite different. . . . She recalls that death was talked about openly in her family during her childhood. Presently, she thinks occasionally about her own death, but quite a bit more frequently than her male counterparts. . . . She believes that religion played a very significant

role in the development of her attitude to death. Possibly as a consequence, she strongly believes in life after death. . . . Her reaction when she thinks of her own death is a feeling of pleasure at being alive. (DaSilva & Schork, 1984–1985, p. 83).

These provocative findings merit further attention. It is particularly interesting to learn that women take from death "a sense of pleasure at being alive," even though most studies find that women also have the higher level of death anxiety. (Unfortunately, these investigators did not include a conventional measure of death anxiety, and so we risk the assumption that the life-loving women in this sample would also have scored relatively high in death anxiety.) The study also suggests powerful differences between boys and girls in early development and socialization within the family, differences that might be linked with adult attitudes toward death. It is also instructive to be reminded by this study that the responses we obtain are strictly conditioned by the questions we ask. Although the Shneidman questions also involved self-report and fixed-choice responses, they approached death concern from a different angle and provided a somewhat wider choice of response alternatives.

It has often seemed to me that "death anxiety" is quite different from *concern* about death. We run the risk of confusing ourselves and others if we take every example of interest in or concern about death as a fear or anxiety equivalent. The women in the DaSilva and Schork study (1984–1985) appeared more likely to think and speak about death. Is it possible that the mere willingness to include the topic of death in our mental life has been misinterpreted as an infallible sign of anxiety? You say, "death." I become anxious. I judge: "*You* are anxious because you brought up the subject of . . . well, you know what."

Is Death Anxiety Related to Age?

All studies bear on age, if only by inadvertence. Administer a self-report instrument to a few samples, and one has at least age and sex to toy with as variables. The investigator who is unable to come up with hypotheses can find something to report simply by examining the relationship between age and anxiety score. We might pause, however, to ask ourselves what relationship *should* be expected and why. Two opposing hypotheses will immediately press their claims.

1. People become *more* anxious with advanced age because of the decreased distance from death.

2. People become *less* anxious because (a) death does not threaten as many of our values; or (b) there is a continued developmental process through which we "come to terms" with mortality.

The first of these hypotheses has an objectivistic and reductionistic slant: Psychological response is regarded as an effect of a nonpsychological causal sequence. The aged person's heightened death anxiety is epiphenomenonal. It is a cognitive and emotional symptom of an underlying biochemical change. Sand slipping through the hourglass is a physical phenomenon that obeys rules not of its own devising. Similarly, the aged person's (hypothetical) agitation signifies merely the behavioral outcropping of a process that is indifferent to human agency and desire.

The second hypotheses meshes well with several life-span developmental theories, such as Erik Erikson's (1979), and with Robert Butler's concept of the life review (1963). Life's last task is to accept the life we have lead including the death by which it is concluded. In Chapter 3 we made our first acquaintance with this increasingly popular view. The "successful maturer" might be expected to experience less death anxiety than when buffeted by the turbulence of youth and identity seeking. One now has a sense of fulfillment or self-actualization. Therefore, death is not the same catastrophic threat that it was when so much of what one valued existed only in the realm of expectation and hope.

Standing apart from these competing hypotheses is the additional possibility that

3. Age per se does not have a strong and predictable influence on our psychological orientation toward death.

Gerontological research across a wide variety of topics has shown that chronological age (within the adult spectrum) is not the all-powerful predictor that one might suppose. Marked individual differences occur at the same echelon—in physiological as well as sociobehavioral functioning. Furthermore, current life circumstances also exert a powerful influence over thoughts, actions, and health status. Perhaps age is but a general index that conceals as much as it reveals. Age might be a valuable piece of information, but it is only one piece in a larger pattern. By implication, then, it would be simplistic to expect a strong and universal relationship between adult age and orientation toward death. (Still another implicit theory will come to light as we examine the data.)

So much for the lovely theories. The data are rather more homely. The first thing to notice is that all the studies are cross-sectional. They do not tell us how the same person regarded death at different ages. The data merely report the death orientations of younger and older people. We can choose to extrapolate. We can choose to regard age *differences* as equivalent to age *changes*. This choice is difficult to defend, however, and invites serious error. Between today's 20-year-old and today's 80-year-old there is more than a difference of six decades. There is a difference in the actual person, in the historical period during which each entered the world, and in the sociocultural circumstances and events with which they contend at every age level. Furthermore, the 80-year-old has clearly demonstrated that he or she is a survivor; this may or may not be true of the 20-year-old whose attitudes toward death were assessed on the same day. Our sample of older adults is always biased by their success in surviving earlier perils—and the odds of survival continue to change with each generation.

At the risk of methodological "overkill," emphasis really must be given to the error of drawing longitudinal conclusions from cross-sectional information. This should be a particular concern for psychology. Philosophers down through the years have often pointed out that we cannot transfer a "cup of consciousness" from one mind to another. Death awareness is but one such cup. We cannot feel much confidence about the relationship between age and orientation toward death if we do not know what changes occur over time in the thoughts, feelings, and values of the same individuals. Overreliance on cross-sectional data leaves us with a kind of psychology *sans* psychology.

What conclusions can be drawn from the available data, then, considering this major methodological limitation? First, it is clear that older people in general do *not* report higher levels of death anxiety. Virtually no support can be found for the general proposition that elderly adults live with an elevated sense of fear, anxiety, or distress centering on the prospect of their mortality. An early study by Jeffers, Nichols, and Eisdorfer (1961) with community-dwelling adults in North Carolina found that many more (35%) reported a lack of death fear as compared with the relatively few (10%) who admitted to such fear. Corey (1960) was among the first to compare young and old within the same study, finding no significant differences in death fears on the basis of a "home-made" projective technique.

Outstanding among the pioneering studies was the sophisticated investigation conducted in the Netherlands by J. M. A. Munnichs (1968). Well aware of the difficulties involved in this type of research, Munnichs conducted in-depth interviews in which the 100 elderly respondents were encouraged to spin out the stories of their lives in considerable detail. More specific questions were then asked about their death-related thoughts and feelings. This seemingly "simple" approach was developed with such insight and care that Munnichs's study remains one of the best research models in this area, although it seems to have escaped the attention of most researchers on the current scene.

His unusually rich findings include several results of particular relevance here. First, clear and important individual differences were observed. As his case histories demonstrate, it would be erroneous to draw up a single profile of *the* older person's orientation toward death. Several basic orientations or strategies were found. Most frequent was *acceptance*, which, along with *acquiescence*, constituted the commonest orientation. About two thirds of the sample expressed a predominately positive conception of dying and preparation for death. Nevertheless, it was not unusual to find *evasion* or *escape* as the dominating strategy. Together with the persistent attempt to *ignore* death, this set of responses characterized about one person in three. There were also interesting variations within as well as between each general type of death orientation.

Another useful finding was an apparent difference between the "young-old" and the "old-old." Men and women just crossing from midlife to "old age" often were actively confronting their finitude. Although they differed in the particular ways in which they contemplated personal mortality, there was a lively cognitive process at work, directed toward answering the personal question: "What should death mean to me at this time in my life?" By contrast, the very old often seemed to have taken their "final stand" and were no longer interested in altering their views. Others at a very advanced age seemed "unable to attach any significance to the end, preferring to evade or ignore the issue." It is unfortunate that this finding by Munnichs has been almost entirely overlooked.

Gerontologists have documented important differences between "young-old" and "old-old" in many domains. Munnichs's study suggests that differences may also be found in the contemplation of life and death as people *continue* to age. At the least, this finding should caution us against sweeping generalizations about *the* old person's view of death. Another hint in his data is that we should perhaps give particularly close attention to contemplations of death in the transition period between midlife and old age.

Munnichs "most important conclusion is that only a small category of old people (7 of 100) were in fear of the end. For the greater part their experience of finitude was of a well-known, a familiar phenomenon (55)" (p. 124).

Most studies in recent years have relied on fixed-choice self-report measures, such as the DAS. Templer et al. (1971) found no significant differences in level of death anxiety among adults in the 19- to 85-year age range. Subsequent studies have either confirmed this "no difference" or have found a *lower* anxiety level for senior adults. Pollak's (1979–1980) literature review concluded that there is no evidence for an increase in death anxiety with increasing adult age, and this conclusion continues to hold true (based on the usual self-report measures).

Is age an unimportant or irrelevant variable, then? Not necessarily. The pattern of findings indicates that simply knowing a person's age does not provide a satisfactory basis for predicting his or her self-reported level of death anxiety. Nevertheless, age may be a useful variable as part of a more complex and realistic approach to understand how and why people contemplate death. A study that illustrates this possibility was conducted by Stricherz and Cunnington (1981–1982). Three samples of normal adults (a total of 258) were asked to express their death concerns: high school students, employed adults (mean age: 42 years), and retirees. This investigation gave respondents the opportunity to indicate the particular type of concerns they had, not just their overall level of anxiety.

Each age echelon had a somewhat different pattern of concerns. The students were most apprehensive about the possible loss of loved ones, death as a punishment, and the finality of death. The working adults expressed their greatest concerns about fear of pain in dying, as well as the possibility of premature death. These midlife people showed the relatively least concern about the possible impact of their deaths on other people. The major concerns of the older adults centered around the fear of becoming helpless and dependent on others—the process of dying rather than the outcome.

A particular fear was of being kept alive in an undignified, semi-vegetative state. They preferred a quick death at the right time to a long, slow deterioration. The senior adults also were concerned about the impact of their dying and death on their loved ones. It should be remembered that this study, like the others, compared different people at different ages. Nevertheless, the results urge us to go beyond *level* of anxiety to discover the specific concerns of an individual or group. In this study, for example, we could probably find an adolescent, a working adult, and a retired adult with the same overall anxiety score—but each might have a very different priority of concerns, and these differences could be decisive in any prevention or intervention effort.

Another informative study was conducted by Kalish and Reynolds (1977), who interviewed more than 400 adults (from age 20 to 60+) in the Los Angeles area. Unlike almost all other studies, these investigators included substantial samples of black, Japanese-American, and Mexican-American respondents, as well as whites. Across these diverse samples, the younger adults were most likely to report "having had the unexplainable feeling that they were going to die." The oldest respondents reported dreaming less often about death, and were "more likely to accept death peacefully. Another age difference was found in response to the question: "How would you like to spend the last six months of your life?" The oldest group tended to prefer contemplation and prayer, whereas the midlifers would not alter their existing life-style, and the young were concerned about the effect of their death on others. It should be noted, however, that there were many questions that were answered in a similar way by all age groups.

We will touch on age again when attention is given to the general pattern of death-anxiety correlates. First, however, let us return briefly to the starting hypotheses.

One hypothesis can be rejected for lack of support (subject, of course, to possible revival by future studies). There is little basis for holding to the view that, "People become more anxious with advanced age because of the decreased distance from death." The wind that blows away this hypothesis leaves us with several benefits. *When a particular elderly person does show elevated death anxiety, this should be regarded as a warning signal.* It is not an automatic or natural correlate of growing old—something else must be happening. In other words, the data encourage an activist orientation, not the passive response that "of course, he or she is anxious—that is just what should be expected." Another benefit is the call for a truly psychological approach. Neither chronological age nor the objective (probabilistic) distance from death are as useful as the individual's own thoughts and feelings.

The third hypothesis receives qualified support. Several studies have shown no adult age differences in death anxiety. The richer studies have also obtained patterns of findings in which there are both similarities and differences in type of death concern. Age has not disappeared as a variable, but it provides a rather limited basis for prediction and understanding. The sensible conclusion, for now, is that we should not attribute cause-and-effect power to chronological age. (A conclusion that an increasing number of investigators have reached in other areas as well.) A more useful approach is to wonder: "What is it about being 20, 40, or 80 that might contribute to an individual's overall way of looking at death?" The answers will probably be more complex but also more useful than those milled out by a simplistic age-causation model.

The second hypothesis has been saved for this later point in the discussion. Do we become less anxious with advanced age, and, if so, does this result from a mixture of reduced threat and matured perspective?

It is not unusual for studies in this area to find that a substantial number of elderly respondents express an orientation toward death that is "something other than anxiety." A case can be made for the reduced anxiety hypothesis. A clear example can be found in the Kalish and Reynolds study (1977) that, along with an interview, made use of a helpful technique devised by Diggory and Rothman (1961) that asks respondents to indicate their relative concern about several aspects of death. One of the items is: "I could no longer care for my dependents." It is not surprising to learn that the oldest respondents considered this to be a lesser concern as compared with the youngest adults in the sample. In other words, the prospect of death was not as strong a threat in at least one respect: The elderly men and women had already discharged most of their responsibilities as parents and caregivers.

This is an example I have recruited to support the reduced anxiety hypothesis. Other concerns do not diminish with age, and some increase. Furthermore, these patterns may change with time and circumstance. For example, I am acquainted with several senior adults who provide substantial care for others and whose values, in fact, are organized around their continuing ability to be nurturant, protective, and useful. There are surely many such people with us today, and their numbers may perhaps be increasing as health and vigor also become commoner among older adults. The octogenarian who supervises the outreach activities of a church or civic group could be more concerned about "who will take my place and provide care?" than some younger people who operate on a self-absorbed basis.

What of the other facet of this hypothesis—that we "come to terms with mortality" in a more seasoned and matured manner with advancing age, a "final task" for psychosocial development? This is one of the more difficult hypotheses to evaluate fairly. There may be a strong inclination to accept the hypothesis prematurely because it has been endorsed by influential theorists—and because we might like to believe it true. A useful way to gain perspective on this attractive hypothesis is to challenge it with a cynical alternative. Here, again, we will draw on the data base.

"Don't think about it. Doesn't worry me." This type of response was noted by Munnichs among some of his elderly respondents. Ignoring, evading, and escaping death-related topics were commoner strategies than out-and-out anxiety. Is it possible, then, that what might pass as serenity should be understood instead as *denial*? As Munnichs observes, it is not always easy to distinguish between a strongly motivated aversion to thinking about death, and the attitude of being "absorbed in the present without worrying about the future." Along with denial is the possibility that "To attach a philosophical significance to the 'end' would be in fact premature." An elderly individual may not be ready to make death his or her number one concern.

The apparently "nonanxious" orientation toward death might reflect, then: (a) *denial*, in which a critical zone of reality has been screened off; (b) *unreadiness*, in which psychological preparations have not yet reached the point of confronting an acknowledged but unattractive aspect of reality; and (c) *acceptance*, in which death has been integrated within a mature life perspective. Many of the available studies provide such limited types of data that one cannot distinguish among these alternatives. Low self-reported anxiety could signify denial, unreadiness, or acceptance—and perhaps other states of mind as well.

There are other reasons to be wary of the hypothesis that maturity naturally brings a reduction in death anxiety. This view assumes that maturity must take essentially the same form and display the same characteristics in everybody. I find this assumption questionable and not well supported (or even examined) by life-span developmental research. There may be truth to the assertion that reduced death anxiety is a key component or outcome of the later phases of adult development. We race far ahead of the facts if we *assume* this to be true, however. There is still much to learn about the general nature of later development and the specific processes through which we come to terms with personal mortality. The denial hypothesis remains an alternative that cannot be ignored at the present time (not that we understand denial that well, either!).

CORRELATES OF HIGH AND LOW DEATH ANXIETY

Three Starting Hypotheses

One person has a relatively high level of death anxiety; another has a relatively low level. In what other ways are these people likely to differ? Age and sex have already been examined. Some studies have attempted to expand the scope of variables that might be associated with differences in death anxiety. We will look at the general pattern of findings that has emerged and at a few selected studies in particular. First, it might be useful to think for a moment about what we might expect to discover. Although most of the studies are essentially atheoretical, an obvious hypothesis does come to mind.

Hypothesis 1

Relatively high death anxiety should be associated with an overall pattern of psychological and perhaps social and physiological distress.

This hypothesis would be consistent with the common view that relatively high death anxiety is a kind of aberration to be overcome, or a mark of psychopathology or immaturity. For an alternative we might consider the next hypothesis.

Hypothesis 2

Relatively high death anxiety is a distinctive response to a distinctive set of circumstances; therefore, the pattern of correlates will have characteristic features that cannot be equated with ordinary psychopathology.

In other words, there is something special about death anxiety, and we must learn precisely what individual and situational factors are associated with extreme levels of response (high or low).

A more peculiar hypothesis can also be suggested, if only to sharpen our powers of observation and analysis.

Hypothesis 3

Relatively high death awareness will be associated with a keener appreciation of life, heightened creativity, and periods of individual and cultural transition and growth.

Perhaps our awareness of death—in fact, of both life and death—is enhanced during risk situations. This could be a survival-oriented phenomenon. The businessperson contemplating a major new venture, the teenaged couple running off together, the cult trekking off to start its own utopian community—in circumstances such as these one may experience an excitement born of both opportunity and risk. The "deathness" of the anxiety might reflect varying components of both symbolic and literal risk. "I will just die if I don't make it!" is not an unknown feeling, whereas transition and growth situations may alter the actual risk of death in various ways.

Demographics of Death Anxiety

There are some weak indications that people in favorable socioeconomic circumstances report relatively lower levels of death anxiety. Being highly educated and enjoying a good income were characteristics usually associated with a relatively low score on the DAS (Lonetto & Templer, 1986). The actual differences were rather small, however, and not all the studies conducted or cited by Lonetto & Templer did find differences. Education and affluence, then, might be regarded as buffers against high death anxiety, if not very powerful buffers. An unpublished study by Farley (1971) that did not come to the reviewers' attention, however, showed a contradictory finding: Among college men, those of higher socioeconomic status also had the higher level of self-reported death anxiety.

The demographic profile of a relatively "low death anxious" person also includes coming from an intact family, and sporting a relatively high IQ (again primarily based on DAS studies reviewed by Lonetto & Templer, 1986). These correlates suggest that growing up in a secure interpersonal environment and possessing strong mental resources for coping with life's problem are factors offering some protection against death anxiety. One must agree with Lonetto and Templer's assessment, however, that these correlations are neither very strong nor entirely consistent. One would not have a difficult time in locating bright, affluent people from intact families who also are experiencing an uncomfortably high level of death anxiety.

Surprisingly, not much attention has been given to marital status. It is well known that marital status is related to longevity and causes of death in several ways. Married people, for example, generally are at a lower risk for suicide. A study designed specifically to examine marital status has found no differences in death anxiety attributable either to having a spouse, or spouse and children (Cole, 1978–1979). Just to keep us from jumping to conclusions, however, it should be noted that another study (Morrison et al., 1981–1982) did find that the never married were more death anxious than the married or widowed.

Ethnic and Cultural Correlates

Does ethnic-cultural group membership have any consistent relationship with death anxiety? Most studies have been conducted with predominately white populations in the United States and Canada. There has been a scattering of studies with more diverse populations, however. Kalish and Reynolds (1976; 1977) found many differences in attitudes toward death among their four Los Angeles samples (Afro-American, Japanese-American, Mexican-American, Anglo-American). These findings seem to have reflected socioeconomic status as well as the particular life-styles favored by each group. This was a much richer study than the usual administration of a self-report death anxiety scale, and is worth reading in its entirety.

One useful lesson from the Kalish-Reynolds findings should be mentioned here, however. The Mexican-American response to death tended to be highly emotional (from an Anglo-American perspective)—but the Anglo-American response tended to be "unduly cold and cruel" from the Mexican-American perspective! In other words, ethnic and cultural styles can have a marked influence on the framework we employ to observe and evaluate death anxiety. The same type and level of response can be seen as either "too anxious" or "not anxious and caring enough," depending on cultural norms. How much our overall view of death anxiety has been distorted by a failure to consider implicit Anglo-American norms is an interesting question that remains to be answered.

Lack of comparability in research design and other difficulties makes it difficult to draw general conclusions about possible differences in death anxiety between Afro-Americans and Anglo-Americans. Pandey and Templer (1972) found no differences, and the other available studies fail to provide a coherent picture.

A set of international studies reviewed by McCordie and Kumar (1984) show slightly lower self-reported death anxiety among college students in India as compared with roughly comparable populations in Australia, Canada, and the United States. What this means, if anything, is not at all clear. One can choose to emphasize either the relatively small differences or the commonalities among these populations. Precisely what is most feared about death, and how these fears are integrated into total personality and behavior are topics that, as usual, remain unexplored in these studies.

Two studies have found that Egyptians report levels of death anxiety that are slightly higher than those of Canadian and U.S. citizens (Abdel-Khalek, 1986; Beshai & Templer, 1978). As the latter investigator notes, however, "the Egyptian and American death anxiety similarities overshadow the differences" (Abdel-Khalek, p. 483). Beshai and Templer prefer to emphasize the differences, though, and suggest that "A developing society such as Egypt is more likely than a society such as the U.S. to find itself in the throes of compounded threats to human life."

There is no shortage of ideas about the ways in which cultural beliefs and practices might affect death anxiety (e.g., Palgi & Abramovitch, 1984). There is, however, a shortage of research designed to explicate the relationship between cultural background and individual thoughts, feelings, and actions in the realm of death concern.

If death anxiety is closely related to the objective or perceived threat of death, then we might expect Afro-Americans in the United States to express more concern than Anglo-Americans because of their less favorable life expectation. A study of responses to a national survey failed to support this hypothesis (Marks, 1986–1987). Because of methodological limitations noted by the author, this study should be considered only as a preliminary exploration.

Religious Affiliation and Belief

Religion could be seen as either a buffer against death anxiety (e.g., salvation and immortality) or a source of special concern (e.g., fear of damnation). It would be naïve, however, to expect any simple relationship to emerge. Religious belief and practice can differ appreciably within the same faith, and the link with emotional response can also be idiosyncratic. I have often worked with aged men and women who maintained an unquestioned belief that they would awaken after death to find themselves in heaven. Yet some were experiencing an anxiety state, whereas others were serene. Religious faith was certainly important to all these people, but did not of itself adequately predit or explain what they were experiencing as death approached.

Templer and Dotson (1970) found no significant relationship between a variety of religious variables and death anxiety in an undergraduate sample. A variety of subsequent studies have come up with almost every kind of finding imaginable—no differences, positive relationships, and negative relationships. There is some indication that "faith" may be associated with a lower level of death anxiety. By contrast a "good works" orientation toward religion has little or no bearing. Possible differences among various denominations remain unclear, although one study indicates that Jews may report somewhat higher levels than Christians.

Another study found that "born again" Christians (by self-classification) reported a slightly lower level of death anxiety as compared with other Christians and non-Christians (Young & Daniels, 1980). In practical terms, however, this difference may not be particularly important—being a "born again" Christian accounts for only a very small percentage of the variation in DAS scores. Saudi Arabians studying in the United States reported a very high degree of (Muslim) religiosity (Long & Elghanemi, 1987). The most religious within this very religious sample reported relatively less fear that significant others would die. Caution is definitely required in drawing interpretations for many reasons, however, including the extremely high religiosity of all the respondents, and the fact that there were many more "no differences." The lack of theoretical rationale in these studies is as crippling in cross-cultural as in domestic research. We have learned little or nothing about the possibly distinctive ways in which Egyptians, Indians, and Saudi Arabians contemplate death on the basis of the available studies.

The soundest conclusion at present is that we know very little for sure about the relationship between religious belief and practice and the individual's personal orientation toward death. This is unlikely to mean that no relationship exists, but rather that religion enters into our death orientations in a complex manner that requires an understanding of individual psychology.

Personality and Life-Style Correlates

Are certain personality or life-style characteristics differentially associated with death anxiety? One major life-style characteristic is sexual affinity. In their norm-building study, Templer & Ruff (1971) included 260 homosexuals (165 men and 95 women) with an age range extending from 17 to 87 years. The overall level of self-report death anxiety fell in the midrange for normal (nonclinical) populations. There was no particular reason to expect any basic differences in death anxiety on the basis of sexual preference (although the male-female discrepancy usually found in heterosexual populations did not show up here).

Today, however, homosexual males have been identified as a population at particularly high risk for AIDS. A variety of psychological problems have been observed for those who have been stricken with the disease (Baker & Seager, 1991). It might also be expected that anxiety has increased markedly among those homosexual men who have not tested positive or shown symptoms. A few years ago, then, homosexual life-style was not associated with a differential level of death anxiety. The emergence of a virulent condition may be having profound and complex psychological effects for those at high risk. In one sense, the homosexual man without any signs of AIDS can be thought of as living his ordinary life: Perhaps he has not and will not contract this disease. In another sense, however, he does live with unusual peril, and this apprehension is likely to affect his thoughts, feelings, and actions in many ways. It is to be hoped that psychological research on those confronted with the heightened possibility of AIDS will not take a simplistic approach. Death anxiety may increase (as, paradoxically, may denial), but it is the individual's total way of interpreting his situation that must be considered whether for research or therapeutic purposes.

Several studies have sought to test the general hypothesis that death anxiety will be associated with other indices of disturbance or ineffective coping techniques. There is some support for this hypothesis, but the differences are often small, and some studies find none at all. College students who reported a relatively higher sense of competence, for example, tended to report lower levels of death anxiety (Farley, 1971; Nogas, Schweitzer, & Grumet, 1974). Although statistically significant, these differences would have little value in any practical circumstance.

Another set of studies showed some support for the hypothesis that people with a clear sense of purpose in their lives and high self-esteem report less death anxiety than those lack purpose or "meaning" (e.g., Davis, Martin, Wilee, & Vorhees, 1978; Durlak, 1972). When the respondents are given an opportunity to consider several types of death concern, however, it was found that "greater perceived purpose in life is associated with a higher ranking of concern for having life's plans and projects end" (Bolt, 1978, p. 160). In general, when differences are found, the higher levels of death anxiety occur among people who see themselves in negative terms, far removed from their ideal selves, and who lack confidence in their own competency and comfort in interpersonal relationships. Furthermore, people with relatively high general anxiety also tend to score higher on death-anxiety measures. This is a consistent pattern, but it would be going too far to say that death anxiety is but another name for generic anxiety. At the most, death and generic anxiety share about a 20% equivalence.

It is also possible, though, that death anxiety measures are simply flawed ways of tapping generic anxiety (Kastenbaum & Costa, 1977). Locus of control (external vs internal) has been studied several times, but with mixed results, perhaps related to the particular populations and instruments involved.[6]

There is another type of finding that has emerged with some consistency and that may prove particularly useful. People with relatively high death anxiety tend to be more open, sensitive, and vulnerable than those with low self-reported death anxiety (e.g., Neufeldt & Holmes, 1979; Thorson, 1977). These are also people who seem more capable of empathy and less invested in aggressive, exhibitionistic, and achievement-oriented activities. This configuration is found among both sexes, but seems to occur most often in women—who, as already noted—comprise the larger proportion of people who select person-oriented and caregiving professions.

The more "armored" orientation of those with lower self-report death anxiety makes it difficult to evaluate one type of person as better adjusted than the other. Is vulnerability, sensitivity, and empathy a positive configuration, if accompanied also by higher death anxiety? Is lower death anxiety a positive characteristic if accompanied by a more self-seeking and emotionally defensive orientation? Or are these but alternative life-styles, each with their advantages and each with their emotional cost?

It should be remembered that we are still dealing here with studies of normal or nonclinical populations. The high anxiety respondents do not appear to be incapacitated by their concerns, nor are the low-anxiety respondents necessarily displaying a pathological degree of evasion or denial. The student of social work with a relatively high level of death anxiety and the student in the college of business with a lower level probably have many other differences in the way they approach life, and it would seem inappropriate to categorize one as "healthy" or "mature," and the other in pejorative terms. It is also worth reminding ourselves that within the normal population there may not be a strong relationship between death anxiety and other indices of concern or disturbance. As quoted in the introduction to this chapter, for example, at least one study has found no strong relationship between fears of death and dying on the one hand, and a sense of depression and hopelessness on the other (Lester, 1985).

Personifications, Imagery, Fantasy, and Dreams

Many of the studies already consulted have relied on direct self-report measures. We now sample some of the studies that have explored imagery and fantasy life.

The tendency to visualize Death as a person has been demonstrated throughout history.[7] *Personifications* had appeared in art, literature, drama, and mythology long before Death starred as a sardonic chess player in Ingmar Bergman's masterful film *The Seventh Seal.* Awareness of this tradition stimulated the pioneering efforts of McClelland (1963) and Greenberger (1965) to explore death personifications as a distinctive source of information in personality theory and research. Nagy (1959) also found spontaneous personifications in her studies with children. We will concentrate here on studies of death personification in adults.

My early research on death personification was summarized in the original *Psychology of Death* (Kastenbaum & Aisenberg, 1972). In the first study, a set of open-ended questions was posed to 240 adults; another sample of 421 responded to a multiple-choice version. Most of the respondents in both samples were college students.

The open-ended version included the following questions:

If death were a person, what sort of a person would Death be? Think of this question until an image of death-as-a-human being forms in your mind. Then describe Death physically, what Death would *look* like. . . . Now, what would Death *be* like? What kind of personality would Death have?

The age and sex imagined for Death was obtained by follow-up questions, if not clear from the first response. Additionally, respondents were asked to indicate their sources for their images of death and the degree of difficulty the task had held.

The multiple-choice version was established after analyzing data from the open-ended version.

1. In stories, plays and movies, death is sometimes treated as though a human being. If you were writing a story in which one character would represent Death, would you represent Death as (a) a young man, (b) an old man, (c) a young woman, (d) an old woman? If other, please specify.

2. Would Death be (a) a cold, remote sort of person, (b) a gentle, well-meaning sort of person, (c) a grim, terrifying sort of person?

Four clear types of personification emerged from these studies. These were labeled The Macabre, The Gentle Comforter, The Gay Deceiver, and The Automaton.

The Macabre was characterized as a powerful, overwhelming, and repulsive figure. The image often was of an emaciated or decaying human, or of a monster with only faint resemblance to human form. The image of a "deathlike death" was also given by some respondents. For example, death would be portrayed as an animated corpse or as an assailant who was himself disintegrating or being consumed. Macabre personifications also tended to be emotionally close to their creators. One young man, for example reported that "a shivering and nausea overwhelms me" when he thinks about the image he has produced. A young woman pictured death as a "gigantic being of superhuman strength. A body to which one would relinquish all hopes of resistance. He would be cold and dark, in such a way that one glance would reveal his mission. He would be always dressed in black and would wear a hat which he wore tightly over his head . . . self-confident with an abundance of ego. He would naturally be callous and would enjoy his occupation. He would get a greater thrill when the person whom he was claiming was enjoying life to a great degree." The Macbre personification often was presented in the form of a hideous old man.

The Gentle Comforter is embued with the theme of soothing welcome. It could be seen as an adult of any age. When presented as an old man, Father Time received much credit as a source. The Gentle Comforter was an image that came readily to many respondents. The idea of a powerful force quietly employed in a kindly way is perhaps at the core of this personification. The respondents often felt they were emotionally close to their Gentle Comforter image, but not in a threatened manner. One woman's response well typifies this type of personification:

> A fairly old man with long white hair and a long beard. A man who would resemble a biblical figure with a long robe which is clean but shabby. He would have very strong features and despite his age would appear to have strength. His eyes would be very penetrating and his hands would be large. Death would be calm, soothing, and comforting. His voice would be of an alluring nature and, although kind, would hold the tone of the mysterious. Therefore, in general, he would be kind and understanding and yet be very firm and sure of his actions and attitudes.

The Gay Deceiver was pictured as an attractive and sensuous person of either sex, often elegant and worldly. Poised and sophisticated, The Gay Deceiver entices its victim, a knowing companion one might seek out for amusement, adventure, or excitement. Those who depict this type of personification often state explicitly that The Gay Deceiver tempts and lures us on, and "Then you would learn who he really is, and it would be too late." That "who he really is" might be a modern dress version of the devil is a possibility, and there are occasional direct references (e.g., "He is a little on the slim side though looks fairly powerful. He has a very dark goatee coming to a point. . . . wearing a dark suit. . . . I see death right now almost in the same way as the devil"). Another respondent imagined death in the following way:

> Death is either a man and/or a woman. This death person is young to middle-aged and very good looking. The man is about 35 or 40 with dark hair, graying at the sides. The woman is tall, beautiful with dark hair and about 30. . . . Both have very subtle and interesting personalities. They're suave, charming, but deceitful, cruel, and cold. . . . Both are really sharp. You like them and they lead you on.

The Gay Deceiver seems to embody characteristics of both an ego ideal (for some people), and a con man. Perhaps on one level, The Gay Deceiver is a character who has stepped out of a morality play—one of the temptations from *Everyman*, or Sportin' Life in *Porgy and Bess*. The explosive rise in use of illicit drugs in recent years (mostly since this study was done) also suggests a connection between the Gay Deceiver and the pusher.

The AIDS epidemic may be an even more potent intensifier of the Gay Deceiver image. "Come with me—what a time we will have!" is not only The Gay Deceiver's lure, but also resonates with the facts of AIDS transmission through sexual intercourse as well as drug injections with contaminated needles. The biological fact is that heterosexual as well as homosexual intercourse can transmit the AIDS virus. The sociohistorical fact, however, is that the first wave of AIDS in the United States was associated with flagrantly promiscuous homosexual activity in several major cities. Among our various personifications of death, The Gay Deceiver is the image most suited to the AIDS epidemic, at least in its early phase.

Perhaps on another level, however, The Gay Deceiver represents the respondents' own efforts to divert themselves from the prospect of death. In effect, one declares: "By immersing myself in all the pleasures that life has to offer, I will have neither the time nor the inclination to admit dark thoughts. The very fact that I revel in sophisticated enjoyments suggests that death cannot really be catastrophic—Am I kidding myself? Of course! But that's the solution I prefer."

The Automaton may be in a class by itself: the image of death as an objective, unfeeling instrument in human guise. The Automaton looks like a normal person but lacks human qualities. Unlike the other personifications, he (usually a male) does not establish a human relationship of any kind. He advances with neither diabolical pleasure nor gentle compassion, but as an automatic—soulless—apparatus. One example from respondents follow:

> He is sort of a blank in human form. I don't know what he looks like. . . .
> Probably he is not very short or very tall or very good-looking or very ugly.
> He is just somebody you would never notice because he just goes his own
> way. He looks angry or sullen, but he really doesn't feel anything. I guess he
> is more like a machine than anything else. You would probably never have
> anything in common with a guy like that. Death, we will not call him Mr., is
> not the frightening person one would imagine, but he is not a jolly sort of
> person either. Physically he is above average height with dark hair and clear
> brown eyes. . . . dressed in a dark suit with a conservative tie. His walk is
> almost military, as if he were a man who is formal in most of his dealings.
> . . . Psychologically, he has no feeling of emotion about his job—either
> positive or negative. He simply does his job. He doesn't think about what he
> is doing, and there is no way to reason with him. There is no way to stop him
> or change his mind. When you look into his eyes you do not see a person.
> You see only death.

A special problem is posed by The Automaton: What are the victims to do with their own feelings? The macabre personifications might terrify, but terror is at least a human condition: One can respond to the terrifying with terror. Even such grotesque personages as the vampire and the werewolf have the reputation of establishing some kind of relationship with their victims. By contrast, one can express nothing to a "blank in human form."

Perhaps The Automaton is a creature of our own times, representing the indifferent, machined termination of a failed apparatus (the human body) rather than a death that holds a spiritual meaning of some kind.

This pair of studies also found that death was most often represented as a man, and as a person of middle or advanced adult years. The Gentle Comforter type of image was the most frequently given—suggesting that "death anxiety" may be alleviated rather than intensified through this fantasy modality for most people. For what it might be worth, funeral directors and students of mortuary sciences were the subsamples with by far the highest percentage of "no personifications," encountering some type of inner resistance to a task most others did not find very difficult. Among less frequent types of personification, the depiction of Death as a shapeless void was noted.

The most systematic follow-up to these studies has been done by Richard Lonetto and his colleagues (Lonetto et al., 1975; Lonetto, 1982). Building a link with more traditional studies, this research team found that women who depicted Death as female had the highest levels of self-reported death anxiety. Men who saw Death as a male were particularly concerned with the sight of a dead body, with the prospect of another world war, and with the shortness of life. Several other findings also contributed to sketching the relationship between the "sex of Death" and the respondent's level and type of death concerns. The Lonetto series confirmed the existence of the types of personification found in our studies, but also found some differences and examined the components in more detail. Although The Macabre image remained less frequent than the others, The Gay Deceiver type of imagery proved the commonest. Does this perhaps reflect some changes in our views of life and death during the decade between the two sets of studies? Or is it perhaps a generational shift—young adults tending to see Death as a tempter when a previous cohort was more likely to call on The Gentle Comforter imagery? Other explanations are also possible, however, so this difference serves only to suggest that there *might* be systematic changes in death fantasies over relatively short periods. In the Lonetto studies, The Gay Deceiver image "was related to the cognitive-affective component of death anxiety; specifically, to fear of dying, appearing nervous when people discuss death, the frequency of death-related thoughts, and being troubled by thoughts of life after death" (Lonetto & Templer, 1986, p. 75).

One unusual contribution of the Lonetto studies was to examine highly specific aspects of the personification imagery (e.g., the hands and feet of Death, how Death walks, what Death is doing, etc.). These elements seem to be important to the respondents as ways of humanizing and communicating with Death. In addition to the common features, each individual's distinctive way of portraying death could provide specific clues to fantasy life and concerns. For example, people whose concerns focused on the swift passage of time and the brevity of life were less likely to depict Death as The Gentle Comforter. It is from this group, in fact, that The Macabre image is most likely to come. One might, then, explore the possible link between "time anxiety"[8] and death concern with individuals who seem to live with their eyes on the clock and the calendar. Another provocative finding appears worth pursuing: "lowered death anxiety was achieved by men and women who did not see death in sexual terms but rather as a spiritual light, a feeling, a great openness, or as a vivid pattern of colors."

McDonald and Hilgendorf (1986) supplemented the personification technique with the DAS and also with the Collett and Lester (1969) Fear of Death Scale. This latter instrument provides specific scores for four types of fear: Death of Self, Death of Others, Dying of Self, and Dying of Others. This study confirmed some of the general findings already reported: Death usually seen as a male, and seldom as a young person, as well as the basic categories of personification type. It was also found, however, that students who elected to enroll in a thanatology course had "more positive images of death and were less fearful of the dying of others" than were students in an introductory psychology class. There was also a general relationship between self-report anxiety and personification: Those who created more positive images of Death had lower death anxiety scores. The strongest relationship with death personifications was with the Death of Self and Dying of Self subscales. An implication noted by McDonald and Hilgendorf (1986) is that understanding the individual's distinctive death imagery could be a valuable tool in psychological assessment and therapy because it seems to represent a highly personal aspect of thought and feeling.

Lonetto and Templer (1987) suggest a research agenda with their conclusion that "Personifications contain within their structures useful information about their nature of symbolization and of the meanings and purpose of life. We need to explore further the extent to which such imagery can be therapeutic and ultimately, curative" (p. 76).

Two cautions might be added, however. Although personifications do tap a different facet of our psychological orientation toward death, we should be careful about assuming that a particular image will necessarily be associated with a particular kind of behavior. Studies linking attitude and fantasy with actual behavior in death-related situations must still be considered a high priority.

Furthermore, we would reduce the likelihood of overinterpreting death imagery if we also studied the individual's imagery, symbolization, and fantasy production in other spheres as well. It could be important to know, for example, whether The Macabre personification is unusual for a particular person, or part of a general tendency toward producing dysphoric and frightening images. Possibly, an exceptionally intense concern with death can have differential effects, depending on the individual's characteristic response to stress. A person who tends to cope with stress by attempting to reduce (or "repress") the intensity of anxiety-producing stimuli might exhibit an overall impoverishment of mental imagery—because any indulgence in imagery could recruit frightening visions of death. By contrast, a person who tends to cope with stress through a "sensitizing" strategy might exhibit a lively overall mental imagery—perhaps an attempt to monitor, transform, and control sources of anxiety.

Death-related fantasies and images may appear either by invitation or unbidden dreams. A variety of methods are available to the investigator: analyze conversations, daydreams, essays, poems, drawings, responses to projective techniques, and so on. There is an abundance of such material already available that could be examined for its possible death fantasy and imagery content.

For example, I remember being shown a drawing made by a 77-year-old woman who resided in a geriatric facility. It was part of a set of drawings she made when asked to draw a map of where she lived and her own place in it.[9] Neither the request nor the drawings would seem to have any particular relevance to death. M. G. chatted as she made the drawings. After sketching the outside of the hospital and her ward area, M. G. started on the drawing in question. Her monologue became more focused and intense. "The Boss is calling me. He wants me in his office. I will go up there real soon. See? Home sweet home!" On the surface, it appeared that she was sketching the office of the hospital's superintendent, situated on the second floor of the facility. I could not resist the thought that she was telling us of her impending death, however, and of being called to an even higher authority. The clinical record and the ward staff both indicated that she was not in any obvious jeopardy; M. G. was one of many frail elderly people at that time who had been admitted to the institution for their custodial purposes, not for any pressing medical condition. And, yes, she was dead within three days of sketching "Home sweet home."

Was this an artful communication of impending death that perhaps could not have been better expressed in any other way? Or a coincidence? This question cannot be answered decisively in this instance, or in most other similar incidents encountered in various circumstances. It does remind us, however, that "death content" can be implicit as well as explicit, and that information from more than one modality (e.g., visual representation and verbal comment) might contribute to our understanding.

Dreams of Death

What about the dream? In folklore, dreams of death or of the dead have often been taken very seriously. One common interpretation, of course, is that such dreams predict a death to come. Abraham Lincoln's dream of his impending assassination is a famous example from American history. (It should be noted, however, that he had already escaped the bullets of at least one assassin and knew that his death was being sought by several dissidents.) With the advent first of psychoanalysis and then of modern sleep and dream research, there have been many more hypotheses advanced about the "meaning" of dreams. Unfortunately, very little has been firmly established about the functions and consequences of death dreams in healthy, normal adults.

An exploratory study involving more than 1,300 undergraduates identified those with the most frequent occurrence of nightmares, particularly those with recurrent themes (Feldman & Hersen, 1967). Biographical information was then collected and the investigators' own death concern scale administered. A significant relationship was found between nightmare frequency and self-reported concern about death. This relationship held true for both sexes, although in the total sample women were the more likely to have reported frequent nightmares with recurrent themes. Those who reported frequent nightmares were also more likely to think often of their own death, to imagine themselves as dying or dead, to think about being killed in an accident—and to have dreams of dying or death. Interestingly, actual death experiences were so few in this undergraduate population that the investigators could not examine the possible relationship between exposure to death and nightmares. The results do suggest, however, that fearful dreams with a death theme do not necessarily depend on actual exposure to death-related situations.

A later report by Hersen (1971) also found a positive relationship between nightmares, death anxiety, and the particular type of dream memories that could be recalled. Another study with college students, employing a different instrument and somewhat different research procedures, did not find a significant relationship between death anxiety and reported frequency of nightmares, however (Lester, 1967).

It might be surprising to learn that dreams of death and dying often have a pleasant rather than a terrifying quality. This phenomenon had come to my attention through the very unsystematic collection of dreams from people with whom I have been in contact over the years. For example, a faculty colleague shared this dream with me.

> While it's still fresh. I was wearing my new beige suit. You haven't seen it because I actually haven't worn it yet. I looked great, except I was dying. There were sea gulls flapping around outside the window, and they were more interesting to me than the committee meeting—imagine, wasting a dream that way! Bad enough I have to go to them when I'm awake. Anyhow, so there I was dying and sort of smiling at the sea gulls, letting them know it was all right, I was ready. Other people get angels—I get gulls! Finally somebody noticed. A guy with a big stack of, I guess, personnel folders. He said, "There goes Elaine," and went back to the folders. I didn't mind. I was happy; I was blissful. Lightheaded all over. So that's how I died last night. Tell me, what does it mean? No—don't tell me.

A recent study by Barrett (1988–1989) has provided more systematic information on dreams of death. Studying healthy young adults, she found most of them to have a pleasant affective tone. One example was quoted at the beginning of this chapter. Barrett worked with almost 1,200 dreams compiled from "dream diaries" kept by her students. These were rated independently by two readers for content and emotional tone. In a second study she worked with a smaller sample of students who reported having had dreams of their own deaths. Dreams of dying were reported by 3% of the total sample, with a tendency for the same person to have more than one such occurrence. Dreams of dying were usually rated as pleasant (86%). Perhaps even more striking is the fact that those not rated as pleasant were considered to be neutral.

Barrett reports that "Not one dream of actually dying was rated as predominately unpleasant." Yet those who dreamed of "almost dying" were very like to have had an unpleasant, unsettling experience (94%). Nobody reported a "nearly dying" dream as being a pleasant experience. We have a new puzzle to consider, then: Why should dream-dying be such a pleasant experience, whereas dream-nearly-dying is quite the opposite? Replication of Barrett's findings would seem to be the first obvious step, followed by a further investigation into the relationship between specific dream content and its emotional tone and meanings.

This study also found two major types of dream-dying (both with positive affect). The slightly commoner type involves dying and then going on into some type of postdeath experience. An excerpt from one such dream follows:

> The clock hands both pointed to twelve and I suddenly had a dizzying, thrilling rush. My mother and I turned into pure energy, pure light. We could go anywhere, free of our bodies. I see my father far below us, drinking his drink. My usual anger at him was diffused by compassion for his fearful, small existence. We soared up to the windows at the top of the ceiling and looked out. Then I incarnated and was walking in the dirt road down below. I knew that I was still dead, but wanted to take a look around at my old self. . . . I knew that death was freeing.

This type of dream has obvious parallels to the NDE, as Barrett notes. The other type of dream-dying is one in which death comes and concludes the episode: "I feel my life gradually slipping away and it feels a bit like fainting only very peaceful and I just let go myself and let myself die."

The explicit death dreams analyzed by Barrett could also be regarded as symbolic of other concerns and processes—as she notes, a Jungian interpretation might well be invoked. This would emphasize the death dream as a symbol of other types of transformation, such as the struggle to become a more mature and individuated person (Herzog, 1969; Jung, 1953).

In opening ourselves to the study of dreams, then, we enter a rich, ambiguous, and complex realm that is far removed from the study of death anxiety by fixed-choice self-report measures. It is much too soon to attempt to draw conclusions; indeed, the more urgent challenge is to improve our methods and gather more information. However, It is also obvious that there is much to learn by considering the dream and other types of mental imagery and fantasy if we really care to know about the human response to death. We will be exploring dreams again when we enter the psychological world of terminally ill and grieving people.

EXPERIMENTAL AND MULTILEVEL STUDIES

Most studies of death anxiety and related topics have been descriptive and correlative. Many have also relied on only one type of procedure, usually a self-report scale (although a few exceptions have already been mentioned). The nature of death anxiety as well as its role in our lives comes into a more adequate perspective when experimental and multi-level studies are sampled.

It is now fairly clear that the normal adult has several levels[10] or modalities of cognitive and affective response to death. A pioneering study by Alexander, Colley, and Alderstein (1957) and his colleagues demonstrated that death-related words (e.g., "coffin") cued off a stronger galvonic (electric) skin response (GSR) than did words with neutral affective tone (e.g., "chair"). This study did not distinguish between death words and other emotionally arousing words, but it did begin to show the split between verbal and physiological levels.

In a follow-up report, Alexander and Adlerstein (1959) retained the GSR measure, but also included a death-anxiety scale, a sentence-completion test, a version of the Semantic Differential technique, and an interview. They found that both religious and nonreligious college students showed heightened emotional arousal to death words. These groups differed in their conscious thoughts and feelings about death, but on a psychophysiological level, all showed signs of stress when required to give verbal associations to death words.

Other studies have confirmed that we tend to respond differently to death on a direct, conscious level and at the levels tapped through projective techniques and psychophysiological measures. When Feifel and Branscomb (1973) asked the title question, "Who's Afraid of Death," they had a clear answer to furnish: "Everybody!" Results of their multi-level investigation indicated that we usually become upset on a psycho-physiological level when encountering death stimuli, no matter what we say or think at a more self-aware level. Surface differences in self-report death anxiety, then, may conceal a universal or near-universal stress response to death stimuli on the gut level.

It is possible, however, that a misleading impression has been generated (inadvertently) by the studies that established discrepancies between response levels. One might rush to the conclusion that this discrepancy always exists because many of us either do not recognize our anxiety for what it is, or smooth it over quickly with well-practiced defenses. The person who can both identify and admit to death-related anxiety, however, might—theoretically—have parallel rather than competing responses on the verbal and the psychophysiological levels. Bernitz (1983) found some men and women who did exhibit this type of intrapsychic harmony. His study, illuminating denial mechanisms through a well-conceived experimental effort, will be reviewed in more detail elsewhere. The main point for now is that we might start to think of the discrepancy between levels of psychological response to death as itself a variable. Some individuals may exhibit greater contradictions and tensions between levels, and some situations may exacerbate these conflicts.

A multilevel Israeli study by Rosenheim & Muchnik (1984–1985) provides the clue that repressors and sensitizers may differ significantly in many ways. On a word-association task, for example, the repressors responded more slowly to death terms, even though on the level of direct self-report they showed a lower level of death anxiety than did sensitizers. We may gradually rediscover here what has been learned in so many other areas of inquiry: We must know something about the person's overall way of meeting life as well as the particular phenomenon at hand. It may also be time to abandon the assumption that we are always at war with ourselves when responding to death-related symbols and events.

What has been learned from the use of death anxiety itself as an experimental variable? There are some preliminary indications that the response to death-related situations is influenced by the prior level of death anxiety. Oranchak and Smith (1988–1989), for example, showed two neutral videotapes, and one consisting entirely of automobile and motorcycle accidents to a group of 52 undergraduates. An independent measure of mood was administered at several points during the experimental process. Those who had previously scored relatively high on the DAS described themselves as more depressed and (generally) anxious after viewing the death video as compared with classmates who had lower self-reported anxiety at the outset of the study. The individual's "basic operating level" of death anxiety, then, predicted the level of depression and anxiety that was experienced after exposure to a death stimulus. This conclusion derives from a clear and fairly specific pattern of findings. Death anxiety did not predict everything, but only what it was expected to predict: depression and anxiety.

A two-part study by Handal (1979–1980) examined the possible effect of death anxiety on problem-solving ability (using the NASA Moon Problem Task). Whether working individually or in groups, the participants' ability to work successfully on this cognitive task was systematically related to their level of self-reported death anxiety. The complex research design and the equally complex findings resist brief summary here. The most provocative finding, however, is that people with *either* high or low levels of death anxiety had more difficulties with some aspects of problem solving than did those with a moderate anxiety level. Handal's interpretation emphasizes the possibility of repressor-sensitizer differences in coping with stress. Of most interest here is the hint that those with either unusually low or unusually high self-reported death anxiety may encounter difficulties in coping with a variety of cognitive challenges throughout life, even though the particular nature of their difficulties may differ (e.g., not taking in enough information or being too distractible).

Pilot studies such as these need to be replicated, refined, and extended. They do begin to suggest, however, that manifest death anxiety can influence the way we respond to the pressures of everyday daily life.

DEATH ANXIETY IN THEORY AND PRACTICE: A FEW SUGGESTIONS

This chapter has explored some of the hypotheses, methods, and findings that have become associated with the concept of death anxiety. For the most part our attention has focused on normal adults who do not appear to be in particular jeopardy for their lives nor beset with clinically significant psychopathology. Several criticisms of this overall enterprise have been noted along the way and need not be repeated.

One further cautionary note should be mentioned, however: We cannot be sure that the responses given by normal adults in relatively safe situations represent their deepest or most acute thoughts and feelings about death. Perhaps an element of real danger or urgent decision making is required before we can know our own minds well. This limitation is most apparent in studies that rely completely on direct self-report measures, but it has not yet been demonstrated that the other techniques completely overcome the tendency to treat death as a distant and impersonal topic when presented within an academic setting. (It is remarkable how well unexpected turbulence at 30,000 feet can recruit feelings that may not be available to us when we are engaged in research on *terra firma*.)

We are ready now to consider a few implications for theory and practice:

1. Most adults seem to function with a low-to-moderate "walking around" level of death concern. There are appreciable individual differences, as well as the fairly consistent differential between the sexes. Nevertheless, we must have additional evidence before concluding that any particular individual is operating on a level that is "too high" or "too low." Instead, it is far more useful to ask: "What differences in life-style are associated with this level of anxiety and this specific configuration of concerns?" With this approach we minimize the likelihood of becoming judgmental and increase the likelihood of helping people to cope with death-related concerns within the structure of their own unique lives.

Is this man too nonchalant about death in a situation that actually holds significant risk? Is this woman too keyed up about death to help a recently bereaved neighbor? Specific questions such as these, respecting the characteristics of specific individuals and situations, can serve as useful guides. It would be less wise to establish an idealized standard for death anxiety by which to judge and manipulate others.

2. A strong *surge* in death anxiety does signify a problem that deserves prompt attention. There is a compelling difference between the moderate responses obtained during most death-anxiety studies and the type of spontaneous anxiety surge described in the chapter opening. The attending physician, J. C. Barker, was so alarmed by this and related experiences that he examined the topic of catastrophic fear in a book aptly titled *Scared to Death* (1968). He develops a theory of what might be called a "hex-prone" individual who flies into a panic when a lethal prophecy seems to be at hand. The terrified man he describes who repeatedly shouted, "I'm going to die! Don't let me die!" might have been caught in this kind of situation.

The important point for us here is not so much Barker's interesting theory but the fact that a sudden upsurge in death-related anxiety can have serious consequences for the individual and his or her family. What we have learned about moderate levels of death anxiety in everyday life does not necessarily prepare us for helping those who suffer intense anxiety episodes. This might be recommended as a high priority research area.

3. The death implications of an anxiety episode are not always self-evident. It is possible to talk death, even to shout death during an anxiety attack, and yet have some other problem that is more directly related to the crisis. Similarly, an anxiety episode can be triggered by a real or symbolic brush with death, and yet there may be no reference to death in the person's troubled thought and speech (Kastenbaum, 1987). Even those psychologists who work primarily with nonclinical populations (such as students, employees, etc.) will find it useful to strengthen their skills in the identification and treatment of acute anxiety syndromes (e.g., Beck & Emery, 1985). Death-related (whether at or below the surface) anxiety can present a very disturbing problem that requires sensitive attention.

4. None of the major theories are firmly supported or disconfirmed by the available data. We can still choose to believe that we are fundamentally incapable of acknowledging our own mortality, or, by contrast, that it is precisely this awareness that is at the root of all our other fears. Irving Yalom (1980), an outstanding contemporary practitioner and writer on psychotherapy, is convinced that "The attempt to escape from

death anxiety is at the core of the neurotic conflict. . . . The neurotic life style is generated by a fear of death; but insofar as it limits one's ability to live spontaneously and creatively, the defense against death is itself a partial death" (p. 146). This significant proposition has not really been touched by the available death-anxiety research.

The developmental-learning hypothesis also still awaits systematic investigation. Continued reliance on cross-sectional descriptive studies will not take us very far.

5. The individual's total way of understanding life must be understood with greater depth and precision if we are to comprehend death anxiety in its actual context. We must know a person's sources of strength and value as well as his or her fears and apprehensions. It would probably be as unlikely to find a person with no fear of death as to find somebody whose only response is fear!

The same person may at times put death to work as a symbol for other phenomena, play jokes on death, defy death, ignore death, think objectively about death, think fantastically about death, resist thinking about death, and resist thinking about anything other than death. Furthermore, this same person may also feel scared, bored, or curious about death; take it to be the central mystery of existence; or feel strangely peaceful and unthreatened by shedding for a moment the burden of a hyperactive little Ego that insists on pursuing its hopes and plans in a universe not made expressly for that purpose. For evidence, I need only consult the experiences of the person writing this book—though I doubt that most readers will have difficulty in recognizing at least some of these quirks from their own experience. We really should not think of "death anxiety" as comprising our entire configuration of thought and feeling, and, with some further effort, we might even be able to examine the broader spectrum of the human response to death through more appropriate types of investigation.

I do not suppose for a moment, however, that the field of psychology as such will ever provide a comprehensive and fully satisfying account of death anxiety. We need, I think, a deeper and more encompassing perspective—one that exceeds the bounds of this book. Consider, for example, that fount of optimistic pessimism, philosopher Arthur Schopenhauer. He anticipated Freud in his view that, fundamentally, we are not rational beings. Instead, all that live are expressions of a "blind incessant impulse" that he called the will (best represented in psychoanalytic theory by "the id"). Schopenhauer (1883/1957) acknowledges his debt to more ancient modes of thought such as Hindu and Greek mythology that see the birth and death of the individual as secondary to "the immortal life of nature." A person who understood and accepted this philosophy might have a very different personal orientation toward death than either the Christian who hopes and fears intensely for salvation or the atheist whose feelings are conditioned by the conviction that "You only go around once." No, I am not trying to recruit a new generation of Schopenhauerians. I am just suggesting that we use the potentials of psychology to the fullest in trying to understand death anxiety—but that we do not limit ourselves arbitrarily to this one approach to a vital human issue.

NOTES

1. Freud reports and analyzes some of his own dreams in *The Interpretation of Dreams* (original work published 1900; several editions now available). Didier Anzieu's *Freud's Self-Analysis* (1986) provides a valuable guide.
2. Rollo May's *The Meaning of Anxiety* (1979) offers a useful historical, comparative, and critical examination of this concept, with particular attention to Kierkegaard. A seminal article by Zilboorg on fear of dying (1943) is also worth attention.
3. The Old Testament, central to Judaism, Christianity, and Islam, emphasized life on earth and unquestioned faith in a Supreme Creator who had revealed himself to Abraham and others. The Pharisee sect and the Jewish Gnostic tradition, however, held the seeds for the eventual Christian and Muslim belief in the triumph over death. In this transition from an ancient world that *feared* death to the devout *longing* for relief from the confines of earthly existence we have one of the major psychological shifts in human history.
4. Other instruments used with some frequency include a brief scale introduced by Boyar (1964) as part of a doctoral dissertation, Handal's (1969) revision of an anxiety scale introduced by Livingston and Zimet (1965), Dickstein's (1976) Death Concern Scale, Diggory and Rothman's Consequence's of One's Own Death (1961), and the Collett-Lester Fear of Death Scale (1969). The Collett-Lester instrument has been favored by those who want to investigate particular areas of death concern as distinguished from the single overall score provided by Templer's DAS. A markedly different conceptual and procedural approach has been developed by Krieger, Epting, and Leitner (1974). The Threat Index (TI) is based upon George Kelly's theory of *personal constructs*. Although also an objectively scored instrument, the TI offers a more cognitive and complex approach. Those interested in studying death anxiety might do well to give this instrument serious consideration.
5. A person completing the widely used Templer DAS could, theoretically, answer no items or all 15 in the "death-anxious" direction. There is no compelling reason to believe that the scale midpoint also represents the "real" midpoint of death anxiety in the population because no clear external crite-

rion has been established. Psychometric instruments in other subject areas have also encountered this type of problem. It is not inconceivable that an average DAS score signifies either a very high (or very low) level of "real anxiety" in the respondent. It might also be argued that there is nothing in the individual's cognitive-affective state that corresponds to the score derived from a fixed-choice, self-report measure. The latter might be a useless or trivial artifice. If we choose to take a face-value approach, however, then it can be said that nonclinical populations generally report a relatively low level of death anxiety. For example, the four normal samples included by Templer et al. (1971) in their norm-building study all had means within the range of 4.85 to 6.84. If the scale scores do reflect something of the individual's "true" death anxiety, then it is difficult to avoid the conclusion that most normal adults experience only low to moderate levels. As to the unanswered question about how much death anxiety is "just right," *why not at least begin by asking the respondents directly?* Is there, in fact, any relationship between a person's death anxiety score and his or her judgment that this is a comfortable or disabling level of concern? Note also that a person might answer only one of the 15 DAS items in the death-anxious direction, and yet be so perturbed about this one aspect of death that he or she disturbed to the point of near incapacity. I have known a few such people. Theoretically, it is also possible for a person to be sensitive to every conceivable facet of death, yet to enjoy an active and eventful life. (Such a person I have not happened to meet yet—have you?)

6. Other studies include those by Sadowski et al (1979–1980); Berman and Hays (1973); Berman (1973), Patton and Freitag (1977); & Hapslip and Steart-Bussey (1986–1987).

7. Death personifications have arisen in many cultures throughout the centuries. Herzog (1966) describes several Death-Demons who appeared in the pre-Greek world and survived in various later forms. Very early in the development of the human psyche it was found necessary to transform the formless shape of death terror (i.e., anxiety) into a being something like ourselves (if also, perhaps, quite alien). The psychological permutations are fascinating but too complex to deal with here. Mother Earth, for example, has often been viewed as both the source of nourishment and the great dark hole that swallows us back up. The Death-Mother is one of the most ancient and pervasive types of personification, though more obviously dominant in ancient times than now. Some aspects of death personification as a response to the catastrophic Black Death in 14th-century Europe were explored in the first version of *The Psychology of Death* (1972). It was suggested, for example, that society's painful recovery from its encounter with megadeath included the strategy of trapping Death in personifications that could then be manipulated, controlled, even mocked. Aries (1981) and Gottlieb (1959) are others who have described some of the historical forms in which the psychological tendency to personify death has taken.

8. "Time anxiety" is a concept that has been invoked occasionally in general personality theory as well as in the realm of death anxiety. "But at my back I always hear / Time's winged' chariot hurrying near" is the way one poet expressed this concern. Another wrote famously about the fear that "I may cease to be / before my pen has gleaned my teeming brain." Less rhapsodic than Marvell and Keats are clinical and research contributions to this subject such as those of Basque and Lawrence (1977); Giroux (1979); Lonetto, Fleming, and Mercer (1979); Vargo and Batsel (1981), and Kastenbaum (1966; 1972).

9. M. G.'s drawings were among those made by geriatric patients at the suggestion of Florence C. Shelton, an environmental psychologist who was a pioneer in exploring the physical and social world of the older person.

10. *Level* is one of those terms that lend themselves well to mischief, both intentional and otherwise. It is easy to suppose that we know precisely what we mean by "level" and that everybody else agrees. When we introduce this concept it tends to influence the ensuing course of investigation and interpretation. A spatial or topological approach is implied, and when the questing eye seeks structures "below" or "behind" the surface, it is often followed by the mind's inclination to regard the "hidden depths" as more "true," or "real." Philosopher Mario Bunge (1969) has described nine forms that can be taken by the concept of level. It is difficult to determine precisely which of these concepts is operative in the various studies of death anxiety and related variables. It might be a useful mental exercise for us to refrain from even mentioning the term "level" until we are prepared to offer a careful and thorough definition.

REFERENCES

Abdel-Khalek, A. M. (1986). Death anxiety in Egyptian samples. *Personality & Individual Differences, 7,* 479–483.

Aday, R. H. (1984–1985). Belief in afterlife and death anxiety: Correlates and comparisons. *Omega: Journal of Death and Dying, 15,* 67–75.

Alexander, I. E., Colley, R. S., & Adlerstein, A. M. (1957). Is death a matter of indifference? *J. Psychology, 43*(2), 77–283.

Alexander, M., & Lester, D. (1972). Fear of death in parachute jumpers. *Perceptual & Motor Skills, 34,* 338.

Anzieu, D. (1986). *Freud's self-analysis.* Madison: International Universities Press.

Aronow, E., Rauchway, A., Peller, M., & Devito, A. (1980–1981). The value of the self in relation to fear of death. *Omega: Journal of Death and Dying, 11,* 37–44.

Axelrod, C. D. (1986–1987). Reflections on the fear of death. *Omega: Journal of Death and Dying, 17,* 51–64.

Badone, E. (1987–1988). Changing Breton responses to death. *Omega: Journal of Death and Dying, 18,* 77–83.

Baker, N. T., & Seager, R. D. (1991). A comparison of the psychosocial needs of hospice patients with AIDS and those with other diagnoses. *The Hospice Journal*, 7, 61–70.

Barker, J. C. (1968). *Scared to death*. London: Frederick Miller.

Barrett, D. (1988–1989). Dreams of death. *Omega: Journal of Death and Dying*, *19*, 95–103.

Bascue, L. O., & Lawrence, R. E. (1977). A study of subjective time and death anxiety in the elderly. *Omega: Journal of Death and Dying*, *8*, 81–90.

Beck, A. T., & Emery, G. (1985). *Anxiety disorders and phobias*. New York: Basic Books.

Becker, E. (1973). *The denial of death*. New York: The Free Press.

Berman, A. L. (1973). Smoking behavior: How is it related to locus of control, death anxiety and belief in afterlife? *Omega: Journal of Death and Dying*, *4*, 149–156.

Berman, A. L., & Hays, J. E. (1973). Relationships between death anxiety, belief in afterlife, and locus of control. *Journal of Consulting Psychology*, *41*, 318.

Bermann, S., & Richardson, V. (1986–1987). Social change in the salience of death among adults in America: A projective assessment. *Omega: Journal of Death and Dying*, *17*, 108–195.

Beshai, J. A., & Templer, D. I. (1978). American and Egyptian attitudes toward death. *Essence*, *3*, 155–158.

Blackman, M. B. (1973). Totems to tombstones: Culture change as viewed through the Haida mortuary complex, 1877–1971. *Ethnology*, *12*, 47–56.

Bolt, M. (1978). Purpose in life and death concerns. *Journal of Genetic Psychology*, *132*, 159–160.

Boyar, J. I. (1964). The construction and partial validation of a scale for the measurement of the fear of death. *Dissertation Abstracts*, *25*, 20–21.

Breznitz, S. (1983). Anticipatory stress and denial. In S. Breznitz (Ed.), *The denial of stress*. New York: International Universities Press.

Brodsky, B. (1959). The self-representation, anality, and the fear of dying. *Journal of the American Psychoanalytic Association*, *7*, 95–108.

Bromberg, W., & Schilder, P. (1938). Death and dying. *Psychoanalytic Review*, *20*, 133–185.

Bromberg, W., & Schilder, P. (1939). The attitude of psychoneurotics toward death. *Psychoanalytic Review*, *23*, 2–25.

Butler, R. (1963). The life review: An interpretation of reminiscence in the aged. *Psychiatry*, *26*, 65–70.

Cautela, J. R., Kastenbaum, R., & Wincze, J. P. The use of the Fear Survey Schedule and the Reinforcement Survey Schedule to survey possible reinforcement and aversive stimuli among juvenile offenders. *Journal of Genetic Psychology*, *121*, 255–261.

Chambers, W. V. (1986). Inconsistencies in the theory of death threat. *Death Studies*, *10*, 165–176.

Chambers, W. V. (1986). Inconsistencies in death threat theory still stand: A rejoinder. *Death Studies*, *10*, 233–238.

Chiapetta, W., Floyd, H. H., Jr., & McSeveney, O. R. (1976). Sex differences in coping with death anxiety. *Psychological Reports, 39*, 945-946.

Ciernia, J. R. (1985). Death concern and businessmen's mid-life crisis. *Psychological Reports, 56*, 83-87.

Cole, M. A. (1978-1979). Sex and marital status differences in death anxiety. *Omega: Journal of Death and Dying, 9*, 139-147.

Collett, L., & Lester, D. (1969). The fear of death and the fear of dying. *Journal of Psychology, 72*, 179-181.

Corey, L. G. (1960). An analogue of resistance to death awareness. *Journal of Gerontology, 16*, 59-60.

Craddick, R. A. (1972). Symbolism of death: Archetypal and personal symbols. *International Journal of Symbolology, 3*, 35-42.

DaSilva, A., & Schork, M. A. (1984-1985). Gender differences in attitudes to death among a group of public health students. *Omega: Journal of Death and Dying, 15*, 77-84.

Davis, S. F., Martin, D. A., Wilee, C. T., & Voorhees, J. W. (1978). Relationship of fear of death and loss of self esteem in college students. *Psychological Reports, 42*, 419-422.

Devins, G. M. (1979). Death anxiety and voluntary passive euthanasia. *Journal of Consulting & Clinical Psychology, 47*, 301-309.

Devins, G. M. (1979). Contributions of health and demographic status to death anxiety and attitudes toward voluntary passive euthanasia. *Omega: Journal of Death and Dying, 11*, 291-300.

Dickstein, L. S. (1977-1978). Attitudes toward death, anxiety, and social desirability. *Omega: Journal of Death and Dying, 8*, 369-378.

Dickstein, L. S., & Blatt, S. J. (1966). Death concern, futurity, and anticipation. *Journal of Consulting Psychology, 30*, 11-17.

Diggory, J. C., & Rothman, D. Z. (1961). Values destroyed by death. *Journal of Abnormal & Social Psychology, 63*, 205-210.

Durlak, J. (1972). Relationship between various measures of death concern and fear of death. *Journal of Consulting & Clinical Psychology, 38*, 463.

Durlak, J. A. (1982). Measurement of the fear of death: An examination of some existing scales. *Journal of Clinical Psychology, 28*, 545-547.

Durlak, J. A., & Kass, C. A. (1981-1982). Clarifying the measurement of death attitudes: A factor analytic evaluation of fifteen self-report death scales. *Omega: Journal of Death and Dying, 12*, 129-141.

Elkins, G. R., & Fee, A. F. (1980). The relationship of physical anxiety to death anxiety and age. *Journal of Genetic Psychology, 137*, 147-148.

Engel, G. L. (1971). Sudden and rapid death during psychological stress. *Annals of Internal Medicine, 74*, 771-782.

Engel, G. L. (1976). Psychological stress, vasodepressor (vasogal) syncope, and sudden death. *Annals of Internal Medicine, 89*, 403-412.

Erikson, E. H. (1979). Reflections on Dr. Borg's life cycle. In D. D. Van Tassel (Ed.) *Aging, death and the completion of being* (pp. 29-68). Philadelphia: University of Pennsylvania Press.

Feifel, H., & Branscomb, A. B. (1973). Who's afraid of death? *Journal of Abnormal Psychology, 81,* 282–288.

Feldman, M. J., & Hersen, M. (1967). Attitudes toward death in nightmare subjects. *J. Abnormal Psychology, 72,* 421–425.

Flint, G. A., Gayton, W. F., & Ozmon, K. L. (1983). Relationship between life satisfaction and acceptance of death by elderly persons. *Psychological Reports, 53,* 290.

Florian, V., & Kravetz, S. (1983). Fear of personal death: Attribution, structure, and relation to religious belief. *Journal of Personality & Social Psychology, 44,* 600–607.

Freud, S. (1953/1913). Thoughts for the times on war and death. In *Collected works,* Vol. IV (pp. 288–317). London: Hogarth Press.

Gesser, G., Wong, P. T. P., & Reker, G. T. (in press). Death attitudes across the life-span: The development and validation of the Death Attitude Profile (DAP). *Omega: Journal of Death and Dying.*

Gilliland, J. C., & Templer, D. I. (1985–1986). Relationship of death anxiety scale factors to the subjective state. *Omega: Journal of Death and Dying, 16,* 155–167.

Greenberger, E. (1965). Fantasies of women confronting death. *Journal of Consulting Psychology, 29,* 252–260.

Halpert, E. (1980). Death, dogs, and Anubis. *International Journal of Psychoanalysis, 7,* 385–395.

Hamilton, S. B., Keilin, W. G., & Knox, T. A. (1988–1989). Thinking about the unthinkable: The relationship between death anxiety and cognitive-emotional response to the threat of nuclear war. *Omega: Journal of Death and Dying, 18,* 53–62.

Handal, P. J. (1969). The relationship between subjective life expectancy, death anxiety, and general anxiety. *Journal of Clinical Psychology, 25,* 39–42.

Handal, P. J., Peal, R. L., Napoli, J. C., & Austrin, H. R. (1984–1985). A relationship between direct and indirect measures of death anxiety. *Omega: Journal of Death and Dying, 15,* 245–262.

Handal, P. J., & Rychlak, J. F. (1971). Curvilinearity between dream content and death anxiety and the relationship of death anxiety to repression sensitization. *Journal of Abnormal Psychology, 77,* 11–16.

Hayslip, B., & Steart-Bussey, D. Locus of control levels of death anxiety relationships. *Omega: Journal of Death and Dying, 17,* 41–50.

Heide, F. J., & Borkovec, T. D. (1983). Relaxation-induced anxiety: Paradoxical anxiety enhancement due to relaxation training. *Journal of Consulting & Clinical Psychology, 5,* 171–182.

Hersen, M. (1971). Personality characteristics of nightmare subjects. *Journal of Nervous & Mental Disease, 53,* 27–31.

Herzog, E. (1969). *Psyche and death.* New York: Putnam's Sons.

Hessing, D. J., & Elffers, H. (1986–1987). Attitudes toward death, fear of being declared dead too soon, and donation of organs after death. *Omega: Journal of Death and Dying, 17,* 115–126.

Hoelter, J. W., & Hoelter, J. A. (1978). The relationship between fear of death and anxiety. *Journal of Psychology, 99*, 225–226.

Hoelter, J. W., & Hoelter, J. A. (1980–1981). On the interrelationships among exposure to death and dying, fear of death and anxiety. *Omega: Journal of Death and Dying, 11*, 241–254.

Hunt, D. M., Lester, D., & Ashton, N. (1983). Fear of death, locus of control and occupation. *Psychological Reports, 53*, 1022.

Jeffers, F. C., Nichols, C. R., & Eisdorfer, C. (1961). Attitudes of older persons toward death: A preliminary review. *Journal of Gerontology, 16*, 53–56.

Jung, C. G. (1953). *Psychology and alchemy.* Princeton: Princeton.

Kalish, R. A. (1963). An approach to the study of death attitudes. *American Behavioral Sciences, 6*, 68–70.

Kalish, R. A. (1986). Cemetery visits. *Death Studies, 10*, 55–58.

Kalish, R. A., & Reynolds, D. (1977). *Death and ethnicity: A psychocultural study.* Los Angeles: University of Southern California Press.

Kastenbaum, R. (1959). Time and death in adolescence. In H. Feifel (Ed.), *The meaning of death* (pp. 99–113). New York: McGraw-Hill.

Kastenbaum, R. (1966). As the clock runs out. *Mental Hygiene, 50*, 332–336.

Kastenbaum, R. (1974). Fertility and fear of death. *Journal of Social Issues, 30*, 63–78.

Kastenbaum, R. (1986). Death in the world of adolescence. In C. A. Corr & J. N. McNeil (Eds.), *Adolescence and death* (pp. 4–15). New York: Springer.

Kastenbaum, R. (1987). Death-related anxiety. In L. Michelson & L. M. Ascher (Eds.), *Anxiety and stress disorders* (pp. 425–441). New York: Guilford Press.

Kastenbaum, R. (1987–1988). Theory, research and application: Some critical issues for thanatology. *Omega: Journal of Death and Dying, 18*, 397–410.

Kastenbaum, R., & Costa, P. T., Jr. (1977). Psychological perspectives on death. In *Annual Review of Psychology* (Vol. 28, pp. 225–249). Palo Alto: Annual Review Press.

Kastenbaum, R., & Sabatini, P. (1973). The do-it-yourself death certificate as a research technique. *Life Threatening Behavior, 3*, 20–32.

Kastenbaum, R., & Teahan, J. (1970). Future time perspective and subjective life expectancy in "hard core unemployed" men. *Omega: Journal of Death and Dying, 1*, 189–200.

Kaufmann, W. (1976). *Existentialism, religion and death.* New York: New American Library.

Kelly, G. A. (1955). *The psychology of personal constructs.* New York: Norton.

Kinlaw, B. J. R., & Dixon, R. D. (1980–1981). Fear of death and fertility reconsidered. *Omega: Journal of Death and Dying, 11*, 119–137.

Klug, L. F., & Boss, M. (1976). Factorial structure of the death concern scale. *Psychological Reports, 40*, 907–910.

Klug, L. F., & Boss, M. (1977). Further study of the validity of the death concern scale. *Psychological Reports, 40*, 907–910.

Klug, L., & Sinha, A. (1987–1988). Death acceptance: A two-component formulation and scale. *Omega: Journal of Death and Dying, 18*, 229–236.

Koob, F. B., & Davis, S. F. (1977). Fear of death in military officers and their wives. *Psychological Reports, 40*, 261-262.

Koocher, G. P., O'Malley, J. E., Foster, D., & Grogan, J. C. (1976). Death anxiety in normal children and adolescents. *Psychiatria Clinica, 9*, 220-229.

Krieger, S., Epting, F., & Leitner, L. M. (1974). Personal constructs, threat, and attitudes toward death. *Omega: Journal of Death and Dying, 5*, 299-310.

Kulys, R., & Tobin, S. S. (1980). Interpreting the lack of future concerns among the elderly. *International Journal of Aging & Human Development, 11*, 111-126.

Kumar, A., Vaidya, A. K., & Dwivedi, A. V. (1982). Death anxiety as a personality dimension of alcoholics and non-alcoholics. *Psychological Reports, 51*, 634.

Kuperman, S. K., & Golden, S. J. (1978). Assessment of attitudes toward death and dying: A critical review of some available methods. *Omega: Journal of Death and Dying, 9*(3), 7-47.

Latanner, B., & Hayslip, B. (1984-1985). Occupation-related differences in levels of death anxiety. *Omega: Journal of Death and Dying, 15*, 53-66.

Lester, D. (1967). Experimental and correlational studies of the fear of death. *Psychological Bulletin, 67*, 27-36.

Lester, D. (1985). Depression and fear of death in a normal population. *Psychological Reports, 56*, 882.

Levin, R. (1989-1990). A reexamination of the dimensionality of death anxiety. *Omega: Journal of Death and Dying, 20*, 341-350.

Livingston, P. B., & Zimet, C. N. (1965). Death anxiety, authoritarianism, and choice of speciality in medical students. *Journal of Nervous & Mental Diseases, 140*, 22-230.

Lonetto, R. (1982). Personifications of death and death anxiety. *Journal of Personality Assessment, 46*, 404-408.

Lonetto, R., & Templer, D. (1983). The nature of death anxiety. In C. D. Spielberger & J. N. Butcher (Eds.), *Advances in personality assessment* (pp. 141-174). Hillsdale, NJ: Lawrence Erlbaum Associates.

Lonetto, R., & Templer, D. I. (1986). *Death anxiety*. New York: Hemisphere Publishing.

Long, D. L., & Elghanemi, S. (1987). Religious correlates of fear of death among Saudi Arabians. *Death Studies, 11*, 89-98.

Marks, A. (1986-1987). Race and sex differences and fear of dying: A test of two hypotheses—high risk or social loss? *Omega: Journal of Death and Dying, 17*, 229-236.

May, R. (1979). *The meaning of anxiety*. New York: McGraw-Hill.

McClelland, D. (1963). The harlequin complex. In R. White (Ed.), *The study of lives* (pp. 94-119). New York: Atherton Press.

McDonald, C. W. (1976). Sex, religion, and risk-taking behavior as correlates of death anxiety. *Omega: Journal of Death and Dying, 7*, 35-44.

McDonald, R. T., & Carroll, J. D. (1981). Three measures of death anxiety: Birth order effects and concurrent validity. *Journal of Clinical Psychology, 37,* 574-577.

McDonald, R. T., & Hilgendorf, W. A. (1986). Death imagery and death anxiety. *Journal of Clinical Psychology, 42,* 87-91.

McMordie, W. R., & Kumar, A. (1984). Cross-cultural research on the Templer and Templer/McMordie death anxiety scales. *Psychological Reports, 54,* 959-963.

Means, M. H. (1936). Fears of 1,000 college students. *Journal of Abnormal & Social Psychology, 31,* 291-311.

Middleton, W. C. (1936). Some reactions toward death among college students. *Journal Abnormal & Social Psychology, 21,* 165-173.

Munnichs, J. H. A. (1968). *Old age and finitude: A contribution to psycho-gerontology.* Basel: Karger.

Myers, J. E., Wass, H., & Murphy, M. (1980). Ethnic differences in death anxiety among the elderly. *Death Education, 4,* 237-244.

Nagy, M. H. (1959). The child's theories concerning death. In H. Feifel (Ed.), *The meaning of death* (pp. 79-98). New York: McGraw-Hill. (Reprinted from *Journal of Genetic Psychology* (1948), *73,* 3-27.

Nehrke, M. F., Belluci, G., Gabriel, S. J. (1977-1978). Death anxiety, locus of control, and life satisfaction in the elderly: Toward a definition of ego-integrity. *Omega: Journal of Death and Dying, 8,* 359-368.

Neimeyer, R. A. (1986). The threat hypothesis: A conceptual and empirical defense. *Death Studies, 10,*   –   .

Neimeyer, R. A., Bagley, K. J., & Moore, M. K. (1986). Cognitive structure and death anxiety. *Death Studies, 10,* 273-288.

Neimeyer, R. A., & Chapman, K. M. (1980-1981). Self/ideal discrepancy and fear of death: The test of an existential hypothesis. *Omega: Journal of Death and Dying, 11,* 233-240.

Nelson, L. D., & Nelson, C. C. (1975). A factor analytic inquiry into the multidimensionality of death anxiety. *Omega: Journal of Death and Dying, 6,* 171-178.

Neufeldt, D. E., & Holmes, C. B. (1979). Relationship between personality traits and fear of death. *Psychological Reports, 45,* 907-910.

Neustadt, W. E. (1982). *Death anxiety in elderly nursing home residents and amount of contact received from staff: A correlation study.* Master's thesis, University of Oregon, Eugene.

Oranchak, E., & Smith, T. (1988-1989). Death anxiety as a predictor of mood change in response to a death stimulus. *Omega: Journal of Death and Dying, 19,* 155-162.

Orbach, I., Feschbach, S., Carlson, G., & Ellenberg, L. (1984). Attitudes toward life and death in suicidal, normal, and chronically ill children: An extended replication. *Journal of Consulting & Clinical Psychology, 52,* 1020-1027.

Orbach, I., Gross, Y, Glaubman, H., & Berman, D. (1985). Children's perception of death in humans and animals as a function of age, anxiety, and cognitive ability. *Journal of Child Psychology & Psychiatry, 26,* 453-463.

Osarchuk, M., & Tatz, S. J. (1973). Effect of induced fear of death on belief in afterlife. *Journal of Personality & Social Psychology, 27*, 256–260.

Pandey, R. E., & Templer, D. I. (1972). Use of Death Anxiety Scale in an inter-racial setting. *Omega: Journal of Death and Dying, 3*, 127–130.

Peal, R. L., Handal, P. T., Gilner, F. H. (1981–1982). A group desensitization procedure for the reduction of death anxiety. *Omega: Journal of Death and Dying, 12*, 61–70.

Persinger, M. K. A. (1985). Death anxiety as a semantic conditioned suppression paradigm. *Perceptual and Motor Skills, 60*, 827–830.

Pettigrew, C. G., & Dawson, J. C. (1979). Death anxiety: "State" or "trait"? *Journal of Clinical Psychology, 35*, 154–158.

Pollak, J. M. (1979–1980). Correlates of death anxiety: A review of empirical studies. *Omega: Journal of Death and Dying, 10*, 97–122.

Ray, J. J., & Najman, J. (1974). Death anxiety and death acceptance: A preliminary approach. *Omega: Journal of Death and Dying, 5*, 311–315.

Reed, P. G. (1986). Death perspectives and temporal variables in terminally ill and healthy adults. *Death Studies, 10*, 467–478.

Rhudick, P. J., & Dibner, A. S. (1961). Age, personality and health correlates of death concerns in normal aged individuals. *Journal of Gerontology, 16*, 44–49.

Richardson, V., & Sands, R. Death attitudes among mid-life women. *Omega: Journal of Death and Dying, 17*, 327–342.

Rosenheim, E., & Muchnik, B. (1984–1985). Death concerns in differential levels of consciousness as functions of defense strategy and religious beliefs. *Omega: Journal of Death and Dying, 15*, 15–24.

Sadowski, C. J., Davis, S. F., & Loftus-Vergari, M. C. (1979–1980). Locus of control and death anxiety: A re-examination. *Omega: Journal of Death and Dying, 10*, 203.

Salter, C. A., & Salter, C. D. (1976). Attitudes toward aging and behavior toward the elderly among young people as a function of death anxiety. *The Gerontologist, 16*, 232–236.

Sanders, T. F., Poole, T. E., & Rivero, W. T. (1980). Death anxiety among the elderly. *Psychological Reports, 46*, 53–54.

Schell, B. H., & Zinger, A. T. (1984). Death anxiety scale means and standard deviations for Ontario undergraduates and funeral directors. *Psychological Reports, 54*, 439–446.

Schopenhauer, A. (1957). The world as will and idea. (3 volumes). London: Routledge & Kegan Paul. (Original work published 1883).

Schulz, R. (1985). Thinking about death: Death anxiety research. In S. G. Wilcox & M. Sutton (Eds.), *Understanding death and dying* (3rd ed.). Palo Alto, CA: Mayfield.

Scott, C. A. (1896). Old age and death. *American Journal of Psychology, 8*, 67–122.

Shady, G., Brodsky, M., & Stoley, D. (1979). Validation of the multidimensionality of death anxiety as supported by differences between volunteers and nonvolunteers. *Psychological Reports, 45*, 255–258.

Shneidman, E. S. (1970, August). Death questionnaire. *Psychology Today*, pp. 67–72.

Smith, A. H., Jr. (1977). A multivariate study of personality, situational and demographic predictors of death anxiety in college students. *Essence*, *1*, 139–146.

Smith, R. B., & Mor, V. (1986). *Aspects of the AIDS epidemic: A literature review*. Providence, RI: Centers for Gerontology and Health Care Research, Brown University.

Stewart, D. W. (1975). Religious correlates of the fear of death. *Journal of Thanatotology*, *3*, 161–164.

Stricherz, M., & Cunnington, L. (1981–1982). Death concerns of students, employed persons, and retired persons. *Omega: Journal of Death and Dying*, *12*, 373–380.

Swenson, W. M. (1961). Attitudes toward death in an aged population. *Journal of Gerontology*, *16*, 49–52.

Tate, F. B. (in press). Impoverishment of death symbolism: The negative consequences. *Omega*.

Tate, L. A. (1980). *Life satisfaction and death anxiety in aged women*. Doctoral dissertation, California School of Professional Psychology, Fresno.

Telban, S. G. (1981). Death anxiety and knowledge about death. *Psychological Reports*, *49*, 648.

Templer, D. I. (1970). The construction and validation of a Death Anxiety Scale. *Journal of General Psychology*, *72*, 165–166.

Templer, D. I. (1971). The relationship between verbalized and nonverbalized death anxiety. *Journal of Genetic Psychology*, *119*, 211–214.

Templer, D. I. (1972). Death anxiety: Extroversion, neuroticism, and cigarette smoking. *Omega: Journal of Death and Dying*, *3*, 126–127.

Templer, D. I., & Dotson, E. (1970). Religious correlates of death anxiety. *Psychological Reports*, *26*, 895–897.

Templer, D. I., & Ruff, C. F. (1971). Death anxiety scale means, standard deviations, and embeddings. *Psychological Reports*, *29*, 173–174.

Templer, D. I., Ruff, C. F., & Ayers, J. (1976). Alleviation of high death anxiety with symptomatic treatment of depression. *Psychological Reportys*, *35*, 216.

Templer, D. I., Ruff, C. F., & Franks, C. M. (1971). Death anxiety: Age, sex, and parental resemblance in diverse populations. *Developmental Psychology*, *4*, 108.

Testa, J. A. (1981). Group systematic desensitization and implosive therapy for death anxiety. *Psychological Reports*, *48*, 376–378.

Thorson, J. A. (1977). Variation in death anxiety related to college students' sex, major field of study, and certain personality traits. *Psychological Reports*, *40*, 857–858.

Thorson, J. A., Horacek, B. J., & Kara, G. (1987). A replication of Kalish's study of cemetery visits. *Death Studies*, *11*, 177–182.

Tobacyk, J., & Eckstein, D. (1980–1981). Death threat and death concerns in the college student. *Omega: Journal of Death and Dying*, *11*, 139–155.

Toews, J., Martin, R., & Prosen, H. (1985). Death anxiety: The prelude to adolescence. *Adolescent Psychiatry, 12,* 134–144.

Tramill, J. L., Kleinhammer-Tramill, P. J., Davis, S. F., & Parks, C. S. (1985). The relationship between Type A and Type B behavior patterns and level of self-esteem. *Psychological Record, 35,* 323–327.

Vargo, M. E., & Batsel, W. M. (1984). The reduction of death anxiety: A comparison of didactic, experiential and non-conscious treatment. *British Journal of Medical Psychology, 37,* 333–337.

Wahl, C. F. (1959). The fear of death. In H. Feifel (Ed.), *The meaning of death* (pp. 16–28). New York: McGraw-Hill.

Wallis, C. L. (1973). *American Epitaphs.* New York: Dover.

Wass, H., & Myers, J. E. (1982). Psychosocial aspects of death among the elderly: A review of the literature. *Personnel & Guidance Journal, 61,* 131–142.

Westman, A. S., & Canter, F. M. (1985). Fear of death and the concept of extended self. *Psychological Reports, 56,* 419–425.

Wilson, G. R. (1902). The sense of danger and the fear of death. *Monist, 13,* 352–369.

Yalom, I. D. (1980). *Existential psychotherapy.* New York: Basic Books.

Young, M., & Daniels, S. (1980). Born again status as a factor in death anxiety. *Psychological Reports, 47,* 367–370.

Zilboorg, G. (1943). The fear of death. *Psychoanalytical Quarterly, 12,* 465–475.

6

A Will to Live and
an Instinct to Die?

If you want to endure life be prepared for death.

—Sigmund Freud, *Inhibitions, Symptoms, and Anxiety*

Freud's tortuous formulations on the death instinct can now securely be relegated to the dust bin of history.

—Ernest Becker, *The Denial of Death*

I want to die.

—An alcoholic doctor to his therapist,
Wallerstein, Forty-two Lives in Treatment

We live. We die. Is it true, helpful, or pleasing to suppose that we also have a "will" to live and an "instinct" to die?

This chapter first examines a controversial theory offered by Sigmund Freud,[1] and then proposes a way of building on his insights without perpetuating untenable assumptions. Instinct theory in general suffered an eclipse soon after Freud proposed his Eros–Thanatos distinction. Although the concept of instinct returned to respectability some years later, it was in a new form that offered little support for the 19th-century view held by Freud and his contemporaries.[2] In our time, the very idea of a death instinct has come to seem anachronistic. One finds little interest in Freud's concept either within the ranks of hospice caregivers or the academic thanatologists. Most clinicians and researchers who have come of age since the end of World War II have only a vague awareness that such a theory was ever proposed, and one cannot say that there is at present any resurgence of curiosity.

Nevertheless, there is much yet to learn from considering Freud's suggestions anew. The years that have passed since publication of *Beyond the Pleasure Principle* (1920) and *New Introductory Lectures on Psychoanalysis* (1933) have brought many events and observations that bear on our relationship with mortality, but—with the possible exception of existentialism—no alternative has arisen that attempts such grandeur of scope or offers such provocative thinking.

Freud's death instinct theory[1] draws biology, philosophy, sociocultural dynamics, and theoretical physics into its ambitious sphere. It also reaches into many diverse areas within psychology, such as normal psychosexual development, war neuroses, and masochism. Furthermore, Freud's death instinct theory was not intended to stand alone. It is integral to his revised formulation of the general psychoanalytic system.

We will try to gain some perspective on death instinct theory by reviewing its origins in the mind of Freud, and the shocks and stresses of the society in which he experienced his later years. As we become better acquainted with this theory we will be able to ask the same questions that are appropriate to address any systematic conception of human nature: Is it true? Is it helpful? Is it pleasing?

The core death instinct theory will first be presented with the assistance of Freud himself. We will next see how and why the theory came into being and what role it was intended to play in the revised formulation of the psychoanalytic system. This will be followed by illustrative applications and critiques of death instinct theory, and finally, by our own evaluation and suggestions.

CORE THEORY

What could be more grim than Freud—ailing, disillusioned, old Freud—discoursing on the death instinct? Yet his most succinct presentation (originally delivered as a lecture) shows the deft touch of an accomplished humorist. He knows we will look askance at such "A queer instinct, indeed, dedicated to the destruction of its own organic home!" (1961, pp. 105–106). Freud declines the support of poets who occasionally write of such things because they are, of course, "irresponsible people." (This remark was hardly meant to be taken seriously, coming from an ardent reader of poetry and other literature.) Teasingly, he slips in the fact that the mucuous membrane of the stomach has a tendency to dissolve itself: Now, how is that for gut level self-destruction? Coyly, however, he does not quite claim this phenomenon as direct evidence for his theory of an underlying self-destructive tendency. He does, however, see to it that listeners and readers are well amused before he comes to the point. Freud obviously knows that the death instinct theory is likely to increase tension and resistance. On this occasion, at least, Freud has mastered the art of reducing discomfort lest it turn into anger directed against himself. Already condemned by some for luring sex out of the closet, Freud was not eager to be targeted as the inventor of death as well.

The death instinct theory he proposed is built on the following basic assumptions:

1. *All* instincts are conservative. They aim to repeat or restore some earlier state of affairs. Freud cites as examples the tendency of many organisms to regenerate lost body parts and of migratory birds to follow the same seasonal routes.

2. This "compulsion to repeat" (Freud's term) rules both our mental and vegetative functioning. It is one of the basic operations built into the logic of our system, to invite the computer analogy. We cannot hope to understand this compulsion by focusing only on the mental or the organic sphere to the exclusion of the other.

3. The compulsion to repeat or restore an earlier condition can take precedence over the usual forms of gratification. Instead of acting so as to experience pleasure, one may actually seek pain and loss to appease the repetition compulsion.

4. "But how can the conservative characteristic of instincts help us to understand our self-destructiveness? What earlier state of things does an instinct such as this want to restore?" Freud offers a bold answer to his own question: "If it is true that—at some immeasurably remote time and in a manner we cannot conceive—life once proceeded out of inorganic matter, then . . . an instinct must have arisen which sought to do away with life once more and to re-establish the inorganic state" (Freud, 1933, p. 107).

5. The death instinct (more accurately although less frequently translated as drive, *Todestrieb*) operates "in every vital process." All living organisms at all phases of their functioning exhibit a tendency toward self-destruction.

6. A strong countervailing force also exists in all living organisms. This force (*Eros*) seeks "to combine more and more living substances into ever greater unities." Eros is dedicated to pleasure, the stimulation of growth, and the promotion of survival.

7. Eros and Thanatos are mingled throughout life, each jousting

with the other in an attempt to achieve its own aims. We are never wholly oriented toward survival and development, and only in the most extreme conditions, if ever, does the death instinct reign without challenge.

8. Death is one of life's most fundamental aims. We live with the intention to die. Life is also an aim of life, however. Both aims are built into the very nature of the living organism. They are to be found at work in processes that occur in every cell of our bodies but also in the powerful tendencies that permeate our (largely unconscious) mental operations.

This is the core of Freud's dramatic theory of the death instinct and its faithful companion, Eros. We consider now some of the problems that Freud hoped to solve with the Eros-Thanatos dyad and the context within which this formulation was offered.

Why a Death Instinct?

As Freud entered his sixth decade of life he might have felt the temptation to step back and allow his extensive output of books and articles to speak for themselves. Psychoanalysis was now an influential international movement. The "Freudian slip" was becoming a part of everyday language, and careers were being made by explaining, extolling, applying, criticizing, or parodying psychoanalysis. Instead, Freud continued his relentless drive toward a more comprehensive, more fundamental and, somehow, more elegant theory of human nature. He was not among those who were satisfied with the existing status of psychoanalytic theory.

It is also likely that his personal experiences prepared him to consider the dark side of life even more intently than before.[3] What had happened in Freud's life before his introduction of the death instinct? A long and deadly war had been waged among nations who considered themselves to be highly civilized. Freud had already given up many of the illusions common to humankind, but he held fast to the conviction that destructive impulses could be eliminated or sharply curtailed by enlightened societies. World War I fractured this assumption. From this point on, Freud would fear for the very survival of the human race. Although the phrase had not yet been introduced, the spector of megadeath started to occupy Freud's mind.

In the immediate postwar years, Freud witnessed and himself experienced further suffering. The flu epidemic was devastating; food was in short supply, and most homes, including Freud's, were unheated much of the time. A mood of sullen destructiveness could be observed among the

defeated Austrian and German people. Freud also witnessed the agoniz-
ing death of a close friend and experienced the threat or reality of death
as a continual presence within his own intimate circle. It hurt Freud, as it
has hurt so many others, to see people younger than himself suffer and
die while he stood by helplessly. He was particularly grieved by the death
of his daughter, Sophie, not long before publishing his death instinct
theory. Furthermore, Freud was already afflicted with physical problems
that would intensify over the years. That Freud would find death a
compelling topic was not at all surprising under the circumstances. That
he would come up with death instinct theory, however, requires attention
to some clinical and developmental phenomena that Freud found puzzling.

Human motivation is founded on the tendency to seek pleasure and
avoid pain. Or is it? This commonsense notion had long been familiar;
indeed, it was enshrined in the philosophical position known as hedonism
and taken for granted by the forerunners of contemporary behaviorism.
It had become evident to Freud, however, that people sometimes act in
such a way that the consequences are heightened pain and anxiety rather
than pleasure. The type of actions that concerned him could not be
dismissed simply as miscalculations—pleasure sought, pain found. Freud
perceived a quality of *compulsion* in these behaviors. People "had to do
it," even though a painful experience was almost guaranteed.

Freud excelled in discovering (or inventing) previously unrecognized
relationships among diverse phenomena. This skill now came into play
again. Some of his own patients showed a stubborn tendency to relive the
past—not simply to remember, but to "go through" painful experiences
repeatedly. This seemed to be a departure from the "pleasure principle"
that Freud had already integrated into psychoanalytic theory as part of
the "primary process" (later symbolized as "The It" or Id).

War neuroses presented an even more disturbing phenomenon. In
the safety of their own homes, some veterans experienced terrifying
dreams related to their war experiences. In fact, it may have been inaccu-
rate to classify all these episodes as dreams. They could also take the
form of waking terrors. (These phenomena have again become familiar in
our own times as some Viet Nam veterans have experienced alarming
flashbacks.) Furthermore, anxiety dreams are not unusual in the ordinary run of human experience. The psychoanalytic contention that even
anxiety dreams represent the operation of the pleasure principle no
longer seemed entirely convincing.

Still another set of unresolved clinical problems pressed on Freud:
the dynamics of sadism and masochism. Some people seemed to need
self-punishment, and some apparently could not enjoy sexual relations

without inflicting pain on others. These phenomena, again, were departures from the usual pleasure principle. Freud's far-ranging mind located still another type of repetition compulsion—the insistence shown by some children in playing and replaying the same game. All the phenomena mentioned here had in common a "daemonic" quality, in Freud's view. There was an intense inner pressure to repeat or restore a *painful* situation.

In puzzling over these phenomena, Freud was influenced by the eruption of raw aggression in the recent war and by indications that these dangerous forces had not been laid to rest by the signing of treaties. His theoretical solution to these clinical problems somehow would also need to reflect the reality of destructive forces in modern civilization, forces that must have their root in human nature itself. The possibility that aggression was a fundamental part of human nature had been rejected by Freud in the past, but now he was ready to reconsider.

The resources Freud would bring to this challenge included his extensive clinical experience, the contributions already made to psychoanalysis, and his prowess as a sleuth, able to piece together small clues until it was possible to solve the case. There was another personal resource available as well. As a young man, Freud had been an avid neurophysiologist, and he made several original contributions to the study of the central nervous system. He therefore possessed a significant background in the organic substrate of thought and behavior, and was also well aware of philosophical views that based their claims on laboratory findings. It was from this mix of problems, influences, and resources that Freud came up with his version of the death instinct.

Death Instinct as Explanation

Freud's revised theory of psychosexual development perhaps should be known instead as a theory of psychothanatosexual development (why stop with five syllables when we can have eight?). Developmental progress involves constant dialectical interaction between the two instincts. Eros is forever urging its sexual cause (in the broad as well as the specific sense of the term), and Thanatos is forever urging the reduction of tension to the inorganic zero point. Death strivings, then, are found not only in the extremis of terminal illness, advanced age, or acute suicidality. The contest between life and death instincts is played out from the very beginning and does not end until the final breath is exhaled. This position is a major departure from his earlier theory of psychosexual development in which aggression was thought to be incidental to the drive for sexual mastery.

What Freud next must explain is how we manage to develop and survive at all, beset as we are by an indwelling drive toward oblivion. Development and survival are accomplished, he tells us, primarily through *fusion* and *redirection*. The two antithetical urges collaborate with each other, if uneasily. The organism's strivings toward development and gratification require vigorous action in and against the world. Eros enlists the aggressive energies of Thanatos for this purpose. It is a double coup when successful. Not only do thanatic-driven energies make it possible for the organism to act aggressively on barriers and challenges in the world, but this assignment also keeps it too busy to turn on its host. One is not far off the mark in thinking of impulse-ridden young toughs who have been sent off to engage in combat on foreign turf instead of staying around to harass the peace-loving folk at home.

In "normal" development, then, the intrinsic urge toward self-destruction is transformed into a variety of aggressive actions directed toward the outside world—including other people. Children are apt to show these dynamics with less disguise. The innocent little boy and girl may alarm and puzzle adults by the enjoyment taken in squashing bugs or tormenting animals. The cruel streak that suddenly manifests itself in otherwise good-natured children can be seen as a strategy for casting the demons of the juvenile death instinct into the sea of life. Killing is fun! And the fun comes, at least in part, from indulging the aims and energies of the death instinct without falling victim one's self.

Because all adults have passed through the vicissitudes of the juvenile death instinct in one way or another, it is perhaps not surprising that the world is crowded with adults who try to manage their own self-destructive urges by developing them on each other. Had Freud attended a professional boxing match, hockey game, or football contest, he could only have nodded gravely as players and officials felt the assault of Thanatos from thousands of hoarse voices. A Little League game attended by highly involved parents could also have had much the same effect on him.

The stadium, however, is not actually a psychiatric ward, and most fans are responsible citizens. The "collective death instinct," if this phrase might be introduced, is usually given only limited opportunities for expression. The "normal" person who is also a rabid fan tempers his or her destructive impulses with the wisdom and charity of Eros. Only a part of the self wishes to crush and eliminate the foe. Eros eventually reassumes command to add a glow to victory, a consolation to defeat, and, above all, *to keep the game going.* The athletes themselves, given half a chance, often feel impelled to honor and embrace their opponents at the end of the contest. Although Freud did not analyze in any detail the phenomena of competitive sports, in this arena the collaboration between Eros and Thanatos is available for all to observe.

Perhaps the most crucial point regarding the role of the death instinct in early development is that aggressive impulses are real and fundamental. They are not just secondary derivatives. True, the infant and child might show increased aggression on being frustrated. This, in fact, is one of the clues to the repetition compulsion in children. Denied the gratifications sought, the child may stubbornly re-create the disappointing situation in the hope of "making it right" or restoring the lost object. Nevertheless, in Freud's revised theory he does not see aggression as only and always a response to frustration or deprivation. Aggression is there from the beginning and represents the claims of Thanatos. From the beginning this aggressive drive threatens the development and survival of the self.

Anna Freud, much more experienced than her father in direct work with children, accepted this view: "In very early phases aggressive energy may find outlets on the child's own body, just as sexual energy (libido) may find outlets in auto-erotic activities. . . . It is essential for the child's normality that the aggressive urges should be directed away from the child's own body to the animate or inanimate objects in the environment" (Freud, 1949, p. 40).

In summary, the infant and young child must quickly find a way of balancing the powerful and contradictory claims of Eros and Thanatos. The basic strategy is to turn the aggressive impulses outward—including vigorous use of muscles and energies. This will be a challenge during the entire life-span as well. Eros must somehow manage to give Thanatos its opportunities, yet prevent catastrophe.

Problems that occur during the individual's early development are likely to have prolonged and accumulative consequences. This is a general rule in psychoanalytic theory. When applied to the vicissitudes of aggressivity and the death instinct, this rule helps to explain otherwise puzzling phenomena (assuming for the moment that Freud's revised theory is essentially correct). A child is angry at a parent. A child is *very* angry at a parent! It might be disastrous to express this anger directly, so the child turns the fierce, murderous anger in on himself or herself. This maneuver has something of a suicidal thrust to it, although without the fatal outcome.

Years later this child, once furious with a parent (almost always the mother, in early psychoanalytic literature) will have strong masochistic urges. Both the mother's aggression and the child's own sadistic impulses have become a permanent thorn in the psyche. Yearnings for intimacy, warmth, and gratification have also gone unfulfilled, further contributing to the buildup of anger. One must be punished, just to survive, just to control the unacceptable rage. (This is a simplification of the actual course of events that would have occurred between child and parent during a critical period.) Furthermore, other patterns of early aggressive and erotic interactions with parents will result in other patterns of adult neurosis. The key point is that whatever interferes with the young child's ability to turn the death instinct outward is also likely to generate enduring problems—especially those expressed by the compulsion to repeat painful and frustrating experiences.

Once this new psychodynamic key has been turned, perhaps other doors could also be unlocked. The problem of suicide had become of more than clinical interest to Freud. Several of his associates in the psychoanalytic movement killed themselves. This compelled increasing attention to suicide on the part of Freud and other psychoanalysts. Perhaps the death instinct could be recruited as an explanation for suicidal actions. Eros had failed in its constant struggle to keep potentially self-destructive forces occupied with other tasks. For some reason—usually associated with problems in early development—the death instinct has slipped its chains. This view also suggested a different way of looking at murder: We take another person's life as a proxy for our own. *"I kill the me in you,"* it might be phrased.

Invoking the death instinct as a partial explanation for suicide also expanded the usual focus. Those in harmony with Freud's concept started to consider the possibility that the death instinct operates through many self-destructive modalities, not only those that are traditionally classified as suicide. This approach was taken up by eminent clinicians such as Menninger (1938) and Farberow (1980). With a sharp eye on self-destructive *tendencies*, one might discern potentially lethal maneuvers of the death instinct even in the absence of obvious suicidality. Both direct suicide and more circuitous paths to self-destruction could be triggered by lapses in ego integrity (e.g., a psychotic episode, a drinking binge, an indulgence in illicit drugs). Given the opportunity, the death instinct ever active in all of us may seize its moment.

The concepts of *conflict* and *ambivalence*, already important in psychoanalytic theory and practice, became even more critical with the introduction of the death instinct. Life *is* conflict. The ego is faced every day (and night) with the challenge of mediating between the demands of Eros and Thanatos as well as between those of external reality and inner drives. Death instinct theory offers a revised perspective: In a fundamental sense, conflicts are never fully resolved; therefore, this is not a feasible aim of therapy or other interventions. The "winner" at last must be death. Therefore, it is the part of wisdom to delay this secular version of the last judgment until one has completed a long and active life. One is reminded of the cynical Stage Manager in Thornton Wilder's classic drama, *Our Town.* He has observed many of the town's inhabitants enact their life stories from the bloom of youth to the cemetery on the hill. The details differ, the ending is the same, and only rarely is the whole story "interesting." Freudian death instinct theory strongly implies that we (ego and Eros) should give Thanatos a long and eventful contest before joining the others on the hill. It is folly—or suicide—to seek a full "resolution" of the Eros-Thanatos conflict in the midst of life and certainly not a realistic goal of therapy.

Other implications of the death instinct for psychotherapy were explored by Freud and subsequent analysts. Freud himself thought that the resistance often shown by clients as psychoanalysis neared completion could be attributed to the death instinct. In "Analysis Terminable and Interminable" (1935), Freud notes that in the later stages of treatment the ego "ceases to support us in our efforts to reveal the id, it opposes those efforts, disobeys the fundamental rule of analysis and suffers no further derivatives of repressed material to emerge into consciousness" (p. 342). The specific types of resistance encountered by Freud struck him for many years as "bewilderingly strange." He came eventually to find the explanation within the "concurrent or opposing action of the two primal instincts."

Unfortunately, here Freud's explication of this relationship lacks the detail and clarity that often characterized his other writings. One seeks in vain for a "missing" section that would present the proported relationship between instinctive drive and resistance in adequate detail. Angel Garma (1971) offers an interesting later attempt to explicate the role of the death instinct in resistance to termination of treatment, but this pathway of inquiry has remained rather obscure.

Other psychodynamic clinicians and researchers have applied death instinct theory to so-called psychosomatic disorders. (This term has been criticized for its implicit mind-body philosophy but retains at least a descriptive utility.) Melitta Sperling (1969) for example, reports that depressed clients with severe migraine headaches actually underwent an "instant somatic discharge of destructive energies." The migraine attacks are said to occur "when there is an acute increase in death instinct and when the inhibitory and defensive functions of the depression no longer suffice in protecting the patient from acute self-destruction" (p. 84). Total organismic distress in infants and children who have been rejected by their parents, ulcerative colitis in adults, and several other life-threatening physical problems have been seen by various psychoanalysts as manifestations of the death instinct slipping its chains.

Smith Ely Jelliffe (1933), a pioneer in this field, suggested that the death instinct, taking the form of sadism against the self, has "operated like a castration or partial death of an organ or of certain functions of an organ and thus brought about the disharmony of function" (p. 124). His case examples include an exceptionally broad range of conditions, such as myopia, hyperthyroidism, kidney dysfunction, and skin disorders. For those inclined to accept Freud's dual instinct theory, it would not be surprising to discover how many forms can be taken by the implacable drive toward cessation.[4]

ASSAULT ON THANATOS

Despite the care he took on many occasions to disarm criticism of death-instinct theory, Freud lived long enough to see this idea attacked fiercely both from within the ranks of psychoanalysis and from the outside. The assault has continued through the years, although recent critics tend to begin with the conclusion that the Eros-Thanatos formulation has been thoroughly discredited, once and for all. One cannot help but imagine that the discarnate spirit of Sigmund Freud (perhaps puffing on a discarnate cigar) would characterize this negative reaction as "resistance" that itself is a deriviative of the sadistic death instinct. Nevertheless, many trenchant objections have been raised to the dual instinct theory, especially to the reality basis and functions claimed for Thanatos.

In sifting through the critical literature one quickly observes that the objections occur on two different levels. These might be termed the philosophical-attitudinal and the clinical-empirical. "I don't agree with the world-view represented by this theory, and I dislike the theory itself— it's so unpleasant" would be an approximate way of summarizing the first level of objections. The second level primarily argues that, "Death instinct theory is false, useless, and misleading as either psychological theory or therapeutic guide."

Philosophical and Attitudinal Criticisms of the Death Instinct

In one of the most searching and influential examinations of psychoanalytic theory and its implications, Norman O. Brown (1959) charged that Freud has bequeathed "complete therapeutic pessimism."

The dual instinct theory is "worse than useless for therapists." This sorry state of affairs follows directly from Freud's insistence that biological forces are responsible for the conflicts we experience at the psychic level. Not in a single 50-minute hour nor in years of intensive psychotherapy can one expect to alter the biological imperatives. If Freud is right, then, psychotherapy is a doomed cause. Furthermore, gloom clouds the more general tidings that psychoanalysis offers to humanity: We are but slaves to our biological makeup. In modern as in ancient times, we struggle with competing instinctual drives. "Progress" is a rather empty concept in this view, for the most sophisticated person alive today must still contend with the brute inner forces that drove our remotest ancestors.

Brown argues that Freud has, in effect, left us with a kind of sick religion. "All organic life is then sick; we humans must abandon hope of cure, but we can take comfort in the conclusion that our sickness is part of some universal sickness in nature. . . . it is true religion" (Brown, 1959, p. 82). All of us are torn with conflict—neurotic, in other words—yet these personal tribulations are also manifestations of a "sick" (conflicted) universe. To put it the other way around: How can any of us expect to be mature and serene when the spirit of the universe is itself conflicted at every level? The motion picture version of Brown's thesis would almost certainly be entrusted to Woody Allen!

Is the dual-instinct theory really so relentlessly pessimistic? Brown recognizes that Freud proposed a more positive option. The ego might call on the instinctual strength of Eros to unify opposites, to reconcile and harmonize the opposing tendencies that contribute to conflict. Just as Thanatos seeks limitation and cessation, so Eros seeks expansion and gratifying activity. Perhaps, then, it is only when we forget about Eros that Thanatos appears as such an inexorable opponent.

This more optimistic facet of Freud's thinking is not persuasive to Brown. Life and death cannot really be unified. Freud has indulged in a redemption fantasy of the genre that had already been familiar in German philosophy and literature since the turn of the eighteenth century. The dual instinct theory perhaps should be read as a late contribution to the romantic movement in literature rather than as a modern psychological thesis. Brown also implies that Freud's is a failed romanticism. There is no possibility of a triumphant ending to the story of our instinctual conflict-ridden lives. Given a choice, then, we would be wise to reject Freud's dual-instinct theory and its burden of pessimism.

Other individuals, although lacking Brown's thorough knowledge of psychoanalytic theory, also reject the death instinct's apparent pessimism. "This is an awfully depressing theory!" is a common first response to its introduction in a university classroom setting. Brown is certainly not the only person who finds Freud's death instinct a most disgreeable companion.

The pessimistic implications of Thanatos are particularly disagreeable because we seem powerless to improve the situation through our own efforts. This intractable characteristic of the death instinct can be seen as one component of Freud's overall conception of human nature and its place in the universe. The death instinct operates in a *deterministic* manner. It could hardly do otherwise, for the universe itself is subject to laws that operate in a deterministic mode. Furthermore, scientific study has *reductionism* as its goal. One explains by reducing the complex to the simple. Determinism and reductionism were powerful guiding tenets of 19th-century science.

Several critics have pointed out that Freud accepted these tenets in his own theory building. Like many other scientists of his day, Freud aimed to reduce the complex to the simple and to explicate a chain of causal relationships. Applying this philosophy of method to the human condition, Freud subjected both waking and sleeping experience to the grind-box of reductionistic determinism. He felt like a real scientist when he could demonstrate cause-and-effect relationships, especially between events and experiences that were usually thought to be unconnected. Death-instinct theory, then, was no exception to his usual approach. It was, in fact, an especially impressive triumph of psychoanalysis as science. Suicidal and murderous thoughts and actions could be reduced, in essence, to instinctual drive. Exercises in reductionistic determinism might make us feel depressed and pessimistic—but perhaps we should instead rejoice along with Freud for this outstanding achievement in meeting the criteria for successful scientific theory construction.

Another of Freud's related achievements—indeed, one of his greatest—could also furnish grounds for criticism. He transferred to psychology the mode of thought he had applied as a young investigator in the neurophysiological laboratory. One might learn a great deal about the nervous system by tracing structures from their earliest form. The *developmental approach* was relatively new and fresh at this time. Even fresher was Freud's application of this general method to the human mind. His first traversal led to a theory of psychosexual development that had a major impact on society as well as psychology. Freud's revised formulation also took the developmental approach. Perhaps the most audacious contention in the dual-instinct theory was his suggestion that every living creature seeks a return to inorganic status—the (hypothetical) starting point for all development. The vicissitudes of Eros and Thanatos in the development history of individuals are also given prominence.

What can be faulted here? Isn't the developmental approach highly relevant to the understanding of human experience and behavior? And isn't it true that a great many other theoreticians and researchers have applied developmental approaches since Freud? It may not seem quite fair to criticize Freud for a bold and radical application of the developmental approach while at the same time giving respectful attention to the more circumspect theories that formed in his wake. I must, nevertheless, add a criticism here. Freud's idea of development emphasizes the power of the past to the near exclusion of other possibilities. Present thought and behavior is driven by instinctual forces and conflicts. The ego labors to keep these inner pressures and conflicts from overwhelming the total organism, simultaneously attempting to cope with the demands of external reality. Poor, beleaguered ego!

There is an alternative position available, however. Gordon Allport, Abraham Maslow, and several other personality theorists have conceived of a more active and creative self that is influenced by but not held captive to the past. The "self-actualization" movement inspired to some extent by Maslow's writings is one of the most obvious examples of this approach. Within the ranks of psychoanalysts there have also been numerous departures from the reductionistic, deterministic developmental approach associated with Freud. Common to these "maverick" views are the following themes: (a) The developing self does organize itself around its basic psychophysiological needs and functions (b) as these interact constantly with the environment (especially the human environment, but (c) the self or ego also has its own resources and agenda that (d) become progressively autonomous as maturation continues, (e) unless held in neurotic bondage to the past. The past-driven determinism that occupies the center of Freud's attention on many occasions can be seen as the outcome of developmental *failure*. The man or woman who has experienced wise, loving, and nontraumatic upbringing is *not* hostage to the past, but instead strives toward a future of his or her own creation.

On this view, one might go so far as to accept the reality of Eros and Thanatos as primitive instinctual forces, but forces that have come under the control of a developed, educated, and competent self-system. Stressful circumstances might stir up the primitive instinctual forces, just as storms might threaten even a well-governed city. Under more benign circumstances, however, Eros and Thanatos lend and blend themselves to the enjoyment of the present and the cultivation of the future. Past-driven determinism rules only for the person under great stress, or the neurotic, or the individual who has suffered exceptional deprivation and trauma in early development. To be sure, enough people exist in these categories to grace every psychoanalytic couch in the world (assuming the financial resources to pay for this privilege). Theoretically, however, *normal* development is characterized by a progressive liberation from instinctual and past-driven determinism. This, at the very least, is a significant alternative formulation of development that would change in many respect the way in which we would think of the death instinct and other (hypothetical) drives.

Freud's death instinct theory is also vulnerable to criticism for its *dualistic* conception of human nature. It is not only Life versus Death. It is also Mind (ego) versus Body (id). It is Man versus Nature. Dualism has a philosophical tradition whose antiquity can be traced beyond Plato and beyond the pre-Socratic thinkers. Those who attempt to construct the mental life of our most remote human ancestors most often conclude that a primitive form of mind/soul-body dualism reigned. Freud was well versed in philosophical traditions, and read extensively in classic and contemporary literature that also emphasized the clash of opposites. He could be seen, then, as "repackaging" dualism.

Again, it is appropriate to ask why Freud should be criticized for espousing one particular philosophical tradition. All philosophical positions are vulnerable to attack—in fact, the most characteristic activity of a philosopher is to either attack another's theory, or defend his or her own! Again, I suggest that there is some merit to the criticism. First, trouble is often invited when we fail to distinguish between philosophical assumption and psychological reality. Freud does seem to *assume* a fundamental dualism within human nature and between ourselves and nature. It is possible that much of psychoanalytic theory would remain of interest even if this dualism were discarded. However, Freud's dualism is, in fact, the overall philosophical context within which the particulars of his theory are to be found. Second, his dualism—so dramatically expressed through the Eros-Thanatos formulation—encourages an adversary attitude toward nature.

A. J. Levin presents this criticism rather vividly.

> The elements, according to Freud, mock at all human control; the earth quakes, burying man and his works; floods submerge all things; storms drive all before them; diseases attack living creatures; and finally there is the "painful riddle of death, for which no remedy at all has yet been found, nor probably ever will." (Levin, 1951, p. 262)

Levin cites many examples from Freud's writings in which nature is perceived as adversary and threat to human life. This attitude, according to Levin, is fundamental to Freud's entire theory and his approach to psychotherapy, "the need to protect oneself *against* stimuli, rather than live with nature." Furthermore, the dualism exists in our relationship with society as well. We must defend ourselves against our own kind, even (or especially) in the social order that presumably exists for mutual support and protection.

You against me! Me against me! All of us against nature! This attitudinal component of Freud's dualism certainly deserves critical attention. It is not the only available attitude toward self and nature. The Navajo, for example, have a long-standing tradition of living in harmony with nature, and do not make the sharp distinctions between human nature and the rest of the universe that are embodied in Freud's dualism. In practical terms, many of us may be so immersed in the competititve, aggressive, and individualistic traditions of Western society that we resonate more to Freudian dualism than to the Navajo sense of harmony. Nevertheless, Freud could be accused of perpetuating and intensifying a vision of universal conflict with our tender little egos caught in the crossfire. To express this criticism in a less than tender form, one might say: Dr. Freud, with your Eros and Thanatos you have tried to solve problems that would not have existed—without your Eros and Thanatos!

The criticisms already expressed here portray Freud as a relentless materialist whose death-instinct theory burdens us with a most unattractive load of pessimism, reductionism, past-driven determinism, and dualism, all unduly influenced by the dynamics of failed (neurotic) development. He towers as one of the last giants in an already dying tradition. Freud's Europe was fast disappearing; science was already undergoing major changes in conceptual and methodological approaches. Among other changes in the air was a drawing away from Big Theory in the grand philosophical tradition. Death instinct theory, then, might have had its greatest impact and best opportunity for acceptance had it been offered to the old world Freud knew when young.

Yet the philosophical and attitudinal criticisms do not end even at this point. At least two more lines of attack have been waiting their turn. Freud himself is the target of one of these assaults, and Ernest Becker (1973) is perhaps his severest critic. Becker examines Freud's life as well as his work to demonstrate that the founder of psychoanalysis carried a "dread of dying" through him from youth to old age. His introduction of the death instinct should not be interpreted as a belated recognition and coming-to-terms with mortality. According to Becker, Thanatos represents a not-very-clever effort to *conceal* death anxiety. To support this interpretation Becker musters several details about Freud's life and habits—invariably patterns and quirks of a negative kind. This selective portrayal helps to build a portrait of Freud as an overcontrolling and driven individual. Death anxiety is proposed as a major explanation for these patterns of personal thought and behavior.

Even those aspects of Freud's personality that some have found admirable are presented as neurotic (the astounding productivity as a writer while also conducting a busy clinical practice, leading the development of psychoanalysis, etc.), or as unremarkable (the courage in living for many years with physical agony). Becker believes "that we can justifiably fish around for some hints about Freud's special orientation to reality and about a "problem" unique to him. "If we get hints of such a problem, I think we can use it to throw light on the overall structure of his work and its possible limits" (Becker, 1973, p. 102). Essentially, Thanatos is Freud's way of avoiding confrontation with the "terror of death." The death instinct is so biological, even cosmic. How much easier it is to contemplate an abstraction such as the death instinct rather than to face one's own dread of mortality! From Freud's life and character, then, Becker (and others) develop the criticism that the death instinct was really intended to control one man's personal anxieties rather than provide a universal law of human thought and experience.

The last criticism to be considered in this section differs markedly from the others and is one of the most interesting. Freud had suggested that the death instinct is a kind of remembrance of the peaceful inorganic status that existed before the emergence of life. We have a fundamental yearning to return to this tension-free state that contrasts so completely with the pressures, strivings, and tumult of impulse-ridden life. It is again Levin who observes that Freud's theory is inconsistent with the knowledge that has been gained about physical matter. There can be no return to what Freud once called the "peace of the inorganic world," not since Einstein "revealed to mankind the tremendous forces locked in 'inert' atoms." The death instinct is, therefore, a fiction.

In the decades since Levin's article there has been a continuing series of revelations about the forces at work in the universe on both the microlevels and macrolevels. Nowhere has been discovered a haven for inorganic matter whose ambition consists of drowsing through eternity. (Black holes are a possible but improbable exception.) Freud's attribution of "peacefulness" to inorganic existence was open to question from the start. Now it appears to be decisively contradicted by modern physics.

Clinical and Empirical Criticisms of Death Instinct

The second set of criticisms is also varied, but has in common the contention that Freud's death instinct theory is either useless or misleading when applied to specific problems.

Freud's introduction of the dual-instinct theory into his account of psychosexual development did not convince many of his followers. The weakness of Thanatos can be seen when compared with Freud's much more familiar account of psychosexual development. Freud could and did refer to such universal features as the mouth, anus, and genitalia. Nobody doubted the reality of these organs. This grounding in consensual reality made it easier for Freud to propose the sequence from oral to genital sexuality. His readers could make their own observations to confirm or contradict Freud's, and could also be somewhat selective regarding the propositions they accepted. As a matter of fact, many clinicians, researchers, educators, and parents have responded differentially to the various component propositions within Freud's original theory of psychosexual development. It is common, for example, to reject much of his account of female development, while finding some of his other ideas palatable.

The first and still most influential theory of psychosexual development also included a major construct that helped to track the vicissitudes. *Libido*—sexual energy—is an idea that has some appeal to the imagination while also suggesting an actual substance or process. Again, Freud could build on the familiar: Sexuality is a quality of life that needs little introduction. It does not ask much of us to consider the possibility that the genitalia, organs obviously specialized for sexual activity, are also a center for sexual feeling and energy. The rest of libido theory does make greater demands on us, but at least it begins with basic consensual reality.

The death instinct was turned loose by Freud without such advantages. Where is the bodily organ for death, equivalent to the genitalia for sex? What process or substance is akin to libido? Freud did consider introducing a "something" that would be Thanato's parallel to libido. He dropped this idea when he could not discover a viable candidate.[5] In discussing the developmental permutations, then, Freud could not offer a vivid and detailed account of the death instinct's adventures. The new concept was remote and abstract. One could see what Freud meant by libido and psychosexual development—not so with Thanatos. This difficulty in describing the death instinct probably contributed much to the initial cool reception it received. Because this difficulty in making the death instinct seem palpable and observable was not subsequently overcome, the first reaction took on a more permanent form.

The problem of suicide might have been expected to be one of the primary beneficiaries of death instinct theory. We kill ourselves when the death instinct becomes all too powerful or our ego resources all too weak. This would be the simplest and most direct implication. The new theory did not seem to make much of a practical contribution to understanding, predicting, or preventing suicide, however. This failure had much to do with the limitation already noted: the somewhat remote and abstract nature of the death instinct concept. How is one to measure or assess the intensity of a given individual's death instinct? Freud, the neurophysiologist and physician, offered no laboratory tests or clinical examinations for this purpose. The researcher's difficulty was no less severe. How is one to operationalize this concept? What criteria could be used? What objective determination can be made of initial value or change?

Death-instinct theory seemed to be useless for either clinical practice or empirical research on the problem of suicide. One has to work as hard with or without death instinct theory to understand, predict, or prevent a suicidal action. Choron (1972) is among those who conclude that Freud did not satisfactorily explain why the death instinct at times is able to overcome our fundamental impulse toward self-preservation. Without a persuasive explanation for the occasional breakthroughs of the death instinct, the concept adds little if anything to the quest for understanding, prediction, and prevention. For example, there is some association between mental illness and acts of self-destruction. One does not need death-instinct theory to support this connection, however, as the statistics speak for themselves. It might be asserted that individuals with a history of mental or emotional disorder are at a higher risk for suicide because their ego strength is less adequate for managing inner tensions. This plausible contention would also fail to demonstrate the value of death-instinct theory. Not all individuals with psychiatric problems complete or even attempt suicide. The clinician and researcher would seem better advised to examine ego strength—a difficult but not impossible concept to operationalize—than to ponder about the intensity of the invisible Thanatos. In practice, specialists in suicide prevention and research take a great many factors into account, environmental, psychological, and biological. Adding the death instinct to an already long list of identified factors does not appear especially helpful.

Major recent books on suicide make only limited reference to death-instinct theory. In his cogent description of *The Suicide Syndrome*, for example, Larry Morton Gernsbacher dispenses with Thanatos after a mere three paragraphs in his introductory chapter. This very brief treatment nevertheless adds still another criticism.

> The endorsement of the death instinct theory would automatically interpret suicide as resulting from an instinctual drive which must be mediated, displaced, or sublimated for survival. But the absence of suicide in all other

living creatures would imply that only human beings—the least instinctually
motivated of creatures—would possess the death instinct. Or it would imply
the equally untenable view that other animals have intellectually learned
better to resist it. (Gernsbacher, 1985, p. 18)

Edwin S. Shneidman, a pioneer of modern suicidology, does not
mention death-instinct theory at all in his most recent book. This is a
particularly significant omission, because Shneidman is quite familiar
with Freudian theory and *Definition of Suicide* (1985) could well be his
own crowning achievement. Freud is mentioned chiefly for the suggestion
that suicide is essentially murder turned inwardly. (This hypothesis,
although consistent with death-instinct theory, does not necessarily depend on it.) One of the many interesting facet's of Shneidman's approach
is the way in which he has used several concepts that have some kinship
to death-instinct theory without making the more philosophical assumptions associated with Freud. *Lethality* is perhaps the most relevant concept here. The term itself has a family resemblance to Thanatos but is
more closely related to practical applications. A lethality rating can be
made on the basis of behavioral observations, interviews, and other
readily available methods. One even comes up with a scaled score for
lethality in the particular situation under investigation—a clear difference from the speculative approach usually associated with death instinct
theory. For Shneidman (1985), "*any* act, deed, or event in the world can
be rated on a lethality dimension" (p. 205). This view nearly rivals Freud's
for universality, but is much more closely tied to observable and verifi-
able phenomena.

All this attention has been given to suicide because it is a significant
human problem, of great concern to Freud and his circle, and one of the
most logical spheres for application of death-instinct theory. The apparent failure—or very limited success—of this theory in explaining, predicting, and preventing suicide could be viewed as a major setback. Furthermore, the conceptual and methodological problems already mentioned
tend to vitiate applications of death-instinct theory in other problem
areas as well.

It has often been concluded by clinicians that death-instinct theory
introduces an unnecessary and unsatisfactory complication. Symons
(1927), for example, judged that Freud's earlier formulations were more
useful in understanding the dynamics of sadomasochism and the repetition compulsion. One did not have to invent a new force that opposed the
pleasure principle. Years later, Galdston (1955) was even more critical of
"Freud's dismal excursion into the realm of death." Galdston contests

Freud's discussion of life-and-death behaviors in the animal kingdom, as well as his view of the metabolic processes involved in the development and survival of organisms. Most critically, the death instinct cannot serve as an explanation of masochistic behavior because "it cannot be validated in experience." What Galdston rejects is Freud's dualistic view of Eros and Thanatos at war with each other throughout life. He leaves room for a revised theory in which the death instinct can be seen as the *fulfillment* of Eros. The normal, healthy adult somehow manages to embrace the painful and threatening side of life, along with the pleasures and gratifications.

Empirical research to test or extend this theory seems to be virtually nonexistent. Clinicians often dismiss the theory as useless or misleading. There is not much point to adding further examples. It is important, however, to acknowledge one of the most powerful and broadly-based challenges that have arisen. This challenge was clearly prefigured in Galdston's insightful but nearly forgotten article. His insider's critique centered around his own belief that "Those who fear to die lack the courage to live." This, in effect, became the rallying cry for the existential challenge. The main thesis of Becker's influential book is captured by its title, *The Denial of Death* (1973). As already noted in connection with his attack on Freud's life and character, Becker sees death-instinct theory as itself a denial of death. Freud was attempting to control his own anxieties by proposing this theory. Becker argues that there is an even more compelling reason to reject the death instinct. The terror of death is central to the human condition. Our "deepest need is to be free of the anxiety of death and annihilation" (p. 66). No abstract speculations about inorganic peacefulness and warring instincts can help us to face our personal anxieties. The courage to live must begin with our recognition that we do, indeed, fear to die.

EVALUATION OF DEATH-INSTINCT THEORY TODAY

It is time now to see what can be learned both from Freud's effort and the critical response. The logical first step is an evaluation of the criticisms described in the previous section. This will be followed by an attempt to envision the kind of approach that might be responsive to the most significant criticisms and yet draw on Freud's insights. In pursuing this task, some attention will be given to material that has remained outside the death-instinct controversy per se.

Critical Review of Response to Death-Instinct Theory

Many other Freudian concepts have received searching criticism and yet survived, if in modified form. Death-instinct theory, however, attracted but a small following after running into a critical barrage that was both immediate and sustained. The battle is over. Twentieth-century psychology has moved on without taking any particular notice of the final theoretical formulation offered by the person with whom it is most identified. With this important caveat in mind, we can look at the actual merits of the major criticisms.

The philosophical-attitudinal response portrayed death-instinct theory as pessimistic, deterministic, reductionistic, past oriented, and dualistic. Were world views available for purchase at the local convenience market, most of us would probably pass up the Freudian product and keep looking. Death-instinct theory has certainly been made to seem unappetizing. Would it really be wise, however, to spurn the theory on these grounds?

Pessimism was one of Freud's traits. It is not difficult to find examples in his life and work. The question that needs to be answered here, however, is whether or not death-instinct theory is so pessimistic that we are left without any constructive courses of action. Notice first the difference between a nihilistic attitude and a recognition of limits. Freud did not try to discourage us from bringing the death instinct under more effective control. This, in fact, became of the highest priority to him. There was a strategic plan involved in his certification of Thanatos as a fundamental instinctual drive. Yes, one could feel pessimistic about human nature if an aggressive, destructive component has such deep roots within us. Recognition of this challenge is a positive step, however, Freud wanted us to realize how much was at stake and what forces we would have to overcome, tame, or sublimate to assure the survival of civilization.

Freud's exchange of letters with Einstein clearly express both the urgency and prominence he gave to the problem, and his guarded optimism for a successful resolution. The correspondence was initiated in 1931 when the League of Nations invited Einstein to contact another intellectual leader of his own choosing for an examination of some topic of great mutual concern. Einstein had already met Freud and read some of his major works. The question he asked Freud: "Why war?"

Interestingly, the distinguished physicist had already arrived independently at an answer that might have come directly from Freud. "How is it possible that the mass of the people permits itself to become aroused to the point of insanity and eventual self-sacrifice . . . ?" asks Einstein, who immediately adds, "The answer can only be: man has in him the need to hate and to destroy." There was urgency, but not pessimism, certainly not nihilism in Einstein's approach to Freud. He thought it might be possible "to so guide the psychological development of man that it becomes resistant to the psychoses of hate and destruction" (Einstein & Freud, 1932, pp. 1–2).

Freud's (1932) response deserves close reading by all who are concerned with the danger of megadeath as well as those specifically interested in the death instinct concept. The most relevant points for us here are the following:

1. The community (society) can acquire sufficient strength to place the rule of law over the more primitive impulse to exercise raw power and force.

2. For the "justice of the community" to succeed, however, requires a key psychological achievement: the recognition of common feelings, a strong sense of bonding with others. The effectiveness of society in controlling aggressive and self-destructive impulses, then, is dependent on the mature psychological development of its citizens.

3. Eros and Thanatos are both real in a sense, but "You recognize that this is basically only the theoretical transfiguration of the universally known contrast of love and hate, which perhaps has an essential relationship to the polarity of attraction and repulsion that plays a part in your field. . . . Each of these drives is just as indispensable as the other; the phenomena of life evolve from their acting together and against each other."

4. War—the expression of the death instinct on a broad scale—can be prevented by "anything that creates emotional ties between human beings." This, in turn, occurs when we are able to identify emotionally with others. Eros is the perfect counterbalance to Thanatos.

Freud and Einstein both express keen awareness of the forces that lead to tension and conflict in society. Furthermore, both conclude that the potential for self-destruction is real and cannot be uprooted from human nature, at least in any foreseeable future. This is a long way from nihilism or the depths of pessimism, however. The deadly, disagreeable dual-instinct theory of Old Man Freud takes on a rather different look when he adds, quite simply, that "Psychoanalysis need not be ashamed when it speaks of love, because religion says the same: 'Love thy neighbor as thyself.'" Furthermore, there is a wide avenue available for those willing to take constructive action because "Everything that leads to important shared action creates such common feelings, such identifications" (Einstein & Freud, 1932, p. 8).

The critics, then, seem to have overlooked the fact that Freud considered Eros to be fully competitive with Thanatos. It is not "sick" to experience conflict. The normal business of life requires the interaction of processes that are opposite in their individual aims, but that together contribute to effective development and functioning. Instead of dismissing Thanatos as leading to "complete therapeutic pessimism," Brown might have just as well accused Eros as leading to "complete therapeutic optimism." Love is as real as hate, anabolism as real as catabolism.

There is a sense in which it might be said that the death instinct eventually triumphs—through death itself. This outcome, however, is not proof of Freud's nihilism nor is it any reason for a mature person to creep through life under depression's dark cloud. We did not need Freud to tell us that life ends in death: Whatever fear or sorrow might accompany our knowledge of mortality was entrenched in our minds well before a Viennese psychiatrist published his latest book in 1920.

There is also a more specific reason to disentangle "bad feelings about death" from Freud's dual instinct theory. We are capable of living full and productive lives, loving and being loved. This potential is best realized by developing a firm sense of self-worth and social responsibility. Thanatos will then play an important but subsidiary role in our lives. Aggression will be channeled in positive directions, free of hostility toward self or others. A society comprised of such people will raise its children in a coherent and loving manner, and will not be susceptible to the primitive temptations of suicide, murder, or—worse of all—war. The person who has lived long and well can face death without terror. The end does not come violently, nor does it destroy the value of what was already achieved in life, still less does this death inflict harm on others, other than normal grief. The actual cessation of life, then, represents as much a victory for Eros as for Thanatos. It was quite a party—now it is time to go!

Admittedly, Freud did not string these thoughts together in quite the way presented here, but this scenario is entirely consistent with his dual instinct theory, and much of his other writings including his letters. The man himself often *was* pessimistic. This attitude certainly had something to do with his own personality development but also had much to do with the troubled times through which he lived. Could he have been a thinking man, and not have found reason for pessimism and doubt? Nevertheless, his overall emphasis remained on the hope that human nature could progressively gain rational and socially responsible control over the destructive side of its impulses. The correspondence with Einstein is one important example, occurring late in Freud's life, that makes it clear he still felt humanity had a chance—death instinct and all! Is it realistic to ask for more?

So much for the pessimism. What about the determinism? Freud did try to see human nature as but one part of the universe and, therefore, subject to scientific investigation that would eventually yield laws and principles. For all scientists, determinism involved an act of faith. Research in Freud's time had not thoroughly demonstrated that the world actually could be understood perfectly in a deterministic framework. One might embrace determinism because it seemed like a rousing banner to carry along the arduous pathway to knowledge. Or one might attack determinism as a reprehensible denial of the vital principle of life and a threat to law and order, religion, morality, and whatever.

In the end, our attitude toward determinism does not count for as much as do the actual results of scientific labors. Either we are able to predict and explain phenomena on the basis of deterministic conceptions, or we are not. When young Freud started his laboratory investigations of the central nervous system, neither he nor any one else knew how far the deterministic credo would take him. When middle aged Freud became simultaneously the first psychoanalyst and the first patient, he again could not have specified the outcome. When old Freud formulated and defended his death-instinct theory, the deterministic credo was once more simply a guide and inspiration. The first of these projects met with modest success; the second (expressed chiefly through *The Interpretation of Dreams*, was a breakthrough; the final effort has been treated generally as a failure.

These differential outcomes were in projects carried out by the same person who maintained essentially the same philosophy of science throughout. Determinism is not a serious "ism" to worry about. The results have never fully justified the deterministic credo in any field of scientific inquiry. Certainly, the psychological and social sciences (not to exclude economics) have remained intractable to all-out determinism, whether of the Freudian or the behavioral type. Furthermore, the whole deterministic enterprise does seem naïve and outdated in light of the theory of relativity and its sequelae. Modern theory building in the sciences tends to be quite different. Field forces and probability have supplanted the mechanical cause-and-effect approach that was still foremost in the 19th century.

Were Freud with us today, he would probably have made these new wrinkles his own. The dual-instinct theory could be modified to be more consistent with current assumptions and theory-building approaches in physics and biology. (Freud had a stubborn streak, especially when under attack: He also prided himself, however, on the scientist's willingness to revise theories and assumptions on the basis of new information.) The critics are right, I think, in faulting Freud for his reliance on determinism. But neither his general theory nor the death instinct in particular are completely dependent on a thorough-going determinism.

In some of Freud's most important passages he seems to have violated (or conveniently forgotten) his own roots in determinism. Once the knowing and flexible ego gains control of the instinctual drives, it (we) are no longer caught up like helpless puppets or slaving machines. If determinism was part of Freud's credo, so was the belief that successful human development gives us some significant measure of choice and control over our own destiny. The person who is still caught in the toils of a past-driven determinism is not the psychologically healthy person who is presently engaged in reading *The Psychology of Death*. No, one who is enslaved by the conflicted passions of the past bears the name "neurotic." The individual whose life reveals a pattern of relentless determinism is an individual who has failed to become fully human.

The reductionistic and past-driven aspects of Freudian theory can be considered together. Both are pendants to the belief that knowledge of the past can lead to prediction of the future. This is hardly a controversial idea. If we want to predict whether a registered voter or a laboratory rat will turn either right or left at the next opportunity, it is obviously useful to have a record of the organism's history of behavior at comparable decision points. Furthermore, we might be very interested in discovering an even simpler (i.e., reductionistic) basis for predicting the choice behavior. A person who is philosophically opposed to the deterministic-reductionistic view would probably still use economic status, age, or gender as a basis for prediction. Most of us do use reductionistic markers from past experience in an attempt to understand, predict, and control future contingencies. This approach is not always successful, of course, but we persist with the effort to construct or discover a strong link between past and future. Freud would have faced even more withering criticism had he abandoned a deterministic-reductionistic approach and asserted instead that what we think, feel, and do tomorrow has no relationship with what he thought, felt, and did yesterday!

The real question is whether or not death instinct theory is crippled by an unjustifiably extreme form of deterministic reductionism. It is possible to read Freud's theory in this way. He tries to convince us that we possess (or are possessed by) powerful instinctual drives that are rooted in forces more universal and ancient than our own biographies. There is place, however, for an alternative interpretation as well. Based on Freud's general contributions to psychoanalytic theory and the way he actually uses the Eros-Thanatos formulation, I propose the following version:

1. It is really *the person in the immediate situation* who determines how the competing impulses will affect his or her life. The past is only *represented* in the here and now.

2. The particular way in which the past is represented depends much on the individual personality and life-style that has formed over time (a thesis that owes much to Alfred Adler as well as Freud). This personality did not yet exist when Eros and Thanatos first began to stir within the young organism, but now the fantasies, competencies, and experiences of a unique human being have much to say about the further adventures of its instinctual drives.

3. More enlightened child-rearing practices, psychoanalytic therapy, and several other modalities can help to produce adults who recognize their own impulses and keep them in a healthful balance. As mature adults, they are no longer driven and determined, but simply *influenced* by the ancient instincts within their organic structure.

4. When the instinctual drives are *represented* in our own mental dramas, they take on a form that is more appropriate to Psyche, the mistress of distinctively human thought. It is *love* and *hate* that features in our waking and sleeping fantasies. Primitive organic urges must transform themselves into more representable characters to gain admission to the theater of our minds. In this significant sense, then, the past conforms itself to the present rather than the reverse.

In summary, what we do tomorrow *can* be linked to critical events in our personal pasts and the operation of instinctual drives—*but* we are helpless in the grip of these forces only if we have failed to achieve mature selfhood. Interestingly, many other theory spinners have also described instinct-driven behavior as rigid or mechanical. This is in contrast to the idealized normal person whose intelligence and experience results in a more flexible and creative approach to life, the instincts still active, but serving higher purposes. Much of what Freud said about instincts was also being said by other investigators and theorists. Distinctive to Freud, however, was his assertion that those who grow up neurotic—or who fail to grow up emotionally—are held captives to instinctual drives they should have mastered.

Freud probably did rely too much on the reductionistic-deterministic credo that was so appealing to scientists of his generation. It is an open question, however, as to whether or not the psychologist of our own times can afford the luxury of condescension. Our journals are filled with raw, or at best, half-baked, empiricism in which multivariate computer statistical packages take the place of searching and reflective thought. It is as though determinism and reductionism have lost some of their power to inspire our efforts, but have not been replaced by any new principle of comparable vigor.

The critics are accurate but selective in characterizing Freud's theory as *dualistic*. Eros and Thanatos are depicted as instinctual drives with opposing aims. Conflict is inevitable and unremitting. This concept is in keeping with his psychoanalytic theory in general, brimming over with steamy pressures and tensions, and demarcated between the dualism of internal and external spheres. It is rather a wicked thing to be a dualist (unless, of course, it is a holy thing, as in Catholic doctrine). Freud's critics have somehow missed John Dewey's (1920) scorching attack on dualistic thinking. In Dewey's philosophical approach, the universe is neither a completely integrated whole, nor a set of rigid dichotomies. Dualistic thinking does untold mischief by allowing us to indulge in glib oversimplifications. Such traditional pairings as "mind" and "body," "means" and "ends," and "good" and "evil" create mental traps that burden society at large as well as individuals. Dewey would probably have found Freud guilty as charged (assuming he could reconcile in his own mind the guilt-innocence dichotomy).

Freud's dualism, however, would not have been possible without an underlying monism! After all, those antagonistic instinctual drives are battling for the same turf, the same resources. It is the same person who either lives or dies, loves or kills (or both). Freud clearly assumes that there is a strong common framework within which the conflicting impulses can have at each other. Those well familiar with his work will perhaps be reminded here of one of Freud's favorite scenarios: the father (ego or superego, depending on the context) facing challenges from rival sons (Eros and Thanatos, if not id and superego).

Conflict between instincts would be pointless unless there was something to fight over (i.e., the self). Furthermore, the antagonism itself is subsidiary to collaboration. We could not function without the reciprocal operation of Eros and Thanatos, any more than we could metabolize without both an anabolic and a catabolic process.

Freud did see conflict as a central fact of life. He did enjoy telling us stories in which the dramatic conflict is heightened. It takes a little discipline on our parts to recognize that all this strife between Eros and Thanatos occurs within the unity of the human soul. If we find it surprising to associate Freud with respect for the "soul," then we have not yet reached Bettelheim's (1983, pp. 9–15) level of understanding.

Two other philosophical-attitudinal criticisms of death instinct theory were presented earlier. Becker has perhaps been the most forceful and persistent in rejecting this theory on the basis of Freud's own personal problems and quirks. Believing he had found a connection between

Freud's anxieties and the development of death-instinct theory, Becker concluded that the theory could therefore be dismissed. It is ironic but no longer unusual for the psychoanalytic approach to be turned against Freud. One may or may not consider Becker's *ad hominum* arguments to be fair play. Far more important, however, is the question of inferential logic. Does knowing (or guessing) the mood and motives of a creator provide a sound basis for judging the product? Would Freud have developed a better theory had he been completely free of death-related anxieties? Or did Freud simply consult his own inner experiences as he wrestled with a significant theoretical issue? I do not consider it a sound procedure to judge the product on the basis of the process that went into its creation. Death-related motivations have been shown to have had major influences on Darwin, Twain, Mahler, and many others whose contributions, like Freud's, ultimately are judged on their intrinsic merits.

Finally, there was Levin's interesting criticism of the physical theory underlying Freud's assumption of "inorganic peace." Freud was wrong about that. The fundamental error was in attributing *any* psychological quality to the cosmos. He was not the first to project human attributes on the heavens; ancient astrologists read personal destinies into the stars, and physicists later spoke of "attractions" and "affinities." Even so, Freud was asking for trouble in building his death-instinct theory on the far-fetched assumption of a primordial inorganic state to which our own instinctual drives owe allegiance. Freud recognized—and perhaps even counted on—the likelihood that this theory was unverifiable. Even as he formulated this theory, however, it was being made to look absurd by major developments in physics, astronomy, and related fields.

If we take the "inorganic peace" component seriously, then, it stands as a classic example of the Psychologist's Fallacy (first identified by William James).[6] The fact that we can analyze or read things into the world (or into each other's behavior) does not make them true. Nevertheless, there are two ways in which one might attempt to rescue this moribund speculation. The more amusing approach would be to argue that inorganic nature feels perfectly at ease with itself, even though the material universe seems committed to racing away from itself at the highest velocity possible. What is velocity, after all, to "matter" that flows in "waves"? The inner life of inorganic nature might be at its most serene under these conditions, for all we know.

Another approach would be to conclude that Freud was just telling us stories again. He could not resist the dramatic impact of making a Big Cosmic Statement—and he did hedge this statement with a variety of disclaimers including characterizing it as a kind of mythology. Freud might have taken us for very dull folk, indeed, if we had accepted "inorganic peace" as a concrete description of reality when all he wanted to do was to prepare us to look kindly on his reformulation of our instinctual life. One can imagine him drawing another puff from his forbidden cigar and sighing, "So they can't take a little joke, can they?"

Central to most of the clinical and empirical critiques has been the difficulty of working with the death instinct in any practical sense. As already noted, the introduction of Thanatos did not provide any "handle" comparable with the sexual instinct's libido, nor could particular organ systems be readily identified as hosts to the death instinct throughout the developmental process. In general, Freud did not offer enough specifics for most clinicians and researchers to find productive use for the death instinct.

There is a predicament here from which we might draw instruction. The hard-headed scientist will not be satisfied until phenomena can be reduced (that word, again) to numbers. Experienced clinicians know that they must deal with inferences. Freud was both the scientist and the clinician. He remained frustrated by his inability to reconcile the goal of quantification with the qualitative and inferential aspects of clinical practice.

He struggled with this problem through a lifetime of work, even beyond *Beyond the Pleasure Principle* (1920/1960). A significant example is his treatment of *Inhibitions, Symptoms, and Anxiety* (1925/1959). This is a clear and insightful contribution to the dynamics of anxiety, with particular emphasis on differences between "normal" and "neurotic" responses to danger. "Differences in intensity" and other concepts that imply quantification are critical to his discussion. Yet Freud still cannot turn the corner and convert the qualitative into the quantitative. This frustration is evident in his presentation of death-instinct theory as well. Freud does want to provide us with a way of assessing the relative strength of Eros and Thanatos, as well as of the ego functions per se. He remains troubled by his inability to do so. Led to expect a tool that we can immediately put to useful work, we walk away in disappointment from the death instinct.

The useful lesson, it seems to me, is that a zone of "best application" exists for most theories and methods. Freud might have continued to employ concepts that imply quantification in his philosophical forays as well as his structural creations in psychology. There is some value, for example, in recognizing that both the forces of repression and the impulses repressed might have variable levels of intensity. This idea might be included in a larger theoretical system even if we never actually measured the forces in any precise way.

It was probably a mistake, though, to build up expectations for measuring the death instinct as though it were a readily observable and palpable phenomenon. Freud would have had to draw back from his grand theoretical project (at least, strategically) and instruct us instead in the art of clinical inference. "Of course, Thanatos is not like the nose on your face, or the whatever on your whatever," Freud might have lectured. "We *infer* the death instinct from certain patterns of speech, action, and communication. If we are good observers, then with the death-instinct concept we will have improved our sensitivity to the inner struggles experienced by our clients. If we are not sufficiently competent or well trained to draw reasonable inferences from keen observations, then we should probably be wrapping herring instead!" (Freud told me so himself in a dream visitation; if you revisit his *Wit and Its Relationship to the Unconscious* (1905/1938), you will find him telling an absurdist joke in which the symbolic relationship between a herring and a bath towel is daringly exposed.)

Had Freud settled for the death instinct as a *hypothetical construct* (in the jargon of a later psychology), and offered us more clues to the processes of observation and inference, we in turn might have given Thanatos a more serious trial as a guide to clinical practice. The master clinician passed up this opportunity to use his expertise in support of death-instinct theory and instead attempted to force "scientific quantification" into an area in which it has seldom been comfortable.

It is also worth remembering that even in a "hard" science such as physics there has been more success in predicting the behavior of the "group" (a large aggregation of molecules in the form of gas), than of the "individual" (a single molecule or subatomic unit). Suicidology from Durkheim (1898) to the present day has also had some success in identifying subpopulations who are at relatively high risk and even in devising a rough quantitative specification of the risk factor.

The quantitative approach, however, still leaves much to be desired in prediction of suicidal behavior by a particular individual. A persistent problem in suicide prevention and research is the large number of so-called false positives. Attention must be given to a relatively large pool of people whose general characteristics have been associated with suicidality, instead of being able to focus down on the smaller number who will actually make attempts on their lives. Freud—and everybody else—has so far had only very limited success in identifying suicidal risk in particular individuals by reliance on quantitative methods alone. Competent clinicians, however, especially with some additional training in suicide prevention, are often able to assess suicidal potential for particular individuals through a variety of observations. Their estimates can even be expressed in a lethality scale or some other predictive instrument, but what gives these formalized techniques much of their power is the clinician's overall sensitivity and competence, not the numbers per se.

Could, then, death-instinct theory be useful if we proceed as clinicians instead of misplaced number crunchers? A logical place to start might be Freud's characteristic emphasis on the importance of early development. Identify the child who has turned anger and aggression inwardly as a basic coping style, and we may have identified a person who is at unusual risk for direct or indirect suicide. Such a person might be said to have organized his or her self around Thanatos. It is as though circumstances impelled this person, while still a relatively helpless child, to conclude: "I will be a self-murderer. This is the only way for me to survive."

It would be useful to observe such at-risk children in their own natural settings and while they are still children, instead of relying on their later adult memories. The death-instinct concept is difficult enough to work with—why compound the problems by limiting therapeutic and investigative efforts to the uncertainties of retrospective analysis? Although Freud had unusual skill in threading his way through the memories and fantasies of adult clients, this is no substitute for more direct observation of the child during its most formative periods.

"I am my death instinct"—or more succinctly yet—"I am death" can serve as a key to therapeutic and preventive efforts, and at a time that such efforts might prove most effective. *From the standpoint of improving quality of life and preventing self-destructive behaviors, it really does not matter whether Thanatos is rooted in cosmic reality or has become an emergent reality for this particular person.* The death instinct is real enough if a life has organized itself around an orientation toward self-destruction.

This line of reasoning could be applied to a variety of configurations, not simply the example given here. I am suggesting an emphasis on direct and timely observations and a liberation of the death instinct concept from its "biocosmic" philosophy. Do we *really* have a death instinct in the same sense that we have bones, muscles, and red blood cells? Who knows? Because the biological sciences do not seem to have provided much support for this concept, we might simply join with Becker and dump Thanatos into the "dust bin of history." If, conversely, we have too uncomfortable a familiarity with the strange turns taken by the history of science, we might be a little more cautious. The notoriously dualistic Freud actually believed in a universe in which physical, biological, and psychological realities had an intrinsic relationship. Scientific knowledge has still not reached the point at which this proposition can be clearly tested. Perhaps eventually Eros-Thanatos will be seen as a preliminary but not entirely erroneous component of a larger world view in which our traditional distinction among physical, biological, and psychological realms has been dissolved or transcended.

Because we cannot be really sure about the ontological status of the death instinct, perhaps we can regard it instead as we do many other concepts that have taken on psychosocial meanings. The "flower child" of the 1960s who smiled appealingly as she inserted a fresh daisy into the barrel of a rifle was telling us something about her hopes, expectations, motives, and beliefs. This was true as well of the young man who went to the trouble of arraying himself in a leather jacket with spiked belt and bicycle chain accessories, perhaps further adorned with a death head's tatoo, and a swastika or two. Would any observer doubt that these people were trying to tell us something? That they had identified with love-peace or hate-violence orientations? There was a psychological and social reality to the concepts embodied in their respective life-styles. The ontological status of the orientations expressed, respectively, by the flower child and the punk was less to the point than the obvious fact that they had organized their lives around certain implied concepts.

The subtle (if, for that reason, sometimes irritating) Freudian approach would have much to offer if we attended to Eros and Thanatos as concepts implicit in everyday life rather than as mythological creatures. We might wonder, for example, what the flower child had done with her death instinct, and in what secret ways love and tenderness expressed itself for the dedicated punk.

There is something about the behavioral dramatics of both the flower child and the punk that suggests the operation of a creative process. The same might be said about the persistent interplay between Freud's suspect pair of instincts. Is it possible that this flawed theory has provided some useful clues to understanding the creative process? Is it possible, then, that an improved understanding of the creative process would enhance our knowledge of the psychology of death? This set of explanations will be explored in our chapter that brings the psychology of creativity and death into the same conceptual framework.

For another possible application of death-instinct theory, let us return to one of the opening quotations. An alcoholic doctor "came to every analytic session with the statement, 'I want to die'" (Wallerstein, 1986, p. 571). He had, in effect, curled himself tightly around the desire to end his life. This man's death resulted from a combination of physical debilitation, viral infection, and substance abuse. Without disregarding the physical bases for the death, his therapist called it "an unconscious suicide." The troubled man had identified with his death instinct. A more obviously deliberate suicide by jumping off a bridge ended the life of a young woman who sent farewell snapshots to her husband and other relatives. "In their last phone conversation, the husband had assured her of his continuing love, and 'she could now die happy'" (Wallerstein, 1986, p. 572).

The final message centered on an interplay between Thanatos ("die") and Eros ("happy"). A person with a long history of unhappiness had somehow put her two instincts together to achieve a sense of resolution— but also, unfortunately, to end her life. These are but two of a great many examples that can be discovered. We do sometimes think, feel, and act *as if* contending with the conflicting claims of Eros and Thanatos. Why not be more observant of these dynamics in our roles of friend, caregiver, and scientist?

There are many specific topics in the psychology of death for which Freud's dual-instinct theory might still provide some guidance. The possible effect of "will" on health and the recovery from illness is one such area. I have often been told by physicians, nurses, social workers, and chaplains that a particular patient either survived or died because "he wanted to." Most of these informants had little or no knowledge of Freud's death-instinct theory. They had noticed something, however, that invites further examination. Would the dynamics of Eros and Thanatos have some value in guiding further observation and intervention?

Just one other example will be mentioned here. There has long been the view that people sometimes "choose" the time of their deaths. *How* does a person choose the day of death, if he or she does choose it? The paucity of explanation invites attention to Freudian theory, although not to the exclusion of other approaches as well.

SOME THOUGHTS IN PASSING

Freud's death-instinct theory has not been demonstrated to be true in any traditional sense of this term. There has actually been very little research devoted to proving or disproving this theory, perhaps because the concept does not readily lend itself to controlled and objective investigation. The prevailing response has been a critical one. Most clinicians and researchers have rejected the death instinct as a true account of human nature. It has also been categorized as useless. Furthermore, the attitudinal or aesthetic response has portrayed the death instinct as a particularly disagreeable component of a most disagreeable world view.

I am not quite ready to dismiss this theory. Why? It is one of the few Big Theories we have. The problem of death is integrated into a broad and rich (if flawed) conception of the human organism. There is something to admire, I think, in the scale, sweep, and elegance of Freud's last theory. At the very least, it is refreshing to work with ideas that confront significant realities—or have you never read a score of typical journal articles in one sitting? There is merit to many of the criticisms. Nevertheless, it seems to me that, collectively, we have been so enamored of the destroyer role, that we have not given comparable attention to what might be heuristic and valuable. Today, we still need all the help we can get. This is why you will find death-instinct theory (in modified form) appearing in various other contexts throughout the book and included as part of the final overview.

For now, we will invite Arthur Schopenhauer to have the (almost) last word. Schopenhauer, like Freud in the next generation, was a deeply pessimistic man who had many optimistic suggestions to offer, all set forth in a beguiling mix of arrogance and humility. He elaborated a concept of the human will as an active, striving force within the cosmos as well as within society. It is not difficult to see a lot of Schopenhauer in Freud. Together, they offer still another psychological construction of death—as a cosmic impulse. This concept was excluded from our chapter on The Psychologist's Death because it required the foundation that is offered in the present chapter and also because it is difficult to find any psychologist today who will espouse this concept in broad daylight.

In his own writings on death (also mentioned in the death-anxiety chapter), Schopenhauer takes us to the misty borderlands where physical reality, propositional logic and mathematics, and myth tend to lose their independent identities.

> Oh! Do you know this dust, then? Do you know what it is and what it can do? Learn to know it before you despise it. This matter which now lies there as dust and ashes will soon, dissolved in water, form itself as a crystal, will shine as metal, will then emit electrical sparks, will by means of its galvanic intensity manifest a force which, decomposing the closest combinations, reduces earths to metals; nay, it will, of its own accord, form itself into plants and animals, and from its mysterious womb develop that life for the loss of which you, in your narrowness, are so painfully anxious. Is it, then, absolutely nothing to continue to exist as such matter? . . . Whatever pertains to the will holds good also of matter. (Schopenhauer, 1883/1957, pp. 260–261)

The Schopenhauer-Freud vision may seem not only unacceptable but utterly bizarre to the empirical psychology of our own day. If we dare to look around, however, we might see a crowd of faces pressed against psychology's window. Who can blame them? They all drawn by the spectacle of grown men and women—PhDs, mostly—who believe the human life-death conflict can be studied "objectively" and as though in isolation from the cosmos that welcomes visiting scholars but grants no tenure.

NOTES

1. Freud is not the only proponent of a death instinct theory. An interesting alternative conception was offered by Elie Metchnikoff (1845–1916). Pasteur's successor and himself a Nobel Price cowinner, Metchnikoff made important discoveries in the areas of phagocytosis, cholera, syphilis, and pathologies associated with aging. In *The Nature of Man* (1903; English translation in 1905), it was Metchnikoff who introduced the terms *gerontology* and *thanatology*, and called for systematic scientific attention to these topics. He considered the fear of death to be the major source of psychological "disharmony" and anxiety. It is natural, he believed, for the old person to desire death as the tired person desires sleep. The mission of science is to prolong the life-span so that people enjoy many years of good health and then await the fulfillment of the death instinct that has ripened within them. Unlike Freud, Metchnikoff assumed that the death instinct expressed itself in conscious experience. Freud's theory is more elaborated and has the special interest of its association with his overall view of human nature as described by psychoanalysis.

2. Instinct theory faded from popularity as new methods of observation and experimentation appeared. A "new and improved" form of instinct theory developed years later, stimulated by the innovative research of Tinbergen (1965) and others.

3. Many biographers and commentators have examined the relationship between the life and work of Freud. The interested reader should consult Didier Anzieu's (1986) book *Freud's Self-Analysis*. This is an unique, thorough, and fair-minded examination that focuses on Freud's own self-discovery efforts. Among other useful contributions may be included the final volume of Ernst Jones's classic biography (1957), and books by Erich Fromm (1959) and Max Schur (1972).

4. It is one thing to observe that psychological factors may be important in the development and outcome of physical disorders, and another thing to demonstrate a causation. Many clinicians since Jelliffe have been impressed by mind-body interactions in health and illness. Such observations, however, do not firmly establish the reality of a death instinct, although they may be consistent with this concept.

5. Knowledge of the central nervous system and its relationship to endocrine functioning has increased significantly since Freud's time. The emergence of computer technology and language also makes it somewhat easier to think of a

"programmed" obsolescence or cessation. There may be new possibilities for linking the Thanatos abstraction with biological processes that are amenable to assessment and experimentation. Perhaps, for example, the death instinct starts to assert itself as soon as the hormones responsible for growth have completed their mission. Or perhaps there is a subtle but powerful change in the rules followed by the autoimmune system that has the effect of marking tissues and organs for destruction. A more psychological pathway might be discovered in the "guided imagery" type suggestions that we give to our bodies, promoting either fitness and healing (Eros) or decline (Thanatos). This avenue of inquiry offers opportunity for experimentation under controlled conditions as well as detailed observation. Although a death instinct parallel to libido could possibly be discovered as our knowledge of psychobiological functioning continues to increase, one can see why Freud did not want to build a case on such uncertain grounds.

6. "The *great* snare of the psychologist is the *confusion of his own standpoint with that of the mental fact* about which he is making his report. I shall hereafter call this "the psychologist's fallacy *par excellence*" (James, 1896, p. 196). How many examples of this fallacy can you discover in *The Psychology of Death*? I may award prizes to those who discover the most, or the most horrific.

REFERENCES

Allport, G. W. (1955). *Becoming: Basic considerations for a psychology of personality*. New Haven: Yale University Press.

Anzieu, D. (1986). *Freud's self-analysis*. Madison: International Universities Press.

Becker, E. (1973). *The denial of death*. New York: Free Press.

Bettelheim, B. (1983). *Freud and man's soul*. New York: Knopf.

Brown, N. O. (1959). *Life against death*. New York: Viking Press.

Choron, J. (1972). *Suicide*. New York: Charles Scribner's Sons.

Dewey, J. (1920). *Reconstruction in philosophy*. New York: Holt.

Durkheim, E. (1951). *Suicide*. New York: Free Press. (Original work published 1897.)

Einstein, A., & Freud, S. (1932). *Why war?* Chicago: Chicago Institute for Psychoanalysis.

Farberow, N. (Ed.) (1980). *The many faces of suicide*. New York: McGraw-Hill.

Freud, A. (1949). Aggression in relation to emotional development: Normal and pathological. *Psychoanalytic Study of the Child, 34*, 37–42.

Freud, S. (1938). *The interpretation of dreams*. New York: Random House. (Original work published 1900.)

Freud, S. (1938). *Wit and its relation to the unconscious*. New York: Random House. (Original work published 1905.)

Freud, S. (1953). Analysis terminable & interminable. In *Collected works* (Vol. 5, pp. 316–357). New York: Hogarth Press. (Original work published 1935.)

Freud, S. (1959). *Inhibitions, symptoms & anxiety.* New York: Norton. (Original work published 1925.)

Freud, S. (1960). *Beyond the pleasure principle.* New York: Norton. (Original work published 1920.)

Freud, S. (1961). *New introductory lectures on psychoanalysis.* New York: Norton. (Original work published 1933.)

Fromm, E. (1959). *Sigmund Freud's mission: An analysis of his personality and influence.* New York: Harper.

Galdston, I. (1955). Eros and Thanatos: a critique and elaboration of Freud's death wish. *American Journal of Psychoanalysis, 15,* 124–134.

Garma, A. (1971). Within the realm of the death instinct. *International Journal of Psychoanalysis, 52,* 145–154.

Gernsbacher, L. M. (1985). *The suicide syndrome.* New York: Human Sciences Press.

James, W. (1896). *The principles of psychology* (Vol. 1). New York: Holt.

Jellife, S. E. (1933). The death instinct in somatic and psychopathology. *Psychoanalytic Review, 20,* 121–132.

Jones, E. (1957). *Sigmund Freud: life and work: Vol. III. The last phase, 1919–1939.* London: Hogarth Press.

Levin, A. J. (1951). The fiction of the death instinct. *Psychiatric Quarterly, 25,* 257–281.

Maslow, A. H. (1968). *Toward a psychology of being* (2nd ed.). New York: Van Nostrand Reinhold.

Menninger, K. (1938). *Man against himself.* New York: Harcourt, Brace.

Metchnikoff, E. (1905). *The nature of man.* New York: Putnam.

Schopenhauer, A. (1957). *The world as will and idea* (Vol. 3). London: Routledge & Kegan Paul. (Original work published in German in 1883.)

Schur, M. (1972). *Freud: living and dying.* New York: International Universities Press.

Shneidman, E. S. (1985). *Definition of suicide.* New York: Wiley Interscience.

Sperling, M. (1969). Migraine headaches, altered states of consciousness and accident proneness: A clinical contribution to the death instinct theory. *The Psychoanalytic Forum, 3,* 69–100.

Symons, J. (1927). Does masochism imply the existence of a death instinct? *International Journal of Psychoanalysis, 8,* 38–46.

Tinbergen, N. (1965). *Social behavior in animals.* London: Chapman & Hall.

Wallerstein, R. S. (1986). *Forty-two lives in treatment.* New York: Guilford Press.

7

Getting on with Life

"What's the use it makes no difference," he said to himself, staring with wide-open eyes into the darkness.

—Tolstoi, *The Death of Ivan Ilych*

How the days can keep coming. And the nights. And the days. That's what I don't understand. How everything can just keep coming on and going on as though a life and a death hadn't happened.

—Father of a child killed by an inattentive driver.

I William Smith Do not want to Live anmore I am sick Mary I want to feel Better:
William Smith
P.S. I want to DIE

—Suicide note, Leenaars, *Suicide Notes*

To say "life" is the same as saying "here and now"

—Ortega y Gasset, *Meditations on Hunting*

Life and death do not wait for our perfect theories, definitive studies, and validated intervention procedures. At any moment we might be called on to—what? To comfort or avoid our grieving neighbor? To respond with statistics or tears to a student's hesitant question? To open a door or build a wall around that symptom we probably should bring to a doctor?

I would have liked to be a less fallible person who could offer a more evolved psychology of death. Nevertheless, it would be wrong to hide behind the limitations of both knowledge base and author. As the Spanish philosopher observes, we do have to get on with life. Here, then, are a few suggestions for a "practical thanatology." I usually avoid this term because *thanatology* sounds so much more impressive than its denoted mixture of clumsy methods and shaky inferences. Recently, however, it dawned on me that thanatology is simply the study of death with life left in. Looked at this way, a practical thanatology would be no more than learning something useful from the reflected-on life experience of ourselves and others. This should be well within our compass. And so we now try to find a little guidance from a psychologically oriented perspective on life with death left in.

THE TOUCHED AND THE UNTOUCHED

The touched and the untouched? This is the most basic and natural distinction that I have observed, whether in a hospital, a classroom, or a community setting. There are people who convey a sense of having been touched by death, and others who behave as though untouched. Becoming aware that the next person we interact with is likely to represent one or the other type of orientation can help us to be more perceptive and helpful, and reduce the probabilities of miscommunication.

External markers can be misleading. Some young children are highly sensitive to the reality of loss and death. Some adults seem to believe that mortality is of no personal relevance. "Death gets you all the attention," a 4-year old tells her father. She is literally so attached to her grandmother, however, that she holds on to the casket at the memorial service and will not let go. Five years later her mind has continued to develop and her attitudes have altered, but she remains a person who has been touched by death. By contrast, a 37-year-old accountant reports that nobody in his life has died ("Not even a cat. Well, I've never had a cat"). Asked about death-related conversations with his colleagues in the office, he responds: "If people have talked about death at work, I wouldn't know. I don't listen to all that office gab."[1]

Age by itself does not determine whether a person acts and feels as though touched or untouched by death. Exposure to death certainly has an influence, but the outcome is variable. For example, some combat veterans seem distant and isolated from mortality even though they have witnessed numerous deaths. Their conversation suggests the persistence of the comforting belief that they were invulnerable or, even better, "born lucky." This psychological shield may well collapse at a later time. Nevertheless, within the same span of time and within the same military unit, one soldier may have become painfully aware of the frailty and vulnerability of life, while another glides along as though unconcerned. We could say that the latter person is "in denial," but this statement too often substitutes for authentic understanding. From an operative, everyday standpoint, this person is just going about his business as though he were going to live forever. And why not? So far, he has!

Similarly, emergency department physicians, nurses, paramedics, fire fighters, funeral directors, and police officers see more than their share of death. It is difficult to remain completely untouched by these experiences. Yet there are marked differences within their ranks. A few minutes of communicative interaction may be all that is necessary to inform us that "This doctor is a robot. No feelings at all," whereas "That doctor is so aware of the thread that each life hangs on . . . it's as though his life hangs upon it, too." Although there is no direct evidence on this point, I have the strong impression that people who have had to cope with the loss of a baby or young child are likely to be touched and remained touched by death. This has certainly been true in our interviews with paramedics—every respondent considered his or her encounters with the death of infants and children to have been the most disturbing of all work-related experiences. Evidences of distress often changed their facial expressions, voices, and breathing patterns as they recalled these incidents in which the reality of death made itself so painfully known.

Here is an example of an adult becoming touched by death in a way that was for him new and powerful.

Officer Draws His Gun

A 36-year-old veteran police officer responds to an interview by a former police officer.[2]

Did you feel any fear for your own life?
I knew he was about to shoot me, but I didn't really feel any shivers. . . . What I felt is that he's pointing a rifle at me and I had to shoot. It wasn't, "Oh, I'm getting scared!" It made me respond . . . from my past training. Afterwards I was scared.
On a scale of 1 to 10 for feeling fear of your own life being taken at the moment prior to shooting, what would you rate yourself?
Probably a 4.
How about immediately afterward, when you had shot?
Probably about an 8 or 9.

So, in other words, after you shot the guy, then you felt that you could have been killed.

Right.

What were you thinking a few minutes prior to the shooting?

I was thinking I didn't want to get shot. I was . . . busy looking for cover, looking ahead of time, and picturing what areas I was going to use for cover. My concentration was on the subject.

What did you think about immediately prior to the shooting?

I was thinking about what I had on hand. Thinking of—if he levels it at me than I have to shoot. Thinking how am I going to respond if he does this.

How about immediately after?

I thought, I felt scared. I felt, I wondered if I did the right thing. I hoped there were witnesses that saw him point the rifle at me. I was hoping I didn't over-react, you know. After the shooting, when I got to the car, then I started thinking about my family. I thought how is my wife going to take this. How is my daughter going to take this, knowing that I shot another man and thinking, golly, he could have shot me and taken it all away from me.

How, if at all, did the incident change your attitudes toward life and death?

That it could be taken away so easily. You always make that—it only happens to the other person. You realize after you shot somebody, how easily they could have shot you, especially in police work. That's when you realize how vulnerable you are. . . . Now that I know it can happen, I'm still scared of death. I was placed in that position two times. I tend to think of my family more when I'm on the street. Now, I think, real quick, I hope this isn't it! Before I didn't think it was going to happen to me.

Are you more/less/same fearful of dying now, then before the incident?

Probably the same in normal life. But when I'm in those situations, I'm more.

What about significant others?

I'm more fearful of you guys dying, of some guy taking my kid's life, a violent type death.

You didn't feel that way before?

I did, not now even more, because I actually saw that somebody could do it.

Rate your current fear of death for yourself.

Probably an 8.

For your family members.

Ten. . . .

Has this change in attitude resulted in any changes in behavior that you are aware of?

Yeah. I'm more cautious when I'm out there. . . . There's not much I can do.

What changes, if any, would you make in the training or handling of officers before/during/after a shooting or close brush with death?

Before a shooting, I would get an officer involved to talk to people and explain his feelings, what you go through, what to expect. During—to keep concentration on what's going on and to realize that you don't have to be a hero. Basically to remember that you are vulnerable.
After?

The only thing is for people to watch their comments to you. Comments such as, "Hope he gets lead poisoning. Hope that son-of-a-bitch dies." To let them know that even though the guy was a bad guy, he was a human. They are only doing it to support you, but you really don't care for the idea of killing somebody.

Learning from Touched-by-Death Experiences

Nobody died in the episode reflected on previously, although the officer, the suspect, and perhaps bystanders were all in danger for their lives. The possibility of death—almost the taste of death—was in the air, however, and had a significant and enduring effect on the officer. Some of the components and consequences of this experience are worth singling out:

1. There was a vital distinction between actions and feelings. The officer had to anticipate possible moves and prepare his responses. During this action-oriented phase, it was more adaptive to concentrate on the practial circumstances than on one's own emotional state.

2. Fear and other emotions broke into consciousness after the immediate danger had passed.[3]

3. This officer had not been untouched by death before this incident. Therefore, it did not awaken him to personal mortality for the first time, but led him to appreciate his vulnerability anew. Instead of a generalized background realization that a fatal incident might occur some day, "Now, I think, real quick, I hope this isn't it! Before I didn't think it was going to happen to me." A theoretical possibility had become as immediate and realistic as the sawed-off shotgun that a robbery suspect had leveled at him.

4. The officer's attitude twoard interpersonal communication had altered as an effect of this experience. He felt the need both to protect others from falling victim to their own sense of invulnerability and to discountenance violent language. Clearly, he did not want to be seen as a person who enjoyed or reveled in shooting another person. Instead, he was concerned about how his wife and daughter might think of him as a potential killer and victim.

5. In rating his current fear of death, the officer differed markedly from the average male respondent on a typical death-anxiety scale. As you might recall, most men receive low to moderate total scores on self-report questionnaires such as Templer's Death Anxiety Scale, which sample a variety of death-related concerns. This officer, however, rated himself as having the highest possible fear for the continued safety of his family, and rated his own fear of death on the high side (8 on an imaginary scale of 10). I think the reason is obvious: He was not responding to a hypothetical catalog of misfortunes as most people do when confronted with such a questionnaire. Instead he was thinking of a specific, highly charged, and consequential experience. Death had been there with him—some place between himself and the robbery suspect—and so this officer had developed a realistic concern for a realistic danger.

There are many other situations in which a person might be touched by death in a way that takes hold. Earlier in this book we quoted Ben Hecht's memory of finally having death break through to him when he stood by his mother's grave. Before this experience, Hecht, then a newspaperman, had witnessed and reported on a variety of deaths without having his own sense of mortality awakened. For Spalding Gray (1986, p. 14) it was as a child that he recalls hearing his mother trying to comfort his brother who was undergoing a middle-of-the-night anxiety attack. His mother sat on Rocky's bed and tried to help him calm down, telling him, "It's all in your mind." Every few minutes, however, Rocky would ask again—and again—"Mom, when I die, is it forever?" "Yes, dear," his mother would reply. And he said, "Mom, when I die is it forever and ever?" And she said, "Yes, dear." And then he said, "Mom, when I die is it forever and ever and ever?" And she said, "Uh-huh, dear." And he said, "Mom, when I die is it forever and ever and ever . . . ?" Gray wrote, "I just went right off to this."

Each of us who has been touched by death has had a distinctive personal history in which this recognition has made itself known to us in a particular way. Furthermore, subsequent experiences can alter our sense of inner relationship to death. For example, Kenneth Ring (1984, 1989) has found that people who report having had NDEs often also report profound changes in their feelings about both life and death. Many if not most episodes in which a person feels touched by death go unnoticed by others (even the dramatic NDE was seldom shared until the recent arousal of public interest in this phenomenon).

It is strange to think that a person who is very close to us may have had a chilling, frightening, deepening, or liberating experience that alters his or her relationship to life and death—and we do not know a thing about it! Again, this is just an impression, but I do not think that the death awareness movement has completely opened up our readiness to communicate about private experiences such as the sense of being touched by death.

A mutual disclosure approach can be helpful. When the situation seems right, we can share one of those moments in which death became something real and personal to us. This can also be done in a small group context. A less demanding variation can be used if we have reason to believe that the others are not quite ready for direct personal mutual disclosure. We can instead tell stories about third persons—Ben Hecht, Spalding Gray, the police officer who fired in self-defense, and so on. By whatever means we choose, it can both quicken and deepen a relationship to share those experiences in which death has made itself known to us in a decisive way. Many people are relieved to learn that even the silent looker-on may derive a delayed benefit. A person who has not yet been touched by death (an "innocent" or a "defender") might draw on the memory of this conversation when, at a later time, he or she finally must come to more direct terms with death. "I guess you can think about it, feel about it, talk about it—they did!"

Defenders and Innocents

In everyday life we interact with people who have been touched by death and know it, others who have been exposed but who shield themselves from the personal realization, and still others who have somehow been spared definitive encounters with loss and death. Many failures in communication result from the difficulties in establishing a common frame of reference when the interactants include defenders and innocents as well as those for whom mortality has become an emotional fact of life.

There is some value in discerning whether we are dealing with a defender or an innocent. Defenders tend to have systems and rituals that keep death at arm's length. Depending on the particular mode through which death awareness seeks entry, the defender may ignore, withdraw from, misinterpret, or trivialize a potential threat. If all-purpose maneuvers such as these prove inadequate, the defender may then resort to more strenuous strategies. For example, the bringer of unwelcome death-related messages may be subjected to anger or mockery, as has often been the fate of a person who bears any kind of bad tidings. Arbitrary statements and impulsive actions may be rushed into the gap to prevent effective communication: "Damn it! I checked the brakes!" (He or she did not.) "Next time, do it yourself!" There may also be some actual denial going on as well. This has often been observed in people suffering from symptoms of a life-threatening disease who do not seem to make the connection between what they are experiencing and what it might signify. Many defenders, however, are not blocking out realities in the blind, massive sense implied by "denial." Instead, they are skilled in avoiding situations that might bring them uncomfortably close to death made plain. Selective attention can also be an effective technique, and truth itself may become a casualty when an impertinent fact threatens to increase anxiety and destroy the illusion of control.

Over the long haul, though, institutionalized systems of communication do much of the heavy work in protecting individuals from naked confrontations with death. Defenders who are positioned within a bureaucracy do not have to rely extensively on their own resources. Death can simply be sent through channels. A man dies in an industrial accident, for example, his body almost totally demolished. This is a harrowing experience for his coworkers and especially for those who are delegated to clean up the scene. But after a step or two has been taken in the organizational communication process, this disturbing death has become an incident that is covered by thus and such insurance provisions, and by wave after wave of paperwork. Even if nobody within the organization takes a blatantly defensive position, the system quietly does its work of transforming a bloody death into documents and procedures.

Some years ago, as director of a geriatric hospital, I attempted to reduce an environmental threat to the lives of our aged and nearly immobile patients, as well as to school children and others in the vicinity. This was a toxic chemical-railroad car situation close to our facility, its hazardous potential having been well established in the preliminary studies we were able to conduct. I contacted agency after agency, official after official. During this process, I did not encounter any clear examples of people intensely, inappropriately, neurotically defending themselves from recognition of this possible environmental catastrophe. They didn't have to! Each agency, each official could simply pass the buck to the next: "Not my department, sorry!" From public health officers to U.S. senators, all those contacted relied on bland institutional responses to avoid dealing with the situation. Individuals can defend themselves from personal encounters with death and remain sweetly reasonable while doing so—as long as they know how to work these bureaucratic levers.

Many variations on this theme occur each day. School systems, governmental agencies, and hospitals have often proved adept at removing death's sting by a sequence of maneuvers that progressively replace the impact of an unique death with the generalized and dulled sensibilities of the bureaucratic organism. Individual comfort levels can be maintained when this organizational pattern runs its course successfully. The basic institutional response to death is most reassuring to those members of the organization who are defenders, people who resist touching death even with the tips of their minds. They do not have to become vehement in denial or clever in evasion. It is a different story for those who have felt and acknowledged mortal twinges in their own lives. A woman in the sales department of a manufacturing company recalls the most recent discussion of death in her workplace. A colleague had died after being hospitalized for what was not thought to be a life-threatening condition. "Most of us learned about it from the bulletin board. The announcement suddenly was just there. It was dignified and all of that, but on the cold side. We were all more than usually polite to each other. That lasted for a few days before things got back to normal. We talked a little about him, but not really. It was all so—well, not false, but not real either. Finally, one night I was able to cry for him, just sit alone and cry for him because he had lost his one and only life and because somebody had to cry for him." Another respondent, also a woman, made a similar comment: "When we have to talk about death at all, we talk about it (here) as though it is just one more thing that happens and then we are supposed to go on as usual. But I know better than that. Death isn't just one more thing, and you don't go on as usual. The one who has died certainly doesn't!"

People who have been touched by death may also take evasive actions to avoid stirring up old sorrows or rekindling underlying fears. Usually, however, they do this with a degree of self-awareness and communicate about it in a forthright manner when given the opportunity. A dignified elderly physician with a reputation for being unflappable quietly asks a younger colleague to take over for him in working with an aged woman. "This old dame reminds me of my mother. And my mother didn't die in a very pretty way. Be a good boy now, and look after her for me; I don't think I can take it." There are tears in his eyes. A person touched by death may avoid reading some books or viewing some movies for fear these will stir up feelings that "don't really need to be stirred up," as the only family survivor of a multiple fatality car accident put it. Being touched by death does not guarantee that a person will handle a particular situation more comfortably or effectively, but it does usually guarantee that the person will feel *connected* with the situation. "My sense of humor has changed and it sometimes makes me feel like I'm not watching the same show or not hearing the same joke. I can't see anything funny in all that bloody, bloody violence that is supposed to be entertaining." As an inner-city emergency room nurse, this student had seen more than enough bloody, bloody violence in real life.

Although sometimes withdrawing from death-related situations, the person whose awareness of mortality has been awakened is more likely than others to recognize others' fear, grief, vulnerability, and danger. This makes the "touched-by-death-person" either an invaluable colleague, neighbor or friend, or a terrible nuisance—depending on one's own frame of reference. For example, in one of our studies we inadvertently discovered a tendency for elderly women to experience vicarious grief (i.e., sorrow and anxiety for the plight of others). Here an elderly woman speaks about the grand-daughter of one of her friends, a young woman who had recently terminated an unwanted pregnancy with an abortion: "She acts like she doesn't feel anything . . . but I know she does, and it's how you feel coming out of anesthesia, but she hasn't come out yet. . . . What she did—the abortion—it doesn't matter I don't approve. Judge not that ye be not judged. But it hurts all the same . . . though I could be the only one who feels it. . . . She will, too. You can, um, you can't have a dead child and not feel it" (Kastenbaum, 1987, pp. 450–451).

Social perceptions of this type may vary in accuracy. The person touched by death might possibly read too much or the wrong thing into another person's situation. Similarly, the impulse to reach out from one's own experience with vulnerability and loss to comfort another may be met with gratitude, indifference, or anger. This is one of the reasons why hospice volunteer directors have learned to be careful in their selection process. Some people who have been touched by death have a tendency to come at others with an alarmingly high level of intensity or to confuse their own emotional agendas with the needs of the clients.

Nevertheless, the most effective counselors and caregivers for people in death-vulnerable situations seem to come from the ranks of those who have themselves been touched by death, whether through significant losses or through empathic intuition. This does not mean that all "initiates" are automatically qualified as caregivers. Whether as a friend, volunteer, or paid professional, one needs also a sense of discipline, balance, and perspective as well as good basic interpersonal skills.

Defenders can be helpful in some situations. They may possess attractive personalities and valuable skills, or control needed resources. For example, a college athlete was famous even to his buddies for his dismissive attitude toward risk and death. Everything would always work out. Nothing bad could ever happen. Death was, vaguely, something that old people do after they have done everything else. Yet Dan was a crucial person while his mother was dying and, later, as his father seemed to become paralyzed with grief. The apple of the family's collective eye, Dan did not have to do much to have a comforting effect. People simply liked to know that he was around. Furthermore, he could say and do "stupid things" without upsetting anybody. Dan's good-natured and oblivious presence helped because, as a younger sister put it, "He just kept doing his normal stuff, and we needed a little normal stuff just about then." Even though Dan remained defended against the personal realization of death, he recognized that his father was now lonely and unhappy, and provided valuable companionship to him.

A person does not always have to understand or relate to the heart of the matter to play a useful role. The anxious defender who senses a crack in his shield can be a source of additional tension and distorted communication. A late-arriving relative, for example, stunned and angered other family members when she tried to turn the situation into a happy little social occasion and seemed to express no awareness that it was an impending death that had brought them together. In trying to insist that others must behave in such a way as to protect *her* from exposure to you know what, she was interfering with their ability to comfort the dying person and each other. The well-defended defender and the defender whose ramparts are crumbling provide different kinds of challenge to those who achieved some kind of working arrangement with their awareness of death.

And what of the "innocent"? This is the person who has not yet awakened to some of life's most fundamental realities. Unlike the defender, this person does not have to invest heavily in either individual or institutional evasions. The "world without death" that we explored earlier in this book is not quite the same as the innocent's own mental representation of a safe universe. In our little exercise, we suspended "natural death," the inevitable cessation of life. This radical alteration is not necessary for the innocent. He or she sees death, hears about death, reads about death, and perhaps even talks about death. It is really just a word, however. There is little sense of inner connection with vulnerability, loss, or finality. It does not make much difference whether death exists or not. To be more specific: It does not make much difference to the person; he or she is *now*.

The psychological makeup of the innocent deserves more attention than can be given here. One set of characteristics, however, helps to define if not to explain this oddly charming relationship to the world. The innocent maintains in good working order the child's endowment for magical and egocentric thinking. "The world operates the way my mind does. Actually, the world is a lot like my mind!" We often see this, for example, in the innocent's attitude toward time, schedule, and obligations. "Things start when I do. Nothing happens when I do nothing.

Anything undone can be done when I'm ready to do it. Anything done that went wrong can be undone. There's always time. . . ."

This egocentricity, with time curved like a rainbow around one's own needs and impulses, makes it possible to survive some challenges and potential stressful situations without quite realizing what has happened. One is innocent not only about death, but about consequentiality in general, as well as the independent existence of other minds and purposes. Cozy narcissism has not yet been surrendered. "The world loves me, and will treat me right." An adolescent boy may be sincerely astonished when he wakes to find himself in an intensive care unit, intubated and swathed in dressings and casts. In an abstract way, he had known that this kind of thing can happen to motorcycle riders. *But not really!* An adolescent girl may be as astonished when she discovers herself to be pregnant. She has known all about sex since forever and even had friends who had become pregnant. Theoretically, this might have happened to her, too—*but not really!*

Freud and some other observers have asserted that none of us can appreciate our own mortality, that, way down deep, we are all innocents. Well, who knows? At levels more accessible to observation and communication, some people go about life as though basically innocent about death and other hard knocks; others either acknowledge these realities or maintain individual and institutional lines of defense.

Innocence, adolescence, and tragic misadventure have long been associated with each other. We need look no further than the death-by-trauma toll on American youth. Accident, homicide, and suicide are the three leading causes of death. Traumatic forms of death are also much in evidence in many other industrialized nations, although none are even close to the U.S. homicide rate. To this carnage we must add the periodic sacrifice of young boys to the gods of war. There are always reasons for war, whether these are dressed up as geopolitical necessities or exposed as diplomatic blunders. Yet regardless of the reasons, the venue, the opponents, and the weaponry, the predictable outcome is always young men killing each other and anybody else who gets in their way.

It seems to me that all this bloodshed owes something to innocence, especially of the male adolescent variety. The urge to exercise one's newly developed strength and satisfy emerging desires often arises before the child's narcissism and egocentricity has fully relinquished its hold. The restless, prancing bull, eager to romp and rage, has not quite realized that life and death are for keeps. Shrewd and unscrupulous adults have frequently recruited these brave young bulls—sometimes in small herds, sometimes by the hundreds of thousand—and offered both a sense of direction and a license to do what they felt like doing anyhow. Compare the letters written by young soldiers (Civil War, World War I, etc.) before and after combat experience. Look at the shrine of impending fulfillment on the faces lined up for the kick-off, and the hurt-to-the-soul lost boy look on the player unable to arise from the field, and just realizing that he cannot make his legs move. Without the lingering caress of childhood innocence, the young male would not be nearly so ready to risk his life and others.

Sexist though it may sound, I really don't see quite this level of doomed innocence in young women. Perhaps women have greater body awareness than men, and more incentive for keeping themselves viable and intact. Perhaps on some obscure biophilosophical level, Nature just doesn't care to have so many young males around at a particular time. Or perhaps young women are spared the lethal connection between innocence, the desire to test themselves in the world, and do-or-die aggressiveness. In any event, innocence is not necessarily an innocent condition. It can lead one all too easily into fatal encounters. Ask 10 million parents of teenagers why they don't sleep well.

It is not redundant to speak of virgin innocence, whether the topic is sex or death. This is the province of the inexperienced, or those on whom experience has not left an impression. By contrast, it is not unusual for people to seek a return to innocence. We try to forget what we know, or we try to reinstate "the way things were." The theme of lost innocence and the search for a new Garden of Eden has expressed itself both in works of art and in the life patterns of less articulate people. Two girls snuggle into the vacated bed of a recently deceased grandparent and report the next morning that it felt good to be close to him, and that the bed and the room were safe places to enter again. Their sense of communion with the beloved elder had somehow removed the strangeness of death and separation. A worldly woman in her middle years is drawn back periodically to visit her childhood home, although she remembers it as a place of tension, unpredictability, and danger. Nevertheless, "Home was what there was before there was anything else. It was before all the trouble started. I can count on having that feeling of peaceful sadness. It's the peaceful part I like."

The return to innocence can take the form of a brief respite. We go back refreshed, to the hard world from which disappointment, loss, mistrust, and hazard cannot be banished. Some plays, movies, books, songs, and games can serve this function very nicely. There is often a "let's pretend; there is no harm to it" quality about such respites. Brief returns to innocence may also remind us that we have been neglecting some of our better personal qualities, such as kindness, patience, and curiosity.

Not quite so harmless is the impulse to return to innocence when it is prompted by desperate, boiling anxiety. We now detect an insistent and driven quality. It is no longer a gentle drift into reminiscences and fantasies. Instead, a group norm or ideal is asserted to which others are expected to conform. The "death meld" approach mentioned in Chapter 3 is a case in point. Death is not death at all. Death is really life. We do not really die. We do not really lose loved ones through death. We should ignore the superficial evidence of our senses (the cold, unresponsive flesh) and the foolish pangs of the heart (yearning for the lost one). A bubble of comfort is created, and we are invited to enter—if we will faithfully obey the rules that keep this delicate apparatus afloat. The rules include rules of language, rules of conflict resolution, and rules of interaction. It becomes more difficult to comfort the grieving, for example, if I have consented to the proposition that grief is unnecessary. So many of our potentially helpful actions and interactions begin with the recognition that a person is facing the pain of loss, separation, and uncertainty. How can I see and understand what you are really going through if I am convinced that there really is no suffering, no loss, no injustice, no basis for doubt? My blissful certitude, my desperately reinvented innocence, might cost our relationship dearly.

Innocence and Awakening: The Sex-Death Connection

Academic psychology has done a number on many of the assertions offered by the psychoanalytically inclined. Freud's theories of psychosexual development and the sexual etiology of neuroses, for example, have not fared well when examined by demanding methodologists. This leaves us holding two bags: The old one is stuffed with appalling and provocative ideas that are difficult to accept; the new one is pretty near empty. More specifically, the mainstream psychology of death has added very little to our knowledge or even to our hypotheses about the sex-death connection. This topic is generally passed over in silence.

I think we must give at least a little attention to the sex-death-innocence connection matter, despite all that we don't know about it. Let us first invite Algernon Charles Swinburne (1942, p. 963) to repeat a few of his lines.

> From too much love of living
> From hope and fear set free,
> We thank with brief thanksgiving
> Whatever gods may be

That no life lives for ever;
That dead men rise up never;
That even the weariest river
Winds somewhere safe to sea

Safe to sea! This passage from *The Garden of Proserpine* sings of a weary journey completed. Having recovered from "too much love of living," one finds comfort in the cool lower depths that are ruled by a queen of darkness. Some of the images implicit in *Proserpine* (1942, p. 967) come to the surface in *The Sea* (1942, p. 967), a poem that seems to complete his thought. Here Swinburne out-Freud's Freud.

I will go back to the great sweet mother,
Mother and lover of men, the sea.
I will go down to her, I and none other,
Close with her, kiss her, and mix her with me.

What are we being offered, then—childhood innocence regained after a long day at play or uninhibited incest? Is death the ultimate mingling, the forbidden and total surrender of which mortal lovers can only dream?

If this were only one poet's excursion into sex-drenched pantheistic mysticism, we might quietly tip-toe away. There were other poets, dramatists, and philosophers at a time when poets, dramatists, and philosophers were actually taken seriously, however. A haunting sense of death-tinged sexuality and sexually tinged death pervades the romantic writings that enjoyed popularity and influence from about the middle of the 18th century until the early years of our own. These were often ardent, first-person, quasi-confessional narratives. The author was usually a young man. Emblematic of these was the German youth, Friedrich von Hardenberg, who wrote under the name, Novalis. Here is an excerpt from a Hymn to the Night.[4]

Suck me toward you, beloved,
With all your force that I may slumber
And love at last.
I am touched by death's
Youth-giving flood. . . .
I live by day
Full of courage and trust,
And die every night
In holy lust.

Not long after writing this poem, Novalis died of tuberculosis, well short of his 20th birthday. In a more restrained manner, another young man dying of tuberculosis, John Keats (1942, p. 768) confesses the following to the nightingale:

> . . . and for many a time
> I have been half in love with easeful Death,
> Called him soft names in many a mused rhyme. . . .

Articulate young men endowed the death they were facing with qualities more often associated with vibrant, throbbing life. Death would somehow give them what life had not. For the doomed young men of early industrial society, especially those marked by "consumption," the disease of the epoch, the void was imagined as lover, mother, fulfillment, escape.

At the same time, the young woman's sexual and mortal destinies were also entwined, as displayed by some of the most influential and enduring cultural representations. This connection shows up clearly in the popular Death and the Maiden theme. Many stories and verses tell this story. From about the same period as Novalis's brief life and death, we have this version by Mathias Claudius.

> *The Maiden:*
> Oh, go away, please go,
> Wild monster, made of bone!
> I am still young; Oh, no!
> Oh, please leave me alone!
> *Death:*
> Give me your hand, my fair and lovely child!
> A friend I am and bring no harm.
> Be of good cheer, I am not wild,
> You shall sleep gently in my arm.

The young maiden was usually depicted as pursued or cornered by the masculine figure of Death. Parallels to a sexual conquest were obvious. Presumably a virgin who had never consummated love in her brief earthly existence, the maiden would now experience something more exciting, more formidable, more all-giving and all-taking. In the theater as well, it soon became a cliché for death to be the alternative if not the outcome of a woman's sexual awakening—the price she pays. In a later generation, *Camille* would die famously in this manner, and so would her operatic counterparts. (Third acts were fatal to a great many soprano leads, especially in Italian operas not by Rossini.) These deathbed scenes recycled into everyday life. The pale, semicadaverous look became fashionably romantic for some time, perhaps anticipating today's anorexia-bulemia epidemic.

From the young person's standpoint, both sex and death qualified as "ultimate experiences." It would not be difficult to get them a little mixed up.

1. A proper young man and a virtuous young woman would have only dared to guess at what pleasures—and anxieties—sex might hold in store for them.

2. Sex did have lethal consequences. Mortality rates were high for infants, young children, and their mothers. "Childbed fever" was a scourge until well into our own century, and still a menace wherever public health precautions are not in place.

3. Venereal disease had become a threat to society as well as individual. There might be a life-time of suffering and disability ahead for a victim of sexually transmitted disease. Furthermore, stillbirths and deaths in the early months of life were occurring as a result of venereal disease. Even more harshly than other causes of infant mortality, syphilis seemed to bring home that terrible warning about "the wages of sin."

In addition to practical factors such as these, it is likely that the themes of sex and death have an intrinsic mutual attraction within our minds: Procreation and decay, excitement and nonresponsiveness, passionate closeness and desolate abandonment. Of course, there is no forgetting the often remarked-on sense of losing ourselves at the moment of sexual climax. Our minds are schooled for a linear, analytical, and discriminant mode of information processing. Under the pressure of strong emotion and the lure of novel circumstances, we may turn to a more mythic, image-making, and poetic way of thinking. It becomes more satisfying to blend and integrate powerful images rather than holding them resolutely apart as incompatible opposite. Death can be sexy. Sex can be deadly.

Perhaps one day psychologists will be able to turn to psychology for elucidation of the sex-death connection. For the moment, we still need our poets.

We still need to sort out our thoughts and feelings about contemporary forms of the sex-death connection. Abortion remains one of the most divisive public topics in the United States today. Sexually transmitted diseases are becoming more prevalent again, with AIDS under-standably causing the most alarm. In women, cancer of the breast and of the reproductive organs, and, in men, prostate cancer present additional challenges to our feelings about the sex-death connection. Also for women, a new generation's commitment to education and career develop-ment has contributed to delayed motherhood. There is increasing con-cern among some women that they will not come to reproductive fruition because of a variety of life circumstances. Alive and healthy as individ-uals, they nevertheless might feel that an essential part of their being has died of neglect. Some husbands share this concern.

These are four very different situations: The decision to end the life of a fetus; sexually transmitted infection of a thus far incurable disease; a cancerous process selecting sexual organs as the site of attack; and the sense of being incomplete and in mourning for a much-desired child. Without blurring their differences, however, we can expect all of these circumstances to stir up vivid themes, fantasies, wishes, and anxieties. Getting on with life can be that much more difficult when we must deal not only with a loss or a threat, but also with the confused signals arising from the mingled claims of sex and death, cessation and renewal.

"Misty-eyed passion" does much to make life exciting. The buildup of excitement and its orgasmic release and quiescent afterglow seem to attract fantasies of dying, death, and a blissful postdeath-orgasmic state. There are moments when it would be out of place to introduce that cold, insistent, and charmless instrument known as analytic thinking. There are other moments, however, when a heated and confused admixture of signals from the realms of sex and death can pose a serious threat to the well-being of ourselves and others. Wagner's *Liebestod* or a track from a *Sex Pistols* album might serve as background music when we choose to meditate on the tragic folly that can result from the acceptance of sex and death as interchangeable images. Death can all too easily become a romance, a solution, or even a pastime.

LET ME LIVE, LET ME DIE

A useful psychology of death would also be a psychology of life. One of its major uses would come into focus when—in ourselves or others—we find doubt where certainty has been taken for granted. I refer to that moment when a person no longer holds fast to the belief that life should and must go on. We have already scrambled over the rough terrain of Freud's death instinct theory and braved the labyrinth of academic death-anxiety studies. Let us begin by drawing one uncomfortable lesson from each of these realms.

1. Human thought and behavior is not always oriented toward avoidance of death. Even if we join the preponderance of critics who have rejected Freud's death instinct theory, we can appreciate that he was not tilting with windmills. There are just too many observations that refuse to be ignored. At times—and not infrequently—we fail to take measures that could improve the chances of survival for ourselves or others.

2. Live anxiety is not a dependable clue or signal to the existence of a realistic death threat. To the extent that the general adult population has been sampled through psychometric techniques, we find that most people go about their daily lives with only a low to moderate sense of death-related discomfort. Sudden peaks of death-flavored anxiety often are related to stress and loss experiences that are not in themselves harbingers of mortality, whereas actual threats and losses may be covered over by a variety of defensive strategies.

There is an obvious inference to be drawn. We would be wise to detach ourselves from the naïve idea that we can depend on a keen sense of danger. There may still be a few special circumstances—such as hunting or being hunted—in which a person will be alert to mortal threats. However, Most of us do not spend most of our time in such situations; instead we interact within scenes that have been constructed from human motives, needs, cognitions, and technological aptitudes. The rules, meanings, and perceptions often are layered and dense. Our responses are mediated by images, symbols, role expectations, and all the paraphernalia common to the postmodernizing mind. In such a world, some people fear death where it is not: We call them neurotics or psychotics. Others continue as though actual death threats did not exist: We call them "normal" because their apparent indifference helps to support our own. It is a major sociocultural event when an actual death threat gains recognition by many "normal" people. We have seen this recently in several spheres, with the heightened campaign against smoking as a major example. We can become aware of actual death threats, and we can reduce our anxiety about being annihilated by threats that are only symbolic. This level of awareness is not a given, however. Hour by hour, I cannot depend on your ability to detect real danger, and you cannot depend on my ability to recognize false alarms for what they are.

By abandoning the belief in an automatic "animal alarm sense," and by recognizing our vulnerability, we can begin to develop more effective ways to detect and deal with those mortal threats that can be controlled.

Were this a "how-to" book, we might now begin with a peppy little section on ways to reconnect live anxiety to realistic threat signals. Here our first set of exercises might well deal with improving our self-awareness of personal feeling states. How do we feel when we feel anxious? What thoughts and images flit through our minds? What actions are we tempted to take? After learning to read our own anxiety states with a higher degree of literacy, we might proceed to improving our ability to detect the signals that tend to set off these episodes. And so on. . . . I am only trying to suggest what direction we might take, once we clearly realize that we cannot depend on an automatic and trustworthy process of detecting and interpreting mortal threats.

Who Lives and Who Dies?

Suicide, parasuicide, spontaneous recovery, and NDEs are among the more striking examples of individual response to the challenge of getting on with life: The college freshman who kills himself after receiving "only" a B+ on an exam . . . The unemployed minority youth who drinks and drives until death obliges him . . . The hacking, lung-diseased smoker who lights up another one . . . The "terminally ill" mother who just will not die—and does not . . . The near-death experiencer who overcomes the sweet temptations of the altered state and decides to return to the responsibilities of life. . . . In their various ways, each of these people has made a statement about getting on with life. Let us look a little closer and see what we might discover about the psychological processes that have been called on. It is possible that these markedly different patterns of action have had a common origin, even though they diverged at a critical point.

Let us try this for ourselves first. Imagine yourself walking along a dusty little road that is hardly more than a path through scrubby woodland. You have not been this way before. It is getting late. The pale sun light is rapidly fading. Now you discover that the road ends at a cliff: Below are rocks and a fog-enshrouded landscape. There is a higher hill that you might choose to climb and that might offer other prospects. The road back is long, darkening, and devoid of comfort. What will you do? Down the perilous cliff? Up the mysterious hill? Back through the long, darkening road?

Never mind the choice! Reflect instead on what has been going on between you and yourself as you visualized this scenario. Did you see yourself trying this way or that? Did you put yourself in the position of moving yourself as though a chess piece or a character in a story? In other words: Did you make the "I-Me" distinction that plays so large a role, if so often unrecognized a role, in life-and-death decisions? As we have pulled back from the end-of-the-road scenario, you may have regained the I-Me unity, at least for a moment. You will have seen, however, how easy it is to divide ourselves into an observing ego with narrative powers and an observed character that can be described and manipulated as we so choose. This is the state of mind—the divided state of mind—in which many consequential decisions are made about getting on with life, or getting off.

Suicidologists have long recognized that some people believe that they will, in a sense, survive their own deaths. This has been evident from suicide notes in which the writer imagines that he or she will be there to observe how others have reacted. We also hear this split-self orientation from some who have recovered from suicide attempts. For example, a college student who had felt rejected by her family recalls, "I could see my mother standing with her mouth open, not knowing for once what to say, and she's thinking, 'Ellen really did it this time. I didn't treat her right and now I won't have another chance.'" Ellen expected to be "in some better place" after her death.

The sense of having taken definitive action can be as important as the outcome itself. "*I* killed *Me*!" This action proves (to one's self) that I am not altogether helpless, not altogether paralyzed or overwhelmed by adversity. It is seldom useful to reduce suicide to a single "cause," but the wish to demonstrate efficacy is often a contributing factor.

Furthermore, there can also be a secret ecstasy. *Me* is dead, gone, finished. But here *I* am! A survivor! The Death of Me has disposed of failure, disappointment, and everything that has become tainted, sanctioned, and unacceptable. *I* can now start off with a clean slate. Innocence reborn.

The inner script differs for particular people in particular situations. For example, suicidal elderly people are less likely to see themselves as observers of their own demise. Usually, the intent is to put an end to a life that is experienced as useless, painful, and not likely to hold further pleasure. There is not nearly the fantasy content that often accompanies suicide in younger people. It is the end of a disvalued life that is desired, not the opportunity to prove something or make somebody else feel bad. Even so, I have often noticed a secret glow of redemption among suicidal elderly people. The old body that has become such a burden will be discarded at last. There will also be an end to worries about money, transportation, crime, and all the frustrations and demands of everyday life.

Yet something does survive. What is this something? Often, it is the image of who he or she has been. It is as though one has reckoned that "I can keep intact the memory of who I was, if I can get rid of who I am becoming." The observing and experiencing self is situated in the past. The contemporary self is seen as a failing enterprise that will be brought to total ruin in the future. The past-situated *I* plans to kill the future *Me*. At the moment this plan wins full attention and at the moment it is ready to be put into operation, the *I* regains control of the present situation. *I* am an active person again, running my own life. When there is no longer a *Me* to produce embarrassment and distress, there will be only the pureness of self remaining. A secret survival. A survival of the fittest (my real, true, or wished-for self). A survival for which the loss of a burdensome, used-up body is rather a bargain.

For another type of example, consider the parasuicidal slow self-destruction inherent in heavy smoking. Health care professionals are accustomed to seeing rampant self-destructive behavior on the part of persons suffering from emphysema, lung cancer, and other respiratory disorders. The patient has been told repeatedly that his or her illness was caused by smoking. The patient has also been told that all further smoking is absolutely forbidden. The doctors, nurses, and respiratory therapists are doing all they can to provide treatment and comfort. It is clear, however, that smoking has destroyed much of the patient's respiratory capacities, and that one can work only for a little longer life with a little less suffering. The patient, however, will not cooperate with the treatment regime—not if this means refraining from lighting up. Given the opportunity, the bed-ridden, emaciated, air-hungry, oxygen-fed emphysema patient will find a way to ignite that next cigarette.

Smoking that next cigarette will undermine the treatment efforts, engender further respiratory distress, and shorten the patient's life. Does this mean, however, that the person has become totally self-destructive? Not at all. The split-self orientation follows a different pattern here. The elderly suicidal person intends to protect something valuable in his or her character and past life by marking the present self for destruction. By contrast, the smoker with advanced respiratory disease is almost completely centered on immediate experience. "Now. I need that cigarette now. That's all I want. That's all I need. Now." Past and future selves appear inconsequential. From an objective standpoint, the patient is continuing to kill himself. Subjectively, though, the smoker is intensely involved with succoring his only self that matters, the *Me-Right-Now*.

The elderly suicidal person and the person with advanced respiratory disease have in common a lack of self-inclusiveness across time. The young suicidal person may have another variation on this theme. If one's future self is threatened, then one's present and past selves count for little. Although healthy and perhaps gifted, the youth may see himself or herself as stillborn or doomed because some circumstance has imperiled the future self-to-be. In these and in other ways, people sometimes develop a state of mind in which self-destruction seems the most attractive choice because the self that is being destroyed is not perceived as a viable edition of one's own true being.

Organizing one's self to preserve a threatened life is a much different proposition. Yet the observer-observed relationship also plays a significant role. A woman who had been severely injured in an automobile accident found herself unable to speak or move as she was wheeled into the emergency room. When she heard a doctor say, "This one's gone," she became furious, however. "I thought, 'Like hell, I am!' as hard as I could, and I forced myself to move something, move anything. I guess some words did come out, and something did move, because the nurse and then the doctor came back and, well, here I am!" (This from a nurse recalling her experience of about 7 years previously.) She had been frightened by her situation, enraged at the doctor, but, mostly, "upset to find myself helpless like that. That's not me."

We do not really understand how some people are able to rally from a life-threatening condition that would usually prove to be lethal. It seems likely, however, that their success includes the ability to reinvest in the endangered self. There may be a period of detachment in which "body and soul" appear to be undergoing a trial separation. At the crucial time, though, there is a decisive reunification. This return to self can also be a journey of discovery. Some reports of NDEs provide illuminating examples, as does Ring's research on personal interpretations and consequences of these experiences.

The more general case may be implicit in *The Problem of Embodiment* (Zaner, 1964). Located at a neglected intersection of anthropology, psychology, neuropsychology, philosophy, and theology, this topic continues to be poorly understood. It may be that our understanding of the *I-Me* relationship in life-threatening situations will continue to be deficient until a thorough examination has been made of embodiment in general. Perhaps we should not assume that it is "natural" for people to feel, literally, at home in their bodies. Philosophers such as Gabriel Marcel (summarized by Zaner) have suggested that much of our lives constitute a quest to discover who we are as owners, servants or inhabitants of a body. According to Marcel, we cannot construct or grasp our own identities until we have also come to terms with the changing, perishable, pleasurable, painful body we inhabit. A life-threatening circumstance, then, might provide us with a fresh perspective on the mysterious nature of what it means to be a thinking body, or a corporeal mind. As a resourceful and creative response to stress, some of us might emerge from the experience with a stronger sense of self. Perhaps this process of realizing ourselves in a new way also contributes to keeping us alive.

There are two worrisome ideas that should linger in our minds after this brief exploration of *I-Me* dynamics.

1. *Self-deception can be fatal.* Take a degree of confusion and uncertainty about where reality ends and fantasy begins. Take a society that drenches us in manufactured symbols and images. Take the disembodiment and decontextualization of human experience as represented in the popular stage theory of dying. Take the temptation to situate the observing ego in a zone of security, while making our real, embodied, at-risk selves but characters in a scenario. And take, perhaps, drink or drugs to further dull the critical senses. The result can be a fatal readiness to solve a problem or to make a statement by treating our actual embodied selves as though inconsequential and disposable manipulanda. "The old person I might become in the future is not real to me as I endanger his existence today. The self I destroy or fail to protect is a kind of fiction; it is only my momentary state of awareness and need that needs be taken seriously. When it comes right down to it, *I* can do without *Me*." This type of psycho-logic takes lives every day.

2. *Dualism can be fatal.* Perhaps the most common pathway of influence is through the preparation and intensification of the *I-Me* dichotomy that has already been discussed. Dualistic assumptions are so enshrined in Western society that we make them part of our own thinking without critical review. Metaphysical dualism asserts that there are two types of reality. Moral dualism asserts that one type of reality is inherently superior to the other. Dualistic assumptions encourage us to ignore and dysvalue some of the actual stuff of our lives. Often we are lured into locating our values in an abstract, symbolic, almost mythic sphere while our imperfect and immediate beingness is, moment by living moment, ticking away.

It is this dualistic streak that makes it so easy to "pack up all our cares and woes" under such rubrics as "failed me," "bad you," or "insignificant them." In turn, this increases our readiness to dispose of "failed me," to destroy "bad you," or to ignore "insignificant them." Compartmentalization, dichotomization, and an illusion of safety tend to follow in the wake of dualistic thinking. Life seems simpler with ambiguities neatly sorted out, and an escape hatch to That Other Realm always available. Life is a scarier proposition for the person who believes that this unique moment *is* life, that there is no insurance against either possibility or risk. "These are our lives, right here, right now" is the reply to the abstracted dualist. Savoring life for ourselves, protecting the lives of others, and knowing how to leave when the time comes might be rooted and authentic experiences for those who have limited dualism to the fantasy hour.

Tomorrow and Tomorrow and—Say What?

We are so accustomed to the ongoingness of life. ("Sunrise and sunset," if you are in the mood for a song cue.) Time becomes spatialized or sequentialized. Second Avenue is followed faithfully by Third Avenue. Mortgage payment coupon 244 is followed, perhaps just a little too faithfully, by coupon 245. Why, then, can't we trust time as well? Continuity lulls us. This perhaps is one of the reasons why familiar places have such appeal. The old neighborhood holds a reservoir of slow, reliable, comforting time. Just thinking about good old places helps to reinstate the sense that time is an inexhaustible resource. In fact, that childhood space-time memory is safe enough, renewable whenever one cares to think about it again. The security blanket starts to slip a little, however, when we expand the image to include space–place–time–person. Those people of childhood memory are not really there any more in the old house, the old neighborhood.

Reminiscence has both a reassuring and an unsettling effect. Time was all right, back then. This suggests that time will continue to be a good-natured, undemanding, ever-available friend. However, the indisputable corollaries of elapsed time hint at problems ahead. The people of our childhood have grown older. Some, perhaps many, have died. We become less trustful. Did we misread the character of time? Or has time undergone a change, becoming now an impatient companion with a rather furtive look about him?

Scanning the future also has both a stimulating and an unsettling effect. Everything we still hope to experience, share, and create will happen—if happen it does—in the future. Everything we fear and dread will also have its opportunity in that future. Ambivalence? Anxiety? Of course.

Furthermore, deaths past and death future tend to arise, join hands, and enact a sort of ghost dance at the fringe of consciousness. Those who have died seem to be calling to those among the living who are most at risk. Each new death returns the gesture by arousing memories of the long departed. Time bends, forming a curve that is weighted down by deaths remembered and deaths anticipated. With his ghosts of Christmas past, present, and future, Dickens tried to alert all of us, not just Mr.

Ebeneezer Scrooge. And so, past, present, and future take on a personal shape for each of us, becoming more than a succession of replaceable moments. "I am going somewhere I have never traveled" and "I am going home" can become noncontradictory psychological realities for some people as they feel their way along their own distinctive lifetime structures. In a parallel manner, some of us sense that increasing age and proximity to death are taking us further than ever away from completion of our being. The nuanced directionality and shaping of personal time becomes an ever-more influential factor in our orientation toward death as we move through life.

In getting on with life, then, each of us has a different path to explore. Death also takes a distinctive shape as each of us views (retrospectively and prospectively) the losses encountered along the way. One towering death from the remote past or one impending death in the near future might dominate a person's thinking. The anniversary of a particular death might endow a day that others consider ordinary with an intense aura of grief and longing. Reaching a certain age may signify the end of one personal era and the start of another.

I no longer assume that people will think and feel a particular way about death just because they have reached the "same" age or have been exposed to the "same" experiences. Instead, I try to learn how each person has constructed his or her own trajectory of passage through life and the distinctive people, places, and events that have become salient. To put this another way: I do not find it all that useful to hear what a person thinks about death—taken as an isolated statement. I would rather know how this person has lived, and what he or she is prepared to make of time past and to come. We have perhaps become a little too preoccupied with death attitudes and cognitions, whose meanings can be illuminated only by understanding all that this person brings to this moment.

The getting-on-ness of life can seem almost routine as long as the world cooperates with our expectations. Here's Third Avenue, just where it should be. There's payment coupon 244. The 11 o'clock news is coming on again at 11 o'clock. Tomorrow? Same thing, of course. And tomorrow, and tomorrow . . .

We can choose to be lulled by the sheer ongoingness. We can choose to be assured by every familiar fact and face that meets our gaze from sunrise to sunset. We can welcome all our mundane reality for its apparent endurance and solidity. How can we, too, and all those we love, not be ongoing as well? The customary sights, sounds, and smells of daily personal life and the prolific stream of mass media images and symbols all insist that our lives are here to stay.

Engrossment in life is a natural opiate for the fear of death. Being entranced by the spell of life certainly seems preferable to spending our days lamenting mortality and rehearsing a deathbed scene.

We might at least grant death a little respect, however. We might nod to the fallen leaves, to the shuttered windows where vanished generations once thrived, to various culture heroes who, though celebrated as "immortal" and "indestructible," have perished along with the rest. And we might remember how a person dear to us went out one promising day into this land of benign ongoingness, and. . . .

Tomorrow is something of a rumor and something of a ruse. Tomorrow is a clever and effective way to keep us going. Tomorrow is a point of focus for thoughts and feelings that might otherwise skirl about aimlessly. For myself, I approve of tomorrow, but I don't much trust it. I would not want to save my life up for tomorrow any more than I would want to burrow myself into the past. Can we have a psychology of death that helps us to find a balance between yesterday, today, and tomorrow? Is there any other psychology of death worth having?

NOTES

1. The young girl's response is reported in a term paper written by her father. The accountant's report is drawn from a pilot study of death talk in the work place, conducted by Tammi Vacha-Haase and myself (Presented at 1991 meetings of Association for Death Education & Counseling, Duluth).

2. This interview is published with the kind permission of D. A. Bodman from her in-progress study of police officers' response to shooting incidents.

3. There may be a useful comparison here with NDEs. I have noticed that NDEs almost always emerge from situations in which people have become victims of circumstances over which they can exercise no effective influence (Kastenbaum, 1991). For example, as a patient who is undergoing surgery, or as an accident victim trapped under an automobile, one cannot *do* anything—and so one escapes into the extraordinary inner world of the NDE. People who do have some course of action available to them in a life-threatening situation, however, almost never report NDEs. Instead, like the police officer in this episode, they respond in a prompt and adaptive manner. Later, when the danger has passed, they often experience an acute anxiety reaction as the realization of their brush with death comes through. Possibly, we have a survival-oriented tendency to give priority to action rather than to experiential focusing when confronted with an immediate danger. Feeling "touched by death" will follow at a later time, unless we have organized ourselves against this awareness.

4. The English translation is by Walter Kaufmann (1976, p. 233) in a collection

of essays that is well worth searching out. Kaufmann, along with Jacques Choron (1963, 1964), was one of the few philosophers to contribute directly to the early phases of the death awareness movement.

REFERENCES

Choron, J. (1963). *Death and Western thought.* New York: Collier Books.

Choron, J. (1964). *Modern man and mortality.* New York: Macmillan.

Gasset, O. Y. (1942). *Meditations on hunting.* New York: Charles Scribner's Sons.

Gray, S. (1987). *Sex and death to the age 14.* New York: Vintage Books.

Kastenbaum, R. (1987). Vicarious grief: An intergenerational phenomenon? *Death Studies, 6,* 447–454.

Kaufmann, W. (1976). *Existentialism, religion, and death.* New York: New American Library.

Keats, J. (1942). Ode to a Nightingale. In L. Untermeyer (Ed.), *A treasury of great poems* (pp. 768–769). New York: Simon & Schuster. (Original work published 1821.)

Leenaars, A. A. (1988). *Suicide Notes.* New York: Human Services Press.

Ring, K. (1984). *Heading toward Omega.* New York: Morrow.

Ring, K. (1989). Near-death experiences. In R. Kastenbaum & B. K. Kastenbaum (Eds.), *Encyclopedia of death* (pp. 193–196). Phoenix: Oryx Press.

Swinburne, A. G. (1942). In L. Untermeyer (Ed.), *A treasury of great poems* (pp. 963, 967). New York: Simon & Schuster. (Original work published 1862, 1906.)

Tolstoi, L. (1960). *The death of Ivan Ilych.* New York: New American Library. (Original work published 1886)

Zaner, R. M. (1964). *The problem of embodiment.* The Hague: Martinus Nijhoff.

Index